The Complexity of Self Government

The Complexity of Self Government represents a revolutionary approach to political science. Bottom-up theory turns political and social analysis upside down by focusing analytic attention not on vacuous abstractions, but on the individual men and women who either consciously or inadvertently create the institutions within which they live. Understanding this practical level of human activity is made possible through complexity theory, recently developed in computer models, but of wider use in understanding everyday human behavior. To this complexity framework the book adds social science to give life and color to the analytical picture: micro-sociology from Garfinkel and Goffman, anthropology from Bourdieu, and nontechnical game theory based on Thomas Schelling's microanalytics, to give rigor and bite. Theoretical examples include India's Mumbai, Iran, the marshes of southern Iraq, Berlusconi's Italy, backcountry China, Zimbabwe, and Nelson Mandela's revolution in South Africa.

Ruth Lane is an associate professor at the American University, Washington, DC, where she teaches methodology and comparative politics. Her research focuses on the computer modeling of bottom-up political processes.

The Complexity of Self Government

Politics from the Bottom Up

RUTH LANE

American University

CAMBRIDGE
UNIVERSITY PRESS

One Liberty Plaza, 20th Floor, New York, NY 10006, USA

Cambridge University Press is part of the University of Cambridge.

It furthers the University's mission by disseminating knowledge in the pursuit of education, learning, and research at the highest international levels of excellence.

www.cambridge.org
Information on this title: www.cambridge.org/9781316615287
10.1017/9781316681657

First published 2017

Printed in the United Kingdom by Clays, St Ives plc in 2017

A catalogue record for this publication is available from the British Library.

Library of Congress Cataloging-in-Publication Data
Names: Lane, Ruth, 1935– author.
Title: The complexity of self government: politics from the bottom up / by Ruth Lane.
Description: New York: Cambridge University Press, 2016. |
Includes bibliographical references and index.
Identifiers: LCCN 2016024245| ISBN 9781107163744 (hardback) |
ISBN 9781316615287 (pbk.)
Subjects: LCSH: Autonomy. | Self-determination, National.
Classification: LCC JC327.L24 2016 | DDC 320.1/5–dc23
LC record available at https://lccn.loc.gov/2016024245

ISBN 978-1-107-16374-4 Hardback
ISBN 978-1-316-61528-7 Paperback

Contents

Preface

Democracy has become a one-word oxymoron, internally contradictory and probably not the culmination of all history, as is sometimes claimed. But if democracy has lost its freshness as a political concept, it gracefully directs attention to an old idea, self government, which opens new human horizons in respect to politics if it is investigated with new methods and a new theory.

Complexity theory directs inquiry to the *bottom* of the sociopolitical world, where new growth is possible in respect to the rights, responsibilities, prospects, and promises of self government because it defines politics as ubiquitous in human affairs, present everywhere and all the time, and not just restricted to far-off, large and important institutions.

While complexity theory started as a computer-based technique and can be highly technical, it is also very simple and accessible as an innovative way of considering the puzzles to which years of stable democratic government have brought its citizens: the disillusion with democratic politicians, policy, and performance that is found in all parts of the political spectrum.

Complexity theory, working from the bottom up, revolutionizes the way people look at their political worlds and opens new territory for the exploration of real self government.

- Complexity theory clears the deck of ideological rhetoric.
- It shows that the political exists in daily life, not just in official institutions and forums.
- It defines politics as including all interactive activity, from the highest to the lowest.

- It explains how justice and injustice arise and why neither is stable.
- It argues that societies create themselves accidentally, when many were inattentive;
- and that for that reason, societies need to think more carefully about what they have done.
- It shows how to explain, and perhaps control, human interactions.

Reformers exhort democratic citizens to vote more regularly as a way of fulfilling their democratic duties of public participation. Complexity theory suggests everyone is already participating 24/7 and might be interested to understand more fully exactly what they are engaged in, for better or worse.

Complexity theory gives new clout to the old phrase, *eternal vigilance is the price of liberty*.

THE GENERAL ARGUMENT

Democracy is a cage; it cuts its citizens off from a rich panorama of personal and sociopolitical life and restricts them to a narrow and increasingly meaningless activity. That one allowed activity is voting, and it occurs in elections dominated by campaigns that range from charade to circus. Granted, elections – regular and fair – are essential to keeping government in line. But they are an inadequate response to the vastness of political reality that surrounds everyone throughout every interaction.

Self government is sometimes mistakenly used as a synonym for democracy, but it is in fact quite different, because democracy, as an official journal of *The American Political Science Association* has recently proclaimed, is actually oligarchy – rule by the few in their own interest. Democracy may be a useful start but it is not the end of the journey.

If self government is to be taken seriously, no one can write a book about it; everyone will have to figure out on their own how to govern themselves; advice from the outside would be insulting. But it may be possible to investigate some of the issues underlying the search for self government, and that is the purpose of this book.

Hibbing and Theiss-Morse (*Stealth Democracy* 2002) have argued that Americans, despite constant exhortation to the contrary, have no desire to participate in government, or even in voting, because they are not interested in politics and simply want the country to be well run. I concur, but because the democratic state is not being well run, by anyone's standards, I take heart from Hibbing and Theiss-Morse's marginal comment that despite Americans' disinterest in the state, everyone loves a good fight: they love contests, athletic competition, "television shows pitting one side against the other." Civics courses, urging volunteerism and civic responsibility, are quite hopeless in this regard (Hibbing and Theiss Morse 2002: 224–225).

What is the alternative to civics? It is politics, properly understood as including both the beautiful and the ugly, and as occurring everywhere people interact, whether they are cooperating or fighting, as the case calls for, attempting to achieve their personal and social goals. Using this broad definition, lessons learned in backyard negotiations with friends and neighbors may be applied to and compared with behavior observed in larger and more official sociopolitical institutions, and may produce a greater appreciation of the *political* in its infinite scope and infinite detail.

The possibility that there is life after democracy has not yet captured the best-seller lists. Europeans seem to be ahead, including Colin Crouch's *Post-Democracy* (2004) and Pierre Rosanvallon's *Counter-Democracy: Politics in an Age of Distrust* (2008). In terms of complexity theory books for the general reader, recently there is *Complexity and the Art of Public Policy: Solving Society's Problems from the Bottom Up* (2014) by David Colander and Roland Kupers. James C. Scott's *Two Cheers for Anarchy* (2012) has something of the same bottom-up flavor, encouraging people to jaywalk occasionally to escape what Max Weber called the cage.

The books that criticize democracy, or try to salvage it, or weep over its failures, or scold voters, are infinite in number but not relevant to the current thesis (some of this literature is included in Chapter 1), which takes all that background for granted and searches for new insights and new perspectives. It is perhaps useful to note that I do not here criticize democracy as a system; it is a beacon when people lack it, and will continue in that role. Yet it would seem a rather dismal conclusion if it were considered the end of the story (Fukuyama 1992).

APPROACHES USED IN THE BOOK

The complexity theory theme pervades the book, first as the rationale for the "bottom up" theme, which argues that the human interactive world *looks* entirely different if viewed from below rather than summarized under vague and often misleading top-down abstractions (such as democracy). Complexity theory also brings together into a single analytic package works from the behavioral and social sciences that utilize micro-sociology and microeconomics but had not been seen as part of a single approach until the new complexity method appeared, potentially revolutionizing approaches to politics and self government.

I

The Simplicity of Complexity

Two errors are typical when it comes to politics. The first error is that politics is a dirty business, having some similarity to the making of sausage, the contents of which are both mysterious and perhaps unpleasant. The second error about politics is that only other people do it, usually people in high places. Neither of these beliefs is true in any thoughtful sense. People standing alone in the shower are political every inch of the way. They have goals, beliefs, values, hopes, passions, and associated strategies that define their political selves in association, benevolent or malign, with other people similarly defined. The result is human existence, and it is political every minute, every hour, every day, everywhere. And from the bottom up, not the top down.

Many professional political scientists choose to ignore the ubiquitous nature of politics, thinking it excessively broadens their task. Democracy is easier to handle; one just needs to lay out a few principles about regular elections and the rule of law and the job is apparently done. But everywhere today citizens of long-standing and stable democratic countries are growing grouchier and grouchier about their governments. Even professional political scientists are in the process of deciding democracies are actually oligarchies, a term the ancients invented to cover a small group of men governing a large group of other people for corrupt and selfish purposes.[1]

Democracy for these reasons begins to seem more like a way station along the long road of political life and experience rather than being a complete solution, and the idea of *self government* takes on new meaning. Perhaps, since every human being is deeply political, they might rise to the challenge of actually governing themselves. Self government is of course ambiguous in its meaning; or perhaps better it can be said to have two meanings that frequently are used interchangeably, without defining just which meaning is intended. One meaning is that an individual might be able to govern himself or herself personally, acting as sovereign over the many dimensions that make up the existential person. The second meaning of self government involves the possibility that such self-governing individuals might be able, as a group, to govern themselves as a group. The two meanings are intertwined.

Self government of a group from within the group as a whole will vary in the skills it requires, depending on the size of the group in question, but it does require special skills, because while we are all political, we are not all equally in charge of our strategic wits. Even with one's dearest friends, negotiation sometimes becomes necessary. And when it becomes a matter of dealing with one's elected officials, some shrewdness may be appropriate if the outcomes are to be widely satisfactory to those at the base of the official hierarchy.

TURNING A PAGE IN DEMOCRACY

Self government, in other words, is not a synonym for democracy. Anthony Downs once provided the minimalist definition of democracy: all sane, adult, law-abiding members are allowed to cast one vote each in elections held periodically with at least two contesting parties; the party that gets the most votes wins and never tries to restrict the rights of the losers, while the losers never try to change the results by force.[2] The definition is invigorating in its simplicity and clarity, but it is not the end of the matter. Perfectly fair elections tend to outrage a great many people because legitimately elected governments often launch policies with which at least 49 percent (and perhaps more) of their members disagree (often vehemently). Sometimes also democratic governments outrage their constituents and their neighbors; perfectly fair elections do not guarantee that the regime's decisions will be either wise or responsible.

Democracy remains a hallowed goal for people who do not have it, but for people who have lived under it for a substantial period of time it has had an unexpected result: it has taught its citizens that democracy may not be the end of history; there may be more options to learn about, more political landscapes to explore. The present work is designed to make itself useful in that exploration, using techniques made accessible by new computer approaches, and bringing under the rubric of the political a variety of social science research that is essential to the craft of self government.

The first step in this reeducation about the shape of the political is to understand that politics runs along a very wide spectrum, covering everything from savage antipathy to selfless devotion. The social scientist who argued this most convincingly, Thomas Schelling,[3] started from the now almost forgotten Cold War and still argued that there is no relation between actors that is so negative that there is not some sliver of agreement, and indeed no relation that is so positive that there is not some sliver of disagreement, between the actors. As an early game theorist, Schelling described his theory as one of "interdependent decision," where whatever acts we take will be helped, hurt, modified, glorified, or brought to naught by other people, many of whom we did not even notice when we worked out our plans.

Schelling would later develop this viewpoint into a model of human "self organization," based on people's tendencies to fit themselves to the circumstances around them, both physical and social, by following simple rules. What was artistic about this concept was the realization that in such self-organizing situations, people were both leaders and followers. They entered an environment and responded to its cues in choosing what action to take; once they had acted, they themselves became part of the environment and acted as stimuli to other people because those other people noticed what they had done and were influenced in turn. Schelling's classic example was housing: people chose to stay or move depending on their neighbors, and once anyone moved, that changed the lives of the neighbors, both those they left behind and those they joined; and the whole process would keep bubbling until and if everyone was content with their environment.[4]

MEETING AT A BRIDGE

This approach would become known as *complexity theory*, and would be pursued in highly technical ways by computer programmers who studied particular patterns of behavior and how they changed under different parametric conditions, seeking to discern the nature and possibility of cooperation between rational people, or the likelihood of changing identities in a mixed geography, or the outcome of hostility and war among combatants.[5] But Schelling's original approach came closer to being a general theory of politics than these narrower exercises would suggest, because he argued that this self-organizing process was in fact the creator of the societies we see around us.

How this self-organizing process works was illustrated in a map Schelling suggested as the basis of a little story about two army airmen who had to bail out of their planes behind enemy lines, were separated from one another, and needed to get together for safety as they tried to rejoin their own forces. They had no communication devices, but each did have a map of the territory, and Schelling uses the situation to show how people "read" natural circumstances to choose their actions.

The map showed a river, a variety of roads crossing in various places, several farmhouses, a fairly large lake, and a bridge. In order to accomplish a meeting, each airman had to figure out where the other man would think he would go; so each looked for some "focal point" on the map. There were several buildings and several crossroads, so they gave no guidance; but there was only one bridge, and this served as a cue to each of the men that the other would expect him to go there if a meeting were to be achieved. The solution was not "fair," because one airman might be far away and have a long tramp to get there while the other was quite near the bridge, but there was no better alternative if a meeting was to be achieved.[6]

Bottom-up politics builds on this simple example. If all societies are organized in this willy-nilly way, with the specific situations of different members having substantial impact on the political outcome, then politics is present from the beginning of human association and politics never goes away because particular people are always at least somewhat discontented with the status quo and are silently or actively working to change it. What we cheerfully call democracy is a top-down label that tries to put a good face on this self-organizing process, but current sociopolitical movements in the United States and many other long-stable democracies indicate that democracy really does not tell much about what is being negotiated at the grassroots. Truths that are inviolate in the system's official definition may not be present in daily experience. Bottom-up politics is a guide to, and a possible strategy for, such ambiguities.

Politics, far from being a dirty business that is carried out by other people, especially in high places, can more helpfully be described as a high calling for people who seek to become self-governed. But it needs to be played well, and the social sciences can contribute to the play.

THE GAME OF LIFE AND POLITICS

Complexity theory makes it possible to look past the standard formulas that are used to evaluate governments of various kinds and move toward a better appreciation of democracy, not as a static label but as an amazing, living phenomenon in which many unexpected, unintended, informal, intricate, and creative processes are involved. To make progress beyond democracy, what is needed is a new perspective on the full scope of political life, not just the campaigns and ballot boxes, but the whole complex reality that a democratic system represents.

Complexity theory has roots in mathematics, physics, and biology but is intuitively simple and directly applicable to the social and political worlds. What complexity theory does is rearrange reality so that familiar things are seen in a new light. Its basic metaphor is the lattice, a potentially infinite checkerboard containing players arranged all at the same level, distributed in different ways across the lattice cells. The individual players have very simple "personal" attributes and conduct themselves according to very simple general "rules." When these simple people and their simple operating rules are dumped into a computer, what emerges are results that can seem wildly complicated and yet can be explained with great accuracy, simplicity, and eloquence by looking down to the bottom at the basic actors and the rules, to see how these actors and these rules unexpectedly interacted to create the reality that people see.

One of the early examples of this intriguing mix of complexity and simplicity was John Conway's famous Game of Life, which took a mathematician's artistry to the central issue of human existence – life and death. On the basic lattice, each cell could be set to be either "live" or "dead" at the beginning, and history was created through miraculously varied patterns as the result of only two rules: (1) a live cell remained alive if it had two or three live neighboring cells; and (2) a dead cell came alive if it had exactly three neighbors, otherwise it stayed dead. The underlying point was that if a live cell had fewer than two neighbors, it died of loneliness, and if it had more than three neighbors, it died of overcrowding. A dead cell came to life only if the mix was exactly right.[7]

What was amusing about the Game of Life to human observers was that the whole lattice was potentially alive and that dead cells would spring to life unexpectedly if certain conditions favored it. The results were not unpredictable, except that human attentiveness is short and not accustomed to such close tracking of every detail. It was the computer that made it possible, for the first time, to think about the world from the bottom up, simply because the computer did the bookkeeping. Where old-time social observers faced complexity unaided, the idea of the *cellular automaton*, as in Conway's model, made it convenient to look for meaning and explanation in simplicity, working from the bottom up.

Rethinking the everyday world in this slightly peculiar way, from the bottom up, has several implications for questions of politics and self government. Its major impact is perhaps to scatter abstract concepts to the four winds. The democratic state, representative government, war and peace, liberalism and socialism, all lose a certain amount of reality because from the viewpoint of a cellular automaton, they cannot be defined in terms of actual human behavior. These abstract concepts, and others like them, will continue to be used in colloquial ways by old-fashioned political commentators, but they do not add to the observer's appreciation of what is actually going on in the world, on a practical level.

One of the insufficiently appreciated maxims of politics in Washington is "don't listen to what we say, watch what we do." A cellular automaton could not have summarized things better. It is also interesting to notice that the lattice eliminates the hierarchical arrangements that are often thought essential to political life, so there is no longer a clear division between citizens and leaders. Such a division is what narrowly restricts the duties of citizens to voting, so getting rid of the distinction is a first step toward self government. Politics is played in every cell in the complexity grid, and the elected official stands elbow to elbow with the ordinary folk. It is a radical vision but quite nonpartisan. The "ordinary folk," both left and right, show a growing appreciation for its possibilities.

LOOKING FOR SUGAR

How far can complexity theory be taken in the social sciences? A full sense of the range of its capacities can be illustrated briefly by an ingenious model, developed by Joshua Epstein and Robert Axtell, which covers all the ground between barren subsistence to whole society formation in a neat logical package.[8] Where does one start in such a heroic intellectual inquiry? The first step is to invent plausible and perhaps incisive ways to describe humankind. Epstein and Axtell accomplish this with two variables: one is whether the agent is near or far sighted, and the other is the agent's metabolism. Eyesight is a useful distinction because it distinguishes agents according to how far they can look in the search for good things; people who see a bigger field are more able to locate the larger rewards and thus become richer.

The agent's level of metabolism is a less obvious factor in motivating human experience, but it is equally important; it is not equivalent to greed, to how much the agent *wants*, but to physical constraints, to how much the agent *needs* to stay in good condition. The first moving step in the model is to take a bundle of people so described and insert them into a field across which they can move at will; the field is provided with sugar distributed about the landscape, and the only rule for the players is "go where the most sugar is and eat." This settles the economy – Adam Smith in a lattice.

Following the Sugarscape model a little further shows how to think about complex systems step by step, so that their analysis remains manageable rather than overwhelming. Agents seek sugar, so one must consider the sugar crop, which is, like the agents, a living object; its growback rates must be specified in the model to distinguish between rich and poor countries. The authors add another point one might have overlooked, that there is pollution at each site where the agents are gobbling up sugar; the choice of what site to choose is therefore modified to include not just the amount of sugar there but also the ratio of sugar to pollution. At each step the agent adds some sugar and loses some to metabolism; spare sugar can be stored, but if the agent runs out entirely, it is removed; others, happily, may live forever on the grid.[9]

Society begins to take shape on the Sugarscape as different agents achieve different levels of wealth, and inequality develops. Seasons are created by modifying the growback rate so that it slows in one area while increasing elsewhere; thus migration enters the model. Eventually Epstein and Axtell introduce a second commodity, spice, so trade can begin. Sex of a simple sort takes the model further in a demographic direction: an actor selects a neighbor at random; if the neighbor is of opposite sex, fertile, and there is a convenient empty cell for the newcomer, a new agent is created. Finally history, in "a very simple caricature," happens when actors settle on two different piles of resources, develop stable societies, then grow and seek to spread and run across their neighbors, whom they may assimilate or fight.[10]

THE PRACTICE OF COMPLEXITY

Complexity theory has a major weakness in that computer people are fascinated by the possibility of setting up algorithmic models that dance around in these interesting ways, but normal people often do not quite see how it all relates to their practical problems of living in the world, much less to governing themselves in that world. It is useful, therefore, to pause and outline some of the potential and actual contributions of bottom-up theories to making the world a clearer place to live in.

- Complexity theory clears the deck of many unexamined ideas that are commonly used but have no concrete meaning and confuse discussion, such as the "public interest" or the "common good," or even apparently practical terms like "efficiency." Taking these words from the bottom up, one is forced to ask *whose* interest, *whose* good, and efficiency for *whose* purposes? It may be that there is one public, but it seems unlikely and cannot be blithely assumed without further investigation. Complexity theory, in other words, recognizes that human experience includes inescapable diversity.

- Complexity theory cuts through romantic myths about perfect forms of government. Once the observer has taken a close look at the people at the bottom of the political system, it becomes obvious that they are too diverse to be neatly unified by *any* form of government. Accepting this fact prepares people (1) to recognize that there may be flaws in their own governments, and (2) to admit that foreign governments may not be as flawed as outsiders would like to think.

- Complexity theory suggests that the politicians about whom everyone complains may be doing a better job than they are given credit for. Considering the contradictions inherent in government, the vagaries inherent in the electorate, and the appalling emergencies that turn up every day, politicians deserve some slack. It is true that they sometimes raise their own salaries while complaining about red ink, but it is also true they face hard policy choices in which none of the options is pleasant. Looking at the world from the politician's point of view might make people more charitable.

- In respect to understanding how institutions work, complexity theory emphasizes the frequently unrecognized point that formal laws, formal regulations, formal offices, and even constitutions are only a fragile superstructure erected like a scaffolding over a flooding river of *informal* political interaction. Whatever the official rules, the players are all inventing personal ways to implement or circumvent them. People matter, everywhere.

- As this implies, institutions cannot be considered sacred but are human creations, made by imperfect individuals trying to implement their own view of the world. That view may be pious or it may be nefarious; complexity theory encourages looking beneath the surface, recognizing the good, recognizing the imperfect, and speaking up for the downtrodden.

- Finally, complexity encourages everyone to notice that they have neighbors, that these neighbors' actions are important to them, and that very likely they do not understand even 1 percent of their neighbors' worldviews, attitudes, opinions, goals, hopes, fears, and dreams.

Complexity theory here does its Socratic duty, providing an intellectual reminder of our own ignorance of each other, and of the dangers inherent in that ignorance.

SOCIAL SCIENCE IN POLITICS

Complexity theory is an honestly new idea in the world, invented by a specific and known group of people from physics, mathematics, biology, and the computer sciences at a specific place and time, and tied to a specific technology, computers, and the algorithmic models they make possible.[11] As with all innovation, however, complexity theory is not entirely without roots in the past, and many of these early ideas are essential to the full appreciation of complexity theory's operation and implications. Fully to carry out the program suggested by complexity theory in the discussion of self government entails assistance from the social sciences, and there are available classic works from the disciplines of economics, sociology, game theory, history, and anthropology that provide a rich background. These works provide frameworks that assist in studying human behavior with a broader focus than computer models allow, and they will provide the background to the chapters in the present book.

The most comprehensive perspective is defined by the work in game theory by Thomas Schelling, *The Strategy of Conflict*, and the later complexity theory in his *Micromotives and Macrobehavior*. His approach to game theory is informally used here to cut through multidimensional human interaction in order to reveal the payoffs at issue any time people come together. Implicit in game theory is micro-sociology, here represented by Erving Goffman's *The Presentation of Self in Everyday Life*, which analyzes the theatrical dimension of behavior and is essential to separating the real and the apparent in political life; and Harold Garfinkel's *Ethnomethodology*, a treatise on human creativity under pressure.

If complexity theory is to prove itself useful in the study of self government, it must guide its students in the understanding of people unlike themselves, with whom they must deal, like it or not, in the process of living their political lives. The present series of essays works toward this goal by providing a sequential set of examples of how bottom-up analysis can make sense of the inexplicable by revisiting case studies of other countries and other regimes and applying relevant concepts from the complexity framework to clarify what is going on and how it can be understood in quasi-logical terms. The analysis works on foreign countries because very few people can be objective about their own home turf, and in the beginning it is more attractive to look at people in other parts of the world. Their unexpected behavior, familiar to travelers, has the effect of creating perplexity, which is the mother of wisdom.

The case studies selected for inclusion have been chosen in some cases because they are inherently puzzling to Americans, in other cases for the depth of detail certain scholars have achieved. The terrain will include Mumbai, India's former city of Bombay, where the nationalist right engages in regular social warfare of great violence; to the country of Iran, which is often pictured as a place of "veils and terrorists" but is in fact a remarkably rich and stable society; to back-country China, where a Peace Corps worker describes the escape of his students into modern lives, leaving behind the misery of their parents; to Italy, where one man made a cultural revolution of vast scope without any outsiders really noticing; to Zimbabwe, where one man continues to make a revolution that everyone notices and the evaluations are sharply skewed; and finally to South Africa where individual and group self government joined in dramatic battle.

The concept that will unify these investigations at an overall level is the idea of *self organization*, which is central to complexity theory. As a general matter, self organization may or may not happen; it is an achievement rather than a guaranteed outcome. It is based on a simple series of steps, starting with *basic agents*, who are usually many in number and are distributed around the *basic lattice* in various patterns, and who act *in parallel* – that is, each actor acts simultaneously, going its own way without waiting for others. This basic setup is why the model is also called *agent-centered modeling,* a term actually more accurate than complexity theory because it gets at the underlying micro-simplicity rather than the macro-results produced.

The central dynamic is that every agent is constantly reacting to its neighbors; this eliminates any reference to an outside governor; and the reaction is in terms of *basic rules*, as just illustrated in the Game of Life and Sugarscape. "Rules" can be misleading here, because the agents are not doing what someone else has dictated but what they themselves think is important. The most vivid illustration between official rules would be a soccer game where the official rules deal in matters such as getting the ball into the goal box, and the unofficial rules suggest that if the referee is not looking, one should attack the opponent's shins.

In agent-based models there are, in effect, no referees, so everyone follows their own behavior preferences, and *sometimes* different people's behavior meshes to create a group, perhaps small, perhaps large. Schelling's approach to game theory brings this process to the macro level by suggesting that whole societies are built through often tacit negotiations that create these informal organizations, which can be transient or sunk in cement.

NOT A SPECTATOR SPORT

Self organization is not the same as self government, because self organization happens thoughtlessly, with at least some of the participants not fully attentive to the interaction despite being a part of it. A simple example of this situation comes from Jean Jacques Rousseau's early exercise of bottom-up analysis when he sought to investigate the origins of inequality. The origin of inequality, according to Rousseau's striking metaphor, occurred as the result of two different actions.

To begin with, there was the man who placed a fence around a plot of the common land and said, "This is mine." The second step was perhaps even more crucial; it was when after the first man fenced the plot of land, with no justification except his own fancy, there was no one to object. Or as Rousseau summarized it: the founder of civil society was the first person "who having fenced off a plot of ground, took it into his head to say *this is mine* and found people simple enough to believe him."[12]

Note that Rousseau's explanation was intended to be a general one, referring not just to everyday inequalities but to the architecture of societal inequalities that build on one another through history. And his central point remains, that government outcomes are the result of two different forces: the folks who act, and the folks who do not act but simply watch. It puts a new flavor into the ancient saying about eternal vigilance being the price of liberty; vigilance not just of the official government but of day-to-day events that may be more important than they appear at first sight.

The present work does not concern itself with definitive diagnoses of the ills of democracy; this has been done brilliantly elsewhere, by scholarly authors and outraged citizens, and the facts seem to be roughly the same whatever side of the fence one is on – that there is serious discontent over democracy, not only among fringe groups but at the steady center, and including politicians themselves.[13]

Nor does the present work seek to suggest system changes that might attract well-intentioned reformers. The giving of advice is almost always fruitless, especially when it is done by critics who locate themselves apart from the social problems in question; it tends to sound authoritarian or elitist, if not inherently tyrannical. Advice giving among adults also entails moral hazard, the risk that people who too readily accept advice lose the happy opportunity to figure things out for themselves – a precondition for self government. Teaching self government contains the inherent contradiction, that if one person tells another how to be self-governed, then that second person is being ruled by the first person, and it is no longer self government.

THE VIEW FROM THE BOTTOM UP

What the present work does attempt to provide, in talking about self government, is a vocabulary based in complexity theory and a social-scientific game paradigm that provides the observer with the tools with which to examine and understand the ubiquitous politics on which human institutions depend. These tools are distinctive in respect to other available vocabularies because complexity theory's tools are designed to be used from the bottom up; they are not grand abstractions, but practical instruments for clarifying what to look for when analyzing the world:

First look toward *people*, whether called agents or actors or players; second ask about the people's *goals* with the recognition that these goals may be different from the observer's goals; third consider the *rules* the people use to map their goals onto the environment they face, remembering that here rules mean not what agents *should* do but what they *actually* do. Finally the agents are surrounded by an *environment*, of which they are aware only locally, as far as their vision reaches but only that far, not to the whole; mistakes will be made, sometimes agents learn from experience and, importantly, sometimes they do not.

From the independent parallel actions of such agents emerges a society, an economy, and a governing system of some sort; all are self-organized, and the form of that organization may vary widely depending on what kinds of actors were present and in what proportions when things got started. If one participant is universally admired, you have George Washington becoming the father of his country; if everyone thinks themselves vigorously equal to everyone else in the lattice, then you may have a Hobbesian world where life is solitary, brutal, and short. The social sciences are helpful in dissecting these outcomes because they provide guides for recognizing the kinds of actions that combine in what kinds of ways to produce the complex results we see in the real world. For example, Chapter 2 includes a discussion of the outrageously titled *The Social Construction of Reality*, which nails down the exact steps by which informal, almost

accidental behavior becomes hard as rock, apparently natural and unas-
sailable but quite fragile if one is sensitive to the logic.[14]

What complexity theory provides, as other methods do not, is an
articulated picture of the many levels of human activity that make up a
political system. Where it may be intellectually convenient to believe that
politics takes place only at the topmost, "official" levels, complexity theory insists on drawing attention to the agents who operate throughout the
system, from the bottom up, agents and interactions that bubble up
through and permeate all the other layers.

The interpenetration of very human individuals into high politics is of
course obvious; when people are appointed or elected to office, they do
not lose all the goals, purposes, and beliefs acquired in long and usually
interesting lifetimes, but bring these values into office with them, to direct
their behavior in areas in which the law does not cover – and perhaps to
interfere where personal motives conflict with the law. Those elected to
public office do not become pure spokespersons for the law, but remain
themselves, and this happens throughout federal, state, and local governments. But because this is obvious does not necessarily make it any easier
to analyze. Complexity theory, in its simplicity, provides a conceptual net
within which to capture some of this obvious behavior and so facilitate
the transition from self organization to self government.

If a new approach to the political world is to be worth considering,
it should endear itself to the world by making some contribution that
is different, interesting, and perhaps startling in respect to traditional
questions in a field. The present introduction to the exploration of self
government therefore turns here to discuss two exemplary analyses of a
very common topic: the state and its operations and origins. Mainstream
analysts frequently define the state in idealistic terms, as perhaps the
manifestation of the people's sovereignty, or as the guarantor of its citizens' rights, liberties, and freedoms. The standard top-down viewpoint,
in other words, is entirely idealistic, announcing what the speaker thinks
the state *should* be rather than what it is.

Such an approach can be seriously misleading, suggesting that the state
should be perfect and that what we have is seriously defective; and the
top-down approach is actually dangerous insofar as it suggests to people
that the state will solve their problems rather than asking that they themselves step up to the plate. The two examples included here each inverts
this top-down perspective, standing it on its head and showing what the
state looks like from the bottom up and how it can be interpreted in
a practical way, making it easier to comprehend and perhaps easier to

wrestle with. James Scott first shows how the state views us, the people, as a neatly planted tree farm, while Charles Tilly explains the state as the slightly accidental result of a gang war.

HOW DOES A STATE SEE?

The result of looking at a large institution from the bottom up can be quite surprising, as shown in James Scott's innovative exercise, *Seeing Like a State*. It is easy to think that bottom-up analysis means one deals only with citizens, the people traditionally and perhaps scornfully placed at the bottom of the administrative hierarchy, but this is wrong. Bottom-up analysis means only that one deals with anyone who is making choices, and that includes everyone from the farmer out digging in his field to the king reigning from his throne; all are equally "agents" from the complexity viewpoint and all have both feet in the lattice, connected to and attempting to cope with the surrounding environment. Scott illustrates this universal application of the bottom-up principle by thinking of "the state" in terms of what it really was, in the old days – simply the king and his counselors.

Scott's analysis begins in a specific year, 1686, with specific people, Louis XIV and one of his ministers, the Marquis de Vauban. The minister fulfills his self-conceived duty to his sovereign by proposing to the king that it would be glorious for the king to know just whom he rules, by an annual census; and more generally to be able from his own office "to review in an hour's time the present and past condition of a great realm of which he is the head, and be able himself to know with certitude in what consists his grandeur, his wealth, and his strengths."[15] This little speech illustrates with what human concerns the grand bureaucratic hierarchy of the modern state begins to be built: a minister wanting to ingratiate himself with his employer by offering a new idea appropriate to the employer's ego, and an acquiescent king who would indeed get satisfaction from feeling the whole realm was at his fingertips.

What is a forest? Beyond counting people, the French state then turned to a more immediate passion – revenues. From this viewpoint, Scott argues that a forest is a fiscal resource, one that would help meet the state's revenue needs. Trees had other uses, such as shipbuilding, construction, and fuel, but "exaggerating only slightly, one might say that the crown's interest in forests was resolved through its fiscal lens into a single number: the revenue yield of the timber that might be extracted annually."[16]

This "heroic" constriction of vision when looking at the forest, as a state looks, left out immense but now irrelevant treasures: foliage for fodder, fruit as food for people and animals, branches for fencing and kindling, bark and roots for medicines and tanning, sap for resins, as well as grasses, flowers, shrubs, vines, birds, insects, and most wild animals, now interesting only to the state's gamekeepers. According to Scott's analysis, the actual tree "was replaced by an abstract tree" representing lumber and the needs of the state; and even these abstract trees were more of a nuisance than their keepers would have preferred.

Traditional forestry divided the land into plots based on the maturity cycle; one plot was harvested each year and then left to grow back for the next cycle. The problem was that the trees distributed themselves unevenly, and with the old method, "the results were unsatisfactory for fiscal planning."[17] To attempt to organize this untidy system, various methods were employed. At first, foresters walked the woods carrying buckets of differently colored nails, which they drove into each tree depending on its size; at the other side of the plot, they counted the nails they had left in their buckets and by subtraction could calculate the amount of actual "timber" represented by that section, the objective being to get a *constant* revenue each year from each plot. This is perfectly sensible, as Scott points out; planning is essential in the state's affairs, and planning is based on a reasonably predictable flow of revenue. Talk to a town or city manager or a mayor today and you will uncover the same obsession with revenue; whether it is Louis XIV or Mayor Mary Smith, the state still sees in the same way.

THE GLORY OF ORDER!

Scott takes us further in the frightening investigation of how the state sees the world around it. Walking the woods with buckets of colored nails did not seem sufficiently scientific to the early foresters, so new practices were developed. Rather than leave reforestation to nature, the next "logical step" in forest management was to grow their own forests by "careful seeding, planting, and cutting, [creating] a forest that was easier for state foresters to count, manipulate, measure, and assess." The result was a neater administrative grid, not only useful with forests but with all state-centered concerns. Underbrush was eliminated, trees were planted in straight lines that were easier to weed and to cut, and the variety of trees was reduced, often just to one species. The intent was to control nature, Scott argues, and it showed up in parallel form in the way army conscripts were transformed from undisciplined peasants into orderly troops.[18]

Under the new planting system, Scott notes, tree cutting no longer required the skills of the older foresters; training protocols could be developed and taught, and unskilled laborers could do the job cheaper than their skilled predecessors. In addition, the greater homogeneity of the logs, all planted at the same time and cared for using similar methods, made them easier to market and easier to work with in manufacturing the final products.

The whole exercise had what Scott describes as an aesthetic impact; forests were judged on their neatness and manageability, and the whole society, quite beyond the forest, began to be seen by the state in the same way, as a triumph of management and routine. The problem was – and this is Scott's deeper concern – that such orderliness worked the first time around but not thereafter, because the artificial forest was vulnerable to nature and its laws. With only one crop, the nutrient cycle was disordered, and "forest death" became a problem; it was then necessary to invent "restoration forestry" to try to restore ecological diversity.[19] But because the state persisted in "seeing like a state," the simplest solution – restoring the forest to its natural foundations, letting the forest recreate itself without outside help – was not used.

Analysis from the bottom up has the collateral benefit of giving the observer some sympathy for the *decision maker* under study; by seeing the world from that agent's point of view, and understanding the nature of that agent's goals and the circumstances as it sees them, behavior that at first seems strange or unacceptable frequently takes on a different light. This may not have occurred in Scott's first instance, since in the present day the reader may feel more sympathy for the forest than for the king, but in his second example it is easier to appreciate the state's predicament when facing an impossibly complicated collection of natural societies. Leaving the woods and turning to statecraft, Scott deals with taxation, which in the early days was "wildly variable and unsystematic" because the state had so little information to go on with respect to where the taxable property was.[20] The state was perfectly capable of getting the information; it was the facts themselves that were chaotic.

THE COMPLEXITY OF THE CUSTOMARY

Consider Scott's sample community and its idiosyncratic arrangements: certain families had the right to use certain croplands during the growing season, but they could only plant specific crops, and every seven years the land was redistributed to reflect new family sizes. After the crops were harvested, all land reverted to common use, for grazing or even off-season crops. Trees and hanging fruit were the property of whoever planted them, no matter who held the land at that time, but fallen fruit belonged to whoever picked it up, according to Scott's synoptic model of village life. If a tree was felled, the trunk belonged to the planter, the branches to the immediate neighbors, and the twigs to anyone who was passing by. In time of famine, the better-off were required to redistribute goods to the worse-off.[21]

In all this carefully arranged particularity, Scott says, consider the poor lawmaker who would like to levy some taxes. He goes village by village, trying to sort out land tenure of the sort just described – and he gives up. Each village is equally complicated and each in an entirely different way. The state responds with a grand simplification: "Accommodating the luxuriant variety of customary land tenure was simply inconceivable," and the standard solution was "individual freehold tenure" a legal individual owns the particular piece of land and all its uses. And the individual can be neatly taxed, just like a forest can be felled.[22]

Scott's little "parable" of the state and how it looks at the world is educational primarily when it is contrasted to the vast academic literature on the state, going back at least to G. W. F. Hegel, if not Plato, where the state is a thing of higher importance than anything in the real practical world. Hegel basically saw the state as the result of a transcendent process whereby an idealist concept of freedom realizes itself in history. Even modern American political scientists, living in a country where there is no clear manifestation of the state as a unified entity, revert to the idea of the state when they wish to emphasize the unity of the American nation, quite apart from red and blue states, partisan infighting, and congressional deadlock.[23]

The state is understood, among most of the people who think about it seriously, as an important top-down concept that reflects the essence and the legitimacy of government. Scott's picture of the king and his ministers leads to a less glorious understanding of the state, but a more practical one. And, as a practical perception, it is apt to give observers a more balanced view of national government. One can recall Ronald Reagan's well-known remark about the most dangerous words in the political language, "I'm from the government and I'm here to help." But on the other hand, there are also highways to be paved and bridges to be repaired. The state has its dangers, but also its benefits, and Scott's bottom-up analysis gives more flavor to this picture than do the more standard, top-down concepts.

BANDITS, PIRATES, GANGS, AND KINGS

The value of complexity theory, with its habit of starting investigation from the bottom of events rather than from the top, must be evaluated in terms of the theory's ability to put the familiar aspects of the world into a new light. James Scott did this as an anthropologist, going back to a king and his helpful minister facing their initially untidy realm. A quite different analysis, based on an equally striking metaphor, is taken from an historian, Charles Tilly, who investigated the origins of the state as it may have been at the beginning, long before historical kings showed up. Working from the bottom, Tilly seized upon a startling comparison, summarized in the title of a brief essay that attempts with some success to capture in a single model a process that infused perhaps all of European history: "War Making and State Making as Organized Crime."[24] The title of the article is slightly more outrageous than the content of the article itself, but it does certainly give support to the idea that complexity theory tends to make people look at the world in new and unexpected ways.

Tilly would not have identified himself with complexity theory; he was an academic historian, primarily specializing in the French but also in European development in general as it brought itself across the centuries and into the modern world. Many years would pass from the time Tilly wrote the article before complexity theory would emerge in the social sciences. Yet Tilly's intuitive perspective on his topic was entirely in the spirit of bottom-up analysis. In seeking to understand the highly organized state of affairs in the European system of nation-states, he went back to a primitive grid where all the actors were washing about in a world largely without structure, with everyone about equal in all things good and bad; from this basic point, Tilly asked himself where power came from.

The answer to this question, in an early world that resembled nothing more than a basic lattice, was not the divine right of kings or sovereign legitimacy or the constitutional protection of the rights of free citizens. The answer was instead violence, and violence in a violent world where everyone in the lattice might be engaged in battle, seeking to destroy everyone else. This appears to have led Tilly to the striking analogy that opens his essay – the similarity between criminal gangs and the nation-state.

The essence of gang "government," as Tilly and most people see the matter, is that it is a protection racket: the gang trashes your storefront and a spokesman comes by to offer you protection from such thugs if you will pay regularly what is called protection money but can as easily be called a tax if the relevant group has some official legitimacy. According to Tilly's analysis, the process of legal taxation takes almost the same form as that of the gang's extortion, because the state offers to protect its residents' property, law, and order if they will pay it some proportion of their wealth in return for these services.

The important question in the case of the nascent state, according to Tilly, is who is causing the violence against which the state offers to protect its people; if the violence comes from outside, then the state is providing an honest, necessary service, but if the state itself is behind the violence, then the state is in the same culpable category as the gang, and both are on the same spectrum, the state being distinguished only by its size.

Tilly postulates this "racketeering" interpretation of the state against more traditional models of the state, such as formation through a social contract between consenting parties, or a marketplace model: he argues that states were "coercive and self-seeking" in the European experience, and only popular resistance mitigated their attempts at "exploitation."[25] Tilly's argument shows another characteristic of complexity theory in concluding that states are to some extent accidents; no one sought them, contrary to the beliefs of Whig historians, and no one deliberately brought them about. Instead the state is a collateral result of men fighting for power simply because power offers benefits to the holder.

RACKETEERING AS LIFE

To explore these ideas in their bottom-up detail, Tilly works his way back to the beginning of European development where he finds that there was no difference between legitimate and illegitimate violence; "many parties shared the right to use violence," and there was a continuum of agents ranging from bandits and pirates at one end to great landed lords at the other end of the continuum. The lattice was full of men each grabbing what he could. Soldiers were encouraged to loot because it was the only way anyone could afford to pay them; when soldiers were demilitarized, they took up the only occupation they had any skill in – banditry. The territories over which these folks warred were held by powerful lords, at least some of which aspired to expand their domains over as many of their neighbors as possible.

The men who sought sovereignty initially used other lords to fight battles for them, then took control and governed alone, substituting bureaucracy and paid police forces for local authorities and their minions. At this stage of development the winners began to systematically collect taxes, and *if* they provided law and order (protection from lesser criminals than themselves), then it qualified them as "legitimate protectors" who should be honored "especially if [their] price is no higher than [their] competitors." If citizens were fortunate, they received "reliable, low priced" protection, and to go along with this benefit, protest against the authorities was no longer tolerated.[26]

Having established states on the basis of complexity theory foundations, Tilly then adds an interesting adjunct explanation about how such states carried out their governing tasks. Staying close to the bottom of the political lattice, and recalling perhaps Scott's emphasis on the state's passion for regular revenue, the analyst might note that rich citizens are much more useful to the state than are poor ones, because there is more revenue among the rich than the poor. This was, in a larger venue, Willie Sutton's explanation about why he robbed banks.

In the earlier formative period, kings tried to destroy their wealthy rivals, but once power had been centralized, it became more profitable to help powerful *economic* groups to expand, in part by making war against their foreign rivals, later through specific alliances with favored social classes. Especially important, according to Tilly, was the point when successful state-makers established property rights "that permitted individuals to capture much of the return from their own growth-generating innovations" – in other words, facilitating the growth of capitalism, which promoted "the accumulation of the wherewithal to operate massive states." From then on, the state and capitalism faced history together, capitalists being the major source of loans for war making, while the state made war to improve the business climate.[27]

Tilly's analysis concludes by suggesting that this simple gangland model also explains why states today have such difficulty in pulling themselves together, or governing well, in contrast to the state-building pattern in Europe of an earlier day. Postcolonial states today in many parts of the world resemble racketeers quite closely, he argues, because the old link with war making has been lost. While earlier states needed to provide some sort of benefits to their people in order to have citizens who were able and willing to be taxed so the state could make war with its competitors, in the present day, money comes from foreign donors who are buying allies in the Third World, and so the old dynamic, which produced states that were forced to uphold citizens' rights, is no longer effective.

Tilly's conclusion needs to be borne in mind in thinking about self government today, because in his historical model, recalcitrant citizens played a major role in keeping the state in line. This current relevance of Tilly's theory is interesting, in suggesting that while it is a very concise model, it has a stiletto quality, common to the complexity viewpoint. The world seen up close can be both unexpected and educational.

THE ARGUMENT OF THE BOOK

Complexity theory, at the present point in time, is a wide tent, welcoming people from both the physical and social sciences and for that reason characterized by a great deal of diversity. It is best described as a method rather than an actual theory; theories ask specific questions, develop hypotheses that may answer those questions, test those hypotheses, and build up an architecture of explanation that allows science to capture and respond intelligently to many of the challenges presented by the world. A method is different from a theory because it is a way of *looking at the world*, prior to even getting started on asking specific questions. The present work uses complexity theory primarily as a method, as a way of seeing the political world more vividly.

The definition of complexity theory, or bottom-up analysis, as worked out in subsequent chapters, is neatly captured by the lattice image, a potentially infinite landscape made up of individual cells each one of which may have a mind of its own and may behave like a fully defined real person with beliefs, goals, habits, and biases that can be described by simple operating principles that are the actor's *personal* rules of the game. A checkerboard with many apparently similar pieces is a better analogy than a chessboard because it is less formalized, but either can serve as a mental reminder of the basic perspective used by complexity theory: there are large numbers of basic pieces, interacting on a structured plane, interacting vigorously in all directions.

On this lattice, individual agents engage only with their own neighborhood, lacking any appreciation of the layout of the whole field, and everyone acts more or less simultaneously and in parallel so that conditions may change rapidly and unexpectedly. Contained within this lattice model is game theory, which focuses on pairs of actors engaged with one another through strategies that result in payoffs to each participant and may have quite different results for each of them. In complexity theory these games are linked together, spatially and temporally, into chains that describe winners and losers as history lurches along, generated by individual decisions.

The argument of complexity theory is that the cascade of events resulting from all this bottom-up activity appears to be complex, but is in fact simple because it can be taken apart and traced back to the individuals whose behavior is causing it. This claim raises many philosophical issues of great resonance, which will be ignored here because they are irrelevant to the book's purpose, which is to explore the actual way complexity theory can be used in the sociopolitical sciences, and what relevance its results might have for persons interested in self government as a step beyond today's democracy.

Subsequent chapters of the book will lay out the major dimensions of bottom-up complexity theory. The first step is to convince everyone that the world is indeed a lattice and that everyone is engaged in political activity constantly, even when alone. Related to this is the point that formal government institutions depend on this underlying layer of activity and cannot operate without it. Also important is that many people do not realize how political is the air they breathe and how they may be vulnerable because of that ignorance. Discussion then moves on to game theory, used as a metaphor for studying interactions between people, and shows how people self-organize with amazing creativity and some wickedness.

One of the major mandates of game theory is the necessity of understanding the people with whom one plays, since otherwise one can neither co-opt nor outwit them. This requirement leads to the introduction of micro-sociological theory and some classic theorists who understood, long before complexity theory was invented, that everything in whole systems of behavior can be traced back to individuals. The power of this insight is then shown in tracing a revolution, a restoration, and a battle royal as examples of complexity analysis. The battle royal also allows observers to study the relation between individual and social self government.

SPECIFIC CHAPTER ROAD MAP

Chapter 2 emphasizes the fundamentally central point of the book, that politics is practiced all the time, everywhere, by everyone, borrowing a term (*haecceity*, pronounced heck-see-ity) from one of the theorists introduced later in the book.[28] To show that top-down concepts do not work, the chapter notes Downs's point (1) that democracy contains a logical contradiction and Condorcet's proof (2) that voting can fail to reflect voter preferences and so cannot justify the democratic system. Further, (3) analysis of the Prisoner's Dilemma shows that top-down analysis creates perplexity where none empirically exists. Two examples are given to show how "official" government is a very thin frosting laid on over this very thick cake of social politics. A hypothetical island of Thomas More shows that even apparently unimportant childhood norms affect political behavior, and a case study of life in the Iraq marshes shows that even at subsistence level, politics is active everywhere in the definition of men and their universes.

Chapter 3 moves to the second stage of the argument, the importance of the *interdependent decisions* studied by game theory, and the way in which whole societies can self-organize themselves on the basis of these tacit games. Thomas Schelling is the major guide here because of his revolutionary approach to the game, bringing it into everyday life and mundane interactions; he also rejoices in the power of irrationality. Schelling's emphasis on focal points pushes analysis toward more social psychological theory because intelligent play requires understanding other players; this leads to his unification of the social sciences, showing that economic game theory cannot be pursued in isolation, but needs sociology to add flesh to the bones. An exotic example of how games can link themselves into ecologically rich tapestries of self organization, quite independent of official institutions, is taken from India's Mumbai and its Shiv Sena organization's bottom-up origins.

Chapter 4 takes Schelling's advice to heart and brings in two sociological classics, written well before complexity theory organized itself as a distinct tool. Erving Goffman invented the theatricality metaphor to describe human interaction, describing how people play roles in society and how these performances build up into complex dramas that define whole lives. Exactly as Schelling would suggest, Goffman argues that these acts are used to control other people and use them for the actor's purposes; this reemphasizes the haecceity of politics. A second micro-sociologist, Harold Garfinkel, took the lesson further, showing how much empty space exists in the everyday world and how people innovate by using clues from their society's invisible culture to survive. This deep understanding of national and group culture is explored in two controversial countries, Iran and China, usually dismissed under top-down stereotypical labels. The chapter concludes with a model of adaptive rationality, useful in social learning where the payoffs cannot be predicted beforehand.

Chapter 5 is an extended lemma on the central concept of self organization with special attention to change and exactly how it occurs, at the bottom of even very large social systems. Using Pierre Bourdieu's anthropological term *habitus* to summarize the point of change, the discussion shows how theorists discussed earlier define a process in which an individual takes a culture and strategically manipulates it to create momentum for movement in an unanticipated direction. The modern nation of Italy is the subject here, described first by a heterodox political scientist as a negotiated game between elites seeking to milk the state, and second by the biographer of Silvio Berlusconi, whose career overturned the existing culture and illustrated vividly all the theories included here under the complexity umbrella: theater, an uncanny ability to see beneath the surface of existing norms, and a no-holds-barred attitude to game theory and the law. The result provides a striking illustration of complexity theory's principle that change is ongoing, never settling into any of the stable forms conventional theory seeks.

Chapter 6 returns to the theme raised first with game theory, that unless one player can understand the other player thoroughly, strategies are impossible to calculate because there is no knowing what will appeal to, or will deter, the other player. Such understanding is central to self government, and the chapter uses both behavioral economics and artificial intelligence to get closer to individual idea systems; here the example is particularly difficult: Robert Mugabe, universally reviled by the West yet still in charge after thirty-five tenacious years as Zimbabwe's leader. After reviewing Tversky and Kahneman's radical destruction of the rationality principle by showing that even trained scientists do not always think logically, the chapter outlines two artificial intelligence models: the Goldwater Machine, which showed how political worlds can be computerized; and the Kaiser and the Tsar model, showing how the exact same set of facts, in the week prior to World War I, were converted into two different worlds. Mugabe's transition from mild schoolteacher to raging tyrant is interpreted in a Garfinkel context, showing that colonial practices created unintended consequences that in fact could have been predicted with complexity theory's aid.

Chapter 7 winds up with self government's two intertwined meanings: government of the self by the self, and government of a whole by self-governed individuals. To provide a wider perspective, the analysis invokes three philosophers who used the bottom-up method of analysis long before it was even a gleam in anyone's eye: Plato, Machiavelli, and Karl Marx. Together they made three points relevant to the present argument: (1) That government necessarily represents the people of whom it is composed, and is neither better or worse than those constitutional people; this should give everyone pause, as they attempt to evaluate their institutions. (2) Every group includes some predators, those who prey on the weak; under the canons of complexity theory, the remedy for this is self-knowledge and self-help, learning to fight one's own wars and to fight them well. (3) As people interact, it may turn out that both sides in a quarrel have good arguments; this is the very definition of politics and emphasizes the need to study strategy; some exemplary game matrices emphasize this point. The intricate mix of all these factors is illustrated by Nelson Mandela's life and role in the bottom-up reconstruction of South African apartheid.

2

The Haecceity of Politics

The importance of expanding the meaning of the *political* is central to the present discussion of the complexity of self government, because only by recognizing that politics is everywhere, like the air we breathe, is it possible to appreciate the infinite possibilities for the exercise of personal government. This wide definition of politics[1] must be especially emphasized because the counter-tendency is so strong; everyone has grown accustomed to restricting the meaning of politics to nation-states, to democracy, to campaigns and elections, in short to civics, the pious and hopeful rules about how the world is supposed to be organized. The narrowing of the political has seriously compromised the public capacity to take a comprehensive view of issues inherent in understanding either government in general or self government in particular.

Three short examples can clarify the way in which narrow definitions of politics are misleading or self-defeating. First there is the well-known but not always thoroughly considered work by Anthony Downs, *An Economic Theory of Democracy*, which in the course of defining democracy showed that it is internally inconsistent; that if leaders and citizens both pursue their rational courses of action, then they logically cancel each other out. His argument is rigorous and convincing, and cannot simply be dismissed or ignored.

The second example bearing on the question of whether the political can legitimately be defined in an entirely narrow way comes from an eighteenth-century thinker, the Marquis de Condorcet, who studied the process of voting with great care and found that voting is not a universally satisfactory solution to the question of how men can govern themselves. Condorcet's analysis showed that when voter preferences are arranged in a particular way, there is no possible voting rule that will give satisfactory results; this occurs because of the possibility that the voters disagree in such a way that no outcome is fair. In other words, sometimes the ballot box, the sacred center for narrow definitions of democracy, simply does not work.

A third and final example showing that *narrow* definitions of the political create trouble in every direction comes from the dilemma of two prisoners, famously hauled in by the sheriff and forced to decide whether or not to turn state's evidence on their buddy in order to escape punishment themselves. The narrow solution outrages conventional people because it says the rational decision for each prisoner is to betray the other, which does not seem a positive result for creating a democratic society. A wider definition of the political dissolves the problem by showing how many and how interesting are the possibilities that arise when looking at the supposed dilemma from the bottom up.

RATIONAL DEMOCRACY

The charm of Anthony Downs's analysis in *An Economic Theory of Democracy* was that it was couched in such rigorous economic terminology and yet applied so obviously and directly to what anyone could observe when looking at the real world that it was almost impossible to argue against him. Using a narrow definition of rationality, that it is everyone's goal to elect a government, without which human life is barbarous, Downs then defined specific rationality for his two major actors, the citizen and the party leader.[2]

The goal of the citizen, according to Downs's approach, is to vote for the political party that offers him or her the greatest payoff, usually designated in monetary terms because these are specific and easier to work with than are more idealistic goals. "Thus we do not take into consideration the whole personality of each individual," nor "allow for the rich diversity of ends served by each of his acts, the complexity of his motives ... his emotional needs"; he is "an abstraction from the real fullness of the human personality."[3]

The calculation for this narrowly defined political individual was summarized in a short citizen formula: the citizen's *expected party differential* is defined by his "expected utility" from one party, compared to his "expected utility" from the other party; and the citizen votes for whichever party's payoff is higher. This solution is unfortunately not as simple as it first appears, Downs noted, since the calculation requires information, and information is costly to acquire, so that *uncertainty* becomes a major difficulty.[4] Uncertainty has many parts, including basic data about what is currently happening, knowledge about the basic scientific dimensions relevant to the particular issue, and intelligence sufficient to handle the processes of logical and causal inference. One would need, in effect, a Ph.D. in several fields to handle the expected-party-differential formula in anything like an adequate way.[5]

THE ESCAPE FROM UNCERTAINTY

With a lightness of step that can only be admired, Downs solved this information difficulty with the introduction of political leadership, which he defined, perhaps unexpectedly, as *relieving people of their uncertainty*. The logic is this: uncertainty is a natural phenomenon based on lack of time or interest, and it divides people into classes, those classes that have more information and those that have less information; and this distinction between classes creates *persuasion*, the attempt by the more certain to influence the less certain.[6]

"Whenever men can be influenced, other men appear whose specialty is influencing them; so it is in our model. Uncertainty renders many voters willing to heed leaders who seem to know the way toward those social goals the voters hold .... Subtler forms of leadership insinuate themselves into the reporting of news, the setting of political fashions, and the shaping of cultural images of good and evil."[7] In passing, it is interesting to notice here that we are back in the complexity-type world where everyone is packed onto the infinite lattice of complexity theory, jostling and pushing and shoving, as everyone reacts to everyone else, trading goals and information levels.

Leaders, the second group in Downs's model, can be divided basically into two groups: those who currently hold office and those who are seeking to oust the current holders. Both sets of leaders have approximately the same definition of rationality and the same working rule designed to achieve it: the goal for all the leaders is the same – "they act solely in order to attain the income, prestige and power which come from being in office," and never out of interest in public policy, which is purely a means to their private ends. Downs states his study's fundamental hypothesis as being that "parties formulate policies in order to win elections, rather than win elections in order to formulate policies."[8]

Such apparent cynicism sometimes shocks those who have never seen it stated so baldly, but the argument is quite consistent with Downs's methodological emphasis on self-interest, and makes sense in addition because of the practical point that one cannot have influence *unless* one is in office, so the exact logic does not matter except that it emphasizes the importance of winning. The parties' political rule is equally simple: find out what the majority wants and do it, or if you are out of office, promise to do it if elected. This strategy is complicated by the fact that some people may not know what they want, while others are quite clear on their demands; and there is a tendency to govern in favor of those who are importunate in their demands, leading to "unequal distribution of income, position and influence," as well as an increasing emphasis on campaigns.[9]

Since on the campaign trail voters would not be inspired by politicians' explanations that they sought office for personal perquisites, *ideology* enters the calculation. Downs accepted what he considered to be the "modern view" of ideologies, that they are not sincere but are weapons in the political battle, and he defined each ideology as "a verbal image of the good society and of the chief means of constructing such a society."[10] Political ideologies must be relatively stable to be credible to voters, but they can be inconsistent and vague because of the need to reconcile different attitudes within the parties.[11]

This problem of ambiguity becomes more vivid when it is transferred to a standard economic model of two stores at each end of a street, where shoppers take their business to the closest one so that the shopkeepers split the business; shortly one storekeeper figures out that moving slightly further toward the center will allow him to attract more shoppers there, while holding on to those at the far end of the street, for whom he is still the nearest store. The other shopkeeper takes the point and also moves a couple of buildings closer to the center of the street; and the two stores shortly find themselves close neighbors at the very middle of the street.[12] Downs accepted that this pattern exactly describes political party rhetoric and then drew a devastating conclusion, that parties cluster at the center where there are few differences between them, and the party officials deliberately try to be as vague as possible about what their platform actually is, since specific positions will inevitably drive off voters who disagree. In this sea of ambiguity, voters cannot calculate their party differential with any real figures; in other words, voters cannot be rational as Downs has defined that rationality.[13]

If party officials favor motherhood, apple pie, and baseball, as is in their rational interest to do in order not to offend voters, then the voter cannot be rational because he or she lacks the information without which voter rationality is impossible. Downs's quasi-solution is to investigate goals and see how different they actually are, but he does insist on avoiding anthropology, an exclusion which is consistent with his narrow definition of the political.[14] The present inquiry into the complexity of self government will take a different course and reach some different conclusions. But if democracy is logically inconsistent, that certainly supports the suggestion that it is time to move beyond it. A second logical analysis makes the same point.

VOTING IS NOT A SOLUTION

His full name was Marie Jean Antoine Nicholas de Caritat, Marquis de Condorcet, and as a minor part of his intellectually and publically rich life in eighteenth-century French society, he invented or discovered a curious paradox that, if taken with full seriousness, undermines most forms of electorally based government, which are frequently based on a belief that voting is the highest principle of decision making in order to ensure fair results and justice to all members of the voting group.[15] Today it is known as the Condorcet paradox and is about as simple as any mathematical paradox can be. It assumes there are three voters, each of which has a preference schedule including three options; the objective is to arrive at a winning choice. The matter is laid out as follows:

Condorcet Paradox

	Voter 1	Voter 2	Voter 3
First Preference	A	B	C
Second Preference	B	C	A
Third Preference	C	A	B

In other words, Voter 1 prefers A to B and prefers B to C; Voter 2 prefers B to C and prefers C to A; and Voter 3 prefers C to A and prefers A to B. Condorcet was interested in finding winners of elections with various candidates, and defined a winner as that individual who defeated every other candidate in pairwise comparisons. The difficulty the Marquis discovered was that in the case shown there is no Condorcet winner: if A is compared pairwise with B, then A gets two voters but not Voter 2; if B is compared with C, B gets two votes but not Voter 3; if C is compared with

A, C gets two votes but not Voter 1. And of course if there is a single vote among all three candidates, no one wins because everyone gets a single vote.

This cyclical majority can be summarized in the unfortunate equation, that A is preferred to B, B is preferred to C, and C is preferred to A, a violation of algebraic transitivity, where if A is greater than B and B is greater than C, then A should be greater than C (not C greater than A as in the paradox). If democracy is going to stand apart from all other forms of government because it assures that social choices, what the group decides, perfectly reflect what the individuals want, then the foundation of democracy is wobbly in Condorcet terms. This reinforces the earlier argument that the definition of the political needs to be very wide, not resting on the head of a single pin.

THE RAT AND THE SUCKER

A third problem, this time from game theory, makes the same point in a different way, showing that artificially narrow definitions of the political are misleading. The Prisoner's Dilemma has become familiar not only in academic circles but in the world at large because the picture it draws is so everyday and the conclusion inherent in the picture is so counterintuitive. The pattern was developed originally in 1950 by Melvin Dresher and Merrill Flood at RAND, in the study of game theory, and was given its name by Albert Tucker, chairman of the Princeton University mathematics department with an unexpected talent for telling stories that made mathematical principles clearer to non-mathematicians.[16]

Everyone tells the dilemma with slightly different numbers, but the basic story is the same; it involves two criminals of some sort who are arrested with inadequate evidence of their having committed any crime; each is placed in a separate cell and given two choices, either to confess or keep silent. If both prisoners keep silent, the sheriff can only get them on minor firearms charges, for perhaps a year in prison; if both prisoners confess, they will get substantial time in jail.

		Prisoner One	
		Confess	Keep Silent
	Confess	−10 / −10	−20 / 0
Prisoner Two	Keep Silent	0 / −20	−1 / −1

The real interest of the game lies in the other outcome, where one prisoner keeps quiet and the other prisoner confesses, effectively turning state's evidence against his former colleague as a way of getting off completely free; the "sucker" role gets sent up the river for a big chunk of time, while the "rat" walks away without any jail time. The game and the payoffs are shown in the preceding table, with the payoffs for the row player in the lower left of each cell and the payoffs for the column player in the upper right.

The problem in appreciating the richness of the game results from the abstract definition of the prisoners and from the abstract rationality each is assumed to use in responding to the dilemma. Bearing in mind that these are two mathematical prisoners with no personal qualities except their capture by the sheriff for looking suspicious in some way, these two very abstract individuals look at the matrix and try to figure out how best to protect themselves.

Prisoner One looks down the column under Confess and sees he will either lose nothing or end up in jail for 10 years; under Keep Silent he sees that he may get 20 years in prison. Prisoner Two looks across the rows and sees the same situation: anything is better than 20 years in the penitentiary. Each therefore "rationally" confesses, and each ends up with 10 years jail time when a little cooperation would have gotten them out in a year. The rational individual choice turns out to be irrational in social terms, since both would have received higher rewards if both had cooperated.

This conclusion is of course provocative, breaching every hope humankind has about governing itself intelligently, but the game itself makes another point important for the present discussion – that when academicians have tried to "solve" the problem, trying to squeeze cooperation from the jaws of perfidy, they have labored in a world where the political is defined as narrowly as possible, insisting that the problem is mathematical rather than sociopolitical and empirical. In such a world, the same nameless players interact with one another repetitively, time after time, with various strategies ranging from reciprocity (Tit for Tat) to forbearance, forgetfulness, provocation, vengeance, and the grim trigger (once betrayed, never again cooperate).[17]

SOCIOLOGY TO THE RESCUE

What is defective in this recondite approach to the Prisoner's Dilemma problem is that its abstractness grossly complicates the analysis by never asking exactly who these prisoners are, and indeed what might be known about the sheriff. An empirical approach, using some sociology and anthropology – in other words, a wide definition of the political – suggests all sorts of possibilities that make the dilemma less problematic. Suppose the two men are members of some local mafia clan and have been schooled in certain rules that pertain to the group; under such a regimen, each knows that if he confesses, he will walk free out the door of the sheriff's office and will be shot before he gets home; under such circumstances, he looks at the matrix quite differently.

Suppose the two prisoners are father and son, or indeed mother and daughter; assume they are in fact guilty of something and wish to continue their criminal careers together as soon as possible; they too will look at the matrix differently. Add some practical factors to the analysis and suppose the two prisoners are the sons of prominent local officials – say, the mayor and the fire chief; the sheriff plays poker with these fathers every Saturday night and has no desire to ruin community harmony; he will not even pose the dilemma but send the kids home with no more than a frown. Suppose the sheriff himself has a somewhat mixed history, only recently turning over a new leaf and entering law enforcement; suppose the prisoners apprise him of a lucrative heist that his connections make possible, and the three run off to a prosperous future together.

THE ROLE OF INVISIBLE POLITICS

Game theorists will consider these possibilities frivolous, which they may be if one is looking for universal truths about human behavior. The search for universal truths may, however, be premature in the social sciences, and inappropriately sought at the abstract level often employed in the search. Complexity theory is distinguished by opening the door to a wide variety of real-world events that make it more convenient to think about interdependent decision, self organization, and eventually self government. The present chapter is designed to bring this wide view of the political onto center stage, by studying in some detail two societies that have very little formal government but a great deal of almost invisible sociopolitical government, the unnoticed habits, customs, courtesies, and maxims that make up the wide range of the political.

The problem with understanding society and the political processes within it is neatly illustrated by the Zen tale of two young fish who were headed upstream and met an elder fish; they exchanged greetings, and the old fish resumed his way with a cheerful farewell, "Enjoy the water!"

The youngsters continued upstream quietly until one turned to the other and said, quite mystified, "What is water?" Political society has that same quality; it is so present that it becomes absent. To bring society and its bottom-up inevitable politics out of obscurity, a good story is useful, and two will be sketched here.

The first of these societies is artificial, invented in the sixteenth century by Sir Thomas More, but its importance here is not at all artificial, because it reveals to the analyst a fully transparent society where one can see, from the bottom up, just what is necessary in political infrastructure to keep a particular institutional pattern together. The second is an entirely natural society, one of the last to be almost beyond the reach of any state, found and recorded by one of the last travelers to visit this politically pristine region, an ancient society organized by itself, almost a perfect lattice, floating on the waters of the rivers that made up the marshes of southern Iraq.

The lesson in both cases is the same, that every nook and cranny of the societies is political, and there is no way to comprehend self government without investigating this whole human web, woven and re-woven day after day in infinitely complex and yet simple ways, proving again and again that politics is more than the ballot box.

The two stories are designed to emphasize one point central to the present discussion of self organization and self government: that political life can only be understood as a layer cake, built up stage by stage from the simple human interactions that make up everyday life, and supported by those interactions. Without this web of almost invisible political interrelations, no political institutions can survive; without an understanding of this web, no self government is possible.

THE ISLAND CALLED NOWHERE

In 2016 it is exactly 500 years since Thomas More published his curious exercise in social theory long before social theory was invented, in the form of a traveler's tale about an island found somewhere in a nameless ocean, discovered accidentally by wandering explorers.[18] More's purposes in writing the work have never been clear; he held a secure position at the heights of the English establishment, but wrote in explicit criticism of all the societies of his day.

In retrospect, Sir Thomas looks quite like the father of complexity theory, showing as he did how everything at the system-wide government level worked in practice only because it was supported by an infrastructure of stable but informal customs, micro-behavioral patterns that covered almost every act each participant did, twenty-four hours a day, from the bottom up. In other words, everything in the human experience was political in the broad encompassing sense of that term, and institutions could only be understood if this underworld were explored.

It is the interest in this transparent infrastructure that motivates its discussion in the present work, not its amusement value as suggesting a better society. In fact, More's title, *Utopia*, means simply "nowhere," and the assumption that it meant "eu" topia, or good-place, is a mistake made by a posterity weak in its Greek vocabulary. To escape this error, the country is here simply called the island. Its brilliance in terms of understanding political society at all its various depths is its transparency; More explains just why people follow each apparently minor custom, and why, without these minor customs, the whole system would collapse.

There is very little official government on More's island: they do not approve of lawyers and write any necessary legislation in simple words that all can understand and follow. There is a small set of officials, one *representative* for every thirty families, and a *senator* for every three hundred families; a prince is elected for life unless there is some serious malfeasance. The representatives largely supervise the workday, making sure necessary tasks have sufficient personnel and that everyone is working their required time.[19]

The senate meets every three days, and two representatives from the lower house are present to ensure oversight, to make sure nothing is secret; the representatives are different at every session so that no conspiracy between them and the senate can occur. The officials serve basically as administrative agents, ensuring steady production, re-allotment of people where there is overcrowding or underpopulation, and defending the realm from invasion. It is a capital crime to discuss public matters except in the assemblies. Crime exists and is punished with bondage, which the residents think is worse than death. Officials get no distinction in society and are recognized only by the sheaves of grain they carry.[20]

This basic political system on the island is similar in its simplicity to Downs's narrow definition of the political discussed earlier, except that More's political system lacks parties, lacks campaigns (it is considered vulgar to ask for a vote), and lacks conflict. Citizens of the modern world may find the absence of competition or hostility between groups unexpected, perhaps explained because the society is supposed to be a perfect one where normal jealousies have simply been assumed away and the whole possibility of disagreement can be dismissed as unreal. But More is quite clear that the inhabitants of his island are no nicer than anyone else; that is why two representatives are sent into the senate every time it meets, because one should not trust the senate or anyone else to stay on the right path.[21]

Residents of the island are in fact so suspicious of even their almost powerless officials that the public treasury is molded into chamber pots for storage. The argument is that if the gold were hidden away in some vault, the common people would continually suspect that someone had spirited it away for their own use; by keeping the storage public and humble (it is also used for chains for prisoners) no suspicion is aroused.[22] The critical question is how More's placid island prospers, given that it is populated with such grouchy, even slightly paranoid citizens.

ESCAPING FROM CHILDHOOD

The particular benefit of More's description of the island society is its completeness; one step at a time he isolates and deals with each of the questions an observer must consider in the course of understanding social politics in its wide definition. Much of what goes on in island society explains how there can be a society with virtually no conflict, and which therefore needs few institutions to control that conflict. An important first point is that the society is an adult society; children are cherished and cared for but they are made aware early in their young lives that they are expected to grow up, as promptly as they can.

Coddled as infants, when they reach the age of five, the children begin to be gently disciplined: they wait patiently behind the adults at the communal dinners until they are handed food; when a little older, they sit with the adults but are spaced out between them so that they are always under supervision and are being watched to see whether they are adapting seamlessly to the group. Scorn for childish things is emphasized in the treatment of the jewels and pearls found naturally lying around the seashore; children are allowed to deck themselves out freely with the pretty stones, but it is made clear that adults would *never* wear such things and the children gladly put them aside, preferring to define themselves by the higher standard.[23]

Beyond these basic socialization patterns, even adult children are the responsibility of their parents, whose permission is needed if they wish to travel to other parts of the island, and whose occupation they ordinarily accept as their own. Yet this arrangement is very flexible; if a child prefers a different type of work, he or she moves to another family that specializes in it. Such a transition is not difficult because the lives of the families are all built on the same pattern. When islanders choose to travel, they need take no luggage or possessions; they will work as usual wherever they end their journey and be entitled to all the necessary supporting materials.[24]

Indeed, children can be redistributed in More's society; where some parents have too many children and other parents have too few, the children are moved around to equalize the numbers. The same is done between cities on the island: if populations grow at unequal speeds people are simply switched around, and if the island as a whole is over-populated, colonies on the mainland are used for the same correction of balances. These redistributions are easy because everyone has been brought up in similar circumstances. Marriage on the island is for life, and norms emphasize the importance of the partners' duty to care for one another; adultery is severely punished.[25]

With five hundred years of perspective, the infrastructure of the island More invented strongly resembles complexity theory's grid. It is divided into fifty-four cities, each of which is at least twenty-four miles apart and no further than a man can walk in a day; each is surrounded by agricultural land sufficient to supply its inhabitants. The urban layout is the same in each city; they are almost square, about two miles along each side, surrounded by high and heavy fortified walls, ditches, and thorn hedges. The streets are twenty feet wide, lined with rows of houses each with a large garden in the rear.[26]

The cities are divided into four quarters, each of which has its own market; there are public halls on each street where the representative lives, and fifteen families on each side of the hall eat their meals there, the women preparing and serving the food, assisted in the heavier work by the bonded servants. Food is distributed free in the markets and supplies are stored in open warehouses where anyone can take what is necessary.[27] Because the islanders all work and their produce is abundant, these provisions elimi-nate the fear of famine or hardship; elimination of fear leads, according to the island's plan, to the elimination of greed and its resulting hostilities.

A WEB WOVEN BY RULES

The island's particular arrangement of its lattice is foundational but less interesting than the remarkable set of rules about how the people's lives are arranged to create the sub-society that supports the more obvious political rituals. Everyone works in agriculture; they are trained in this occupation from childhood on, both in school and in the field. Each person also has a trade, in wool, linen, masonry, metalwork, or carpentry. Since everyone works, no one need work for more than six hours a day – three in the morning and three more after a two-hour lunch. Every two years there is a rotation of people between the city and the country, although people may choose to remain in the country longer if they wish. Those living in the city change their houses by lot every ten years.[28]

All property is therefore held in common and everyone's role and place in society is common; even clothing is all the same: simple comfortable garments of undyed materials appropriate to the season. The results are striking in that poverty has been conquered, there is a two-year supply of food and necessities in storage in case of weather or crop problems, and there is a surplus that they sell to friends on the mainland, from which comes the gold they store as chamber pots until it is needed for war. One-seventh of their exports are given to the mainland poor, and in general they have so little need for gold that they sell on credit and do not call in their debts except in case of emergency; they think it unethical to take anything that is useless to them.[29]

Beyond the provision of a stable economy, the island community devised by More devotes itself to its major goal, human happiness, which the people define not as a short-term pleasure but as long-range balance and wisdom in the conduct of life. They allow every pleasure that has no negative effects, and spend their spare time in various sorts of education, literature, and chess-like games; even such niceties as incense are allowed, since it is pleasant and does no harm. The islanders object to war, which they think is detrimental to their goal; they avoid danger rather than seek glory.[30]

If an aggressive enemy threatens their territory, they first offer bribes for delivery of the enemy's king, preferably alive; they also offer bribes for defection by the enemy. If this fails, they try to weaken the enemy by encouraging its people to engage in civil wars, or incite old enemies to new quarrels. Next they hire mercenaries, arguing piously that this reduces the number of dangerous people on the mainland. Only if all these practical but ignoble strategies fail do they go into battle, each fighter taking his own family to provide support and to ensure that the fighter never retreats because he can see exactly what he is fighting for. Island priests also roam the battlefield, urging both islanders and the enemy to exercise mercy. It is interesting that the islanders make no treaties; they argue that if nature does not make friends, no words will.[31]

There is a form of slavery on More's island and this needs special attention in light of the sensitivity of the topic; it also emphasizes how the pinning of top-down labels on social events of this sort can be utterly misleading. No one is born into slavery in More's country; rather, it is the result of having committed some crime, or having been captured in war. That there is crime on the island makes an important point in understanding the society; these people are not perfect, and if their society works, it is not because it is made up of good people; rather, there is a constant and silent educational process that is intended to keep people well governed, even if they would not do this when left entirely to themselves. The islanders do take into account this excellent upbringing in evaluating members who break the rules, and feel that people who have grown up on the island are especially to be condemned for bad behavior since they, among all people, should know better.[32] Among outsiders who become slaves on the island, More says, some foreigners actually chose slavery, because life in bondage on the island was preferable to freedom on the mainland where there was poverty and injustice. If those in bondage bore it patiently, the penalty could be lightened.

Religion on More's island was encouraged, although it was religion of a very minimal sort; basically they thought it socially necessary to believe in life after death and a final judgment on one's sins; otherwise there seemed no basis for morality. Their insistence on the threat of final judgment is a tribute to their suspicion of natural human behavior, since they believed that only this threat keeps people in line; in other words, no one is naturally good. Islanders believed no one should fear death, because fear suggested one's record might be flawed. For the old and the very ill, euthanasia was allowed but only with the considered permission of the political and religious officials. The island people were particularly tolerant of each other's beliefs; God might prefer variety, they argued. But proselytizing was forbidden; one could believe what one wished but should not attack others with it.[33]

THE SIMPLE LOGIC OF COMPLEXITY

More's miniature country is exemplary in its logic, and provides a graphic introduction to the problem of understanding whole societies as created by politics from corner to corner, all the way across the variously organized lattices of the real world. What was going on among the people who were said to inhabit this nonexistent island? The observer can pick out specific activities at the bottom of the whole system: everyone worked, supervisors arranged matters efficiently, the cities were all laid out the same, the treasury was stored as chamber pots, the people lived together and ate together, they studied new languages for fun. How does this fit together?

Postulate that More had two major goals that he thought must be served if a society in 1516 was to prosper equally for everyone. The first goal was physical survival, meeting human needs for food and water, shelter, and regularizing agriculture sufficiently that there was a sufficient supply that emergencies were not destructive. Along with these arrangements went various fortifications to defend against enemy invasion. The second goal was to provide for human happiness, which was based on comfortable physical circumstances but also included provision for the emotional and intellectual pleasures important to human beings.

Achieving the first goal, the provision of sufficient goods and arrangements to amply meet the islanders physical needs, would not have been possible without the control of underlying conditions. More constantly emphasized that on the nearby mainland there was poverty, famine, overwork for the many and luxury only for the few; somehow this had to be avoided or the problem was impossible to solve. His solution was to eliminate greed, or in other words, to eliminate the desire of people for having too much of anything; greed naturally led to scarcity and undermined the island's major goal.

How is greed eliminated? Two principles were structured into the island's political life. Greed is, on the one hand, created by the fear of want; if people fear for the future, fear that they will not have access to physical necessities, they will take more than they need and pile it up; they will take from others, leading to scarcity and poverty. This motive was eliminated on the island by storehouses that were full of goods and open to all, so that there was no need to hoard. This provision is helpful but not decisive, for if people want *more goods, more wealth than other people*, greed will flourish anyway. More's society therefore deliberately stamped out false values by making jewelry a prize only for children and by making gold into an ordinary metal, used for ordinary chores.

Provision of human happiness, the second major goal, was slightly more complicated because it in part overlapped with the elimination of greed; but the politics was obvious. The island removed all lifestyle differences among the people: they all worked part time in agriculture, they all lived in the same houses – literally in the same houses, since tenancy rotated – they all wore similar clothes, using materials taken from the unlocked warehouses, and meals were taken in common. There was nowhere for conspicuous consumption to flaunt itself, given these arrangements, which therefore contributed to extinguishing the greed problem, and the lack of greed made the economic prosperity of the island possible because nothing was wasted in idle emulation.

The completion of the human happiness goal came in the provision of many ways to exercise the individual islander's physical and intellectual pleasures, with plenty of spare time because everyone contributed his or her share of work and no one was idle. Using this ample time for their own choice of purposes allowed the islanders to make whatever innovations amused them in terms of games, sports, travel, literature, languages, and the useful sciences such as meteorology, which also helped in knowing when to plant crops.

There is, however, more to extract from More's little island's society, because he also concerned himself with the possibility that the whole mechanism could be thrown out of balance by human conflict. Since he was an almost exact contemporary of Niccolo Machiavelli, and understood the dangers of politics – Thomas More would one day himself be executed by his sovereign, Henry VIII – he made multiple provisions toward ensuring that the island could govern itself happily and safely.

The first set of strategies involved reducing the differences between people; this has come up before, in the physical arrangements, but was amplified by social norms and customs on the island. First the islanders lived in public, and were therefore constantly observed by one another in the workplaces, at meals, and at leisure activities; children were socialized into obedience to their elders, and the elders were attentive to make sure the process was effective.

More's suspicions that conflict might arise even despite this social observation and training were shown in his simple but firm public institutions, which were designed to avoid any appearance of irregularities among the leaders and to quell any conspiracy theories on the part of the citizenry. Public deliberations were conducted publically, and discussion of such matters outside the assemblies was forbidden. In addition, the warehouses were all open and the gold was all stored in public. With such transparency, even congenitally skeptical citizens might find themselves satisfied.

The logic of More's island is laid out with a particular clarity because it is an invention, but as the present chapter and indeed the book suggest, all societies have their own, individual logic. The contribution of complexity theory is to encourage observers to become aware of this logic and consider its implication in terms of self government. If in a real society there are problems such as poverty or crime or inequality, it is common to deal with the problems on the surface. If there is crime, then more police are needed; if there is ignorance, then blame the school system;

if there is inequality, then tax the rich. What More's analytic exercise suggests is an alternative strategy, the study of the whole society and its bottom-up arrangements that lead to larger problems. Complexity theory provides tools that may make this kind of analysis more accessible, and Thomas More gives us a sample of how it can be done.

A BOTTOMLESS POLITICAL WORLD

It is not always easy to see one's world as a lattice, with oneself as a cell surrounded by neighbors, with everyone simultaneously a unique individual and an important part of a local or even a larger society, and to understand this complex field as political in its constant allocation and reallocation of values as people pursue their goals, values, and purposes. The discussion therefore moves from a plausible if fictional realm to an empirical society that makes these abstract ideas into a concrete image.

To search out the ways in which individual politics permeates even everyday human interactions, which seem on the surface nonpolitical, it may seem sensible to pick a simple society, in order to limit the task; but of course, no society is simple, and any apparent simplicity is an illusion created by our ignorance, as external observers, of how much is really going on under a quiet surface.

But while there are no simple societies, there are small ones, complete in community terms but living closer to the natural foundations on which human existence depends, and among these small societies, until fairly recently in historical terms, there was a community made up of the Iraq marsh Arabs, whose traditional bare-to-the-bone existence can serve as an example of the way in which individual women and men conduct their political lives in a world where there appears to be no politics.[34]

The lives of these people were documented by a visiting Englishman, who was untrained in the social sciences but had an intelligent eye for studying other people, and who entered the unknown vastness of this geographic area with a kindly interest in figuring out how it worked. These marsh communities can serve as a second illustration of human lattices and how political lives are lived in such worlds, using the wide interpretation of politics around which this chapter centers. Perched on the living surface of the waters of the marshes created by the Tigris and Euphrates rivers, these ingenious people lived full political lives in the barest of circumstances and are a case study of the intricacies of this existential lattice.

The classic account of this exceptionally natural political world comes from Wilfred Thesiger, a visitor who deliberately sought to escape from the "civilized" world to discover people he thought still retained the integrity and indeed nobility that he believed the modern world had lost. He learned to live among them, largely on their terms, and finally wrote down his experiences of a society that was built literally on water and entailed physical challenges few outsiders were willing to face.[35] Thesiger, born in 1910 in Addis Ababa, son of the British consul general to Ethiopia, reveled in the life of traditional societies as they slipped swiftly into the past.

The marsh society described by Thesiger was a pure subsistence economy; what its members produced they used themselves and generally had no contact with markets either in the marshes or outside. Their houses were constructed of common reed (phragmites) and were built on floating islands made of the same material – a tall thin reed that grew everywhere and could be cut, layered, and pounded into a firm surface.[36]

On these floating platforms the people built houses and kept buffalo for milk and meat, along with chickens and other animals. Rice grew in the areas made available by the eccentricities of the rivers' flooding patterns. The rest of their nutrition came from the marshes themselves, through hunting and fishing. All transportation was by canoes of various sizes, depending on social status; ranging from skiffs made from phragmites through the aristocratic *tarada* canoes with sweeping high-curved prows.[37]

These marsh people were isolated by their environment and by their own behavior. Outsiders were loath to even visit areas where living conditions were so desperate: flies and mosquitoes alone were so thick that even the buffaloes suffered. The isolation was increased by the fact that the marsh people were dangerous; they had acquired firearms by looting during World War I, and officials who traveled alone in the area were likely to disappear without a trace. Even the sheikhs who governed the tribes thought Thesiger was mad to want to live in the marshes, but he saw virtues in the people called Madan that others missed: stoicism, courage, and strength in the people, and a living coherence in the community.[38] His history provides an almost experimental case for studying the ubiquitous politics on which self government is based.

THE IRRELEVANT STATE

In probing a society to explore the dimensions of its political landscape, it is easiest to start with the most obvious locations and work downward into the deeper reaches of the lattice. What was the role of the Iraqi state in these marsh societies? In the period of Thesiger's travels, the state's impact had effectively been reduced to zero; it could not control the people because when it tried to track troublemakers they disappeared into the impenetrable labyrinths of reed; the state therefore left government to the sheikhs, leaders of great tribes of marsh residents, who claimed to own the land and paid taxes on it, and who exercised political power at their will.[39]

The state officials resented this, according to Thesiger, but could do nothing about it, at least in part because lower-level officials refused to live in the marshes because of the dismal conditions. The state had a law that all males must serve two years in the army, but when the recruiters turned up, sheikhs would report that most names on the list were either dead, had moved away, or were too young to serve. Occasionally a conflict in the marsh would be taken to government officials, but for the most part the common people preferred informal adjudication by the sheikhs, who were autocratic but fair, and at any rate were familiar. In state courts the tribesmen had to pay bribes and the city lawyers overcharged them.[40]

The next step in the search for the political, in order to see how deep and fine it ran in these apparently nonpolitical marshes, is with the tribal leaders. There were two major sheikhs reported in Thesiger's account, and they did the usual things: taxed the rice crop, forced villagers' participation in building dams and other infrastructure, made occasional rules about which tribes could fish in which waterways, and adjudicated quarrels and misdemeanors, carrying out their own verdicts. The sheiks were excellent farmers because they had lived in the marshes since childhood and knew the waters and the weather; in self-interest, also, they wanted the highest production and understood just how to achieve it, directing the waters strategically. Outsiders would simply have given water to those who bribed them, ruining the harvest.[41]

The sheikhs were autocrats but responsible ones; if one of their designated officials got out of hand and tried to exploit travelers for personal profit, the official would be dismissed instantly, without appeal. Thesiger reported that the sheikhs seemed essential in economic terms, since when left to themselves the common villagers would talk a problem to death but never get around to taking concerted action. This too is self organization from the bottom up: some people will take more authority than others, and those others will let them. In other words, it takes two to create autocracy.[42]

Having dispatched the state, which traditional political science would criticize for failing to govern the society it was formally required to control and perhaps modernize, and having taken notice of the tribal leaders, which traditional political science would dismiss as typical of such leaders everywhere, students of politics from the conventional top-down perspective would consider their task at an end, feeling their duty was done. In the narrow sense of politics, not much was going on in the marshes of the Madan people.

Yet such a high-handed framework would miss everything of real interest in the marsh communities where every hour of every day was political in the wider sense of allocating values among the various members. Justice was political, the family was political, religion was political, education was political, recreation was political, entertainment was political, food was political, clothes were political, circumcision and even urination were political. Tracing this network, this filigree of political relations in the march communities, can sensitize observers of more familiar societies to the wealth of politics in their own backyards.

SELF ORGANIZATION AT THE BOTTOM

Consider first the family, the central organizing principle in the marshes, a blood relationship that defined for everyone his or her natural allies and natural enemies, from the day of birth to the day of death and even afterward. Family considerations entered every individual's personal calculus in that they provided rules for behavior, and punishment – sometimes severe – for violations. Living up to these rules, the individual maintained the family's honor, its place in political society.[43]

It is an outsider's mistake to think of honor as an ethical or an abstract principle for these people; rather, it was a raw political strategy with specific practical uses. If a family member was assaulted in some way by an outside tribe, his relations would fight at his side to avenge the insult; or more accurately, they would fight for him *if he was in good standing*, if his family honor was intact, if he followed the political rules inherent in family society.[44]

If a villager had failed in this responsibility, he stood alone in his time of trouble; the state was indifferent, and the sheikhs had other demands on their time. Maintaining one's allied network was therefore crucial. The most notable example here was sexual morality; at the slightest whiff of impropriety (and life was very public in the marshes, with flimsy shelters and thin walls), the woman was killed by the family. In a closed community where flight was not a viable option, this meant that everyone, including the men, respected the rules that would of course, when they eventually married, benefit themselves.[45]

Gender relations in the marshes, once one got beyond this harsh basic rule, were political in a more interesting sense as a web of protection and accommodation in which women's preferences played a major role in the workings of the lattice. In respect to marriage, family elders had certain rights to be consulted, but many marriages appear to have been based on affinity of the partners. This was emphasized by several cases in Thesiger's history where young, discontented wives exercised their right to leave their husbands and go back to their original families where they were welcomed by fathers or brothers who supported their decision. Such decisions of course had wider implications in that bereft husbands would demand back the bride price, and in subsistence economies this might be difficult to produce.[46]

Particularly indicative of the way in which gender roles were open to political negotiation rather than being set in social cement was the situation in which marsh society recognized some women as men; such women were called *mustarjil* and were given rights normally allocated only to men, allowed to engage in war activity, and honored for service in this way. Some *mustarjil* married but were exempt from typical women's work around the home. Conversely, Thesiger records a case of a woman with full male genitalia who felt herself to be female and worked without any difficulties side by side with other women, who willingly accepted her. Such decisions were political in that they defined values, and it should be remarked that it was a benign politics, cooperating with rather than repudiating people who did not fit the expected roles.[47]

Justice was also defined by the family and was largely a bottom-up political activity in that wrongs were defined by the participants rather than by written law, and that culpability and restitution were worked out, sometimes minutely, by the persons involved. Settlement generally entailed exchanges that would in some sense restore the conditions of the victim's family prior to the crime. For a young woman accidentally killed when a householder shot into the woods at night, blood repayment required six women, at least one of which was a marriageable virgin. Even dogs could require blood money if killed, according to Thesiger. But the process could sometimes be evaded by flight, where the culprit fled to another marsh community sufficiently distant and hostile that the victim's family could not pursue him. In such cases the culpability shifted to the criminal's nearest relative, whose property and life might come under threat.[48]

Bottom-up justice was particularly political in the Iraq marshes in every man's personal imperative to defend his life and property on an entirely individual basis. Even positions of authority did not protect leaders when traveling or even at home. Sheikhs could be shot and killed, or their property blatantly stolen, while the perpetrators melted into the obscure waterways of the marshes, lost to retribution. Travelers in the marsh were welcomed to food and a night's lodging in the guest houses provided for that purpose, but the host would have to place a son or a retainer on armed guard over the guests all night while they slept, to protect them from thieves. Thesiger remarks in this regard that it was also well for travelers to sleep on their guns, since even their hosts could not be trusted.[49]

Theft was not always grand; anyone who arrived by canoe to share a meal with a villager carried his canoe paddles inside with him to lunch, lest they be gone when he returned. Horses were hobbled with iron cuffs rather than rope because chains could not be cut so quickly by marauders.[50] This battle for self-protection, constant and inescapable in the marshes, made the villagers' lives existentially political in a sense most members of stable societies have forgotten. But the counters at modern hardware stores, full of locks, are a silent tribute to this daily protection-oriented politics, in all societies.

BOTTOM-UP THEOLOGY

Religion was also political in the Iraq marshes, in that quite aside from theology, religion entails legislation concerning the proper or orthodox way to carry out various procedures and that villagers may have their own reactions to officially promulgated doctrine, as do religious communicants everywhere. While the old men of the community prayed regularly as required, the able-bodied worked throughout the day and negotiated with the rules, living with small rebellions that made life easier without seriously challenging doctrine.

In respect, for instance, to the preparation of food, especially the killing of birds and animals, with the farmyard animals the rules were generally followed, but hunting was a major contributor to the marsh diet, and by the time carcases were retrieved by the hunters it was too late to kill them in the proper way. In a tacit negotiation with religious authority, therefore, the local people slit the prey's throats after they were dead – a procedure that was technically incorrect but an accepted political compromise.[51]

Religion was also political in the marshes in that it could be used for self-advancement, much in the manner described by Downs as rational maximization. Religious eminence was designated by the style and color of the head coverings worn, marking either descent from the Prophet or pilgrimages to any of various religious sites. Yet when a family was seized by social ambition without the possession of the proper credentials for high religious rank, it was common for the head of the family to simply change the color of his turban, making a political claim that the neighbors recognized as inappropriate but to which they still deferred. Thesiger points out correctly that shortly everyone would forget how the new status had been acquired and the ranking would be seen as proper and legitimate. In fact, of course, the change was purely political, a tiny but gratifying coup d'état.[52]

Formal education in the Iraq marshes was rare; while people were wise in the ways of adaptation to nature (they could recognize different species of fish by the wake left behind in the water), they were not literate. The decision to educate their sons was political in origin, based on the need to have someone in the family able to cope with official documents, but the ramifications were political in an entirely negative way. "Few boys who had been at school were content to remain in their village"; their teachers hated tribal life and taught them that people in the marshes lived "like animals." If they could escape, they joined the unemployed masses on the streets of the upland towns; if they stayed in the village, they were discontented and bitter.[53]

The provision of services was also political in the marshes, and it would be unrealistic to hope that this does not also happen in more modern societies. Health among the marsh Arabs during Thesiger's travel period was Darwinian in that the strong survived and the weak did not. The marsh people feared the hospitals on the mainland where caregivers despised them and extorted bribes for what little treatment they could be persuaded to give; even local dispensaries were useless, as the officials overcharged for medicines that did not have any impact on the disease or injury for which they were prescribed.[54]

The society made up for this outside indifference to their health by having a total acceptance of their disabled or crippled members as fully participating members of the community; the blind, the lame, the crippled were integrated into common life with a surprising generosity that illustrates high politics, the willingness to give complete acceptance to people who were disabled through no fault of their own. The people could also be callously indifferent to others' injuries; in one case Thesiger angrily reported that a man gored by a boar on a hunting expedition was allowed to suffer alone while the rest of the party had a leisurely lunch.[55]

While the marsh villagers largely lived their lives without medical intervention, religion imposed one requirement where it was essential. Male circumcision was, by the time Thesiger arrived, almost unobserved despite the religious injunction because the lay practitioners did such a bad job of it, using rusty razor blades and no attention to cleanliness during the operation. The way these mal-practitioners held on to their trade among at least some of the villagers was by an ingenious political strategy, the invention of a series of prohibitions, that after surgery the boys should not smell baking bread, nor eat fish, curds, or watermelon. If the wound did not heal properly, the victims were blamed for violating the sanctions and thus causing their own problems.[56] Indeed, there are no simple societies! This pattern of strategic escape from facing one's own failures is a fully sophisticated game and another interesting example of the irregularities inherent in self organization.

POLITICS, PUBLIC, AND PRIVATE

Thesiger's own political contribution temporarily solved the circumcision problem for the marsh Arabs. With minimal training but with clean instruments and basic medicines, he became the primary provider of free medical treatment; in some houses when word of his arrival got around, so many people turned up that the reed rafts on which the houses were built sank several inches into the water. His medical services provided him with political bonds throughout the marsh communities, illustrating another of the many meanings of politics, that of providing services as a way of attracting friends. At one point he brought with him an air rifle that the people delighted in using to kill the bats and sparrows that filled their open guest houses, and Thesiger remarks dryly that "You can usually get on terms with people by helping them to kill something."[57]

The consumption of food was also political in the marshes, in that it was given and received under strict unspoken rules that defined status, respect, rights, and duties among the participants. All villagers were required to offer food to visitors; it was not a matter of friendship or of generosity, but of strict custom; reciprocally, the recipient did not say thanks for such hospitality because this would have misinterpreted the situation. One person thanks another for a freely given gesture, but not for a mandatory one. In a related act of local courtesy, the host did not help his departing visitors carry their equipment to the canoes; to do so would have suggested the host was glad to get rid of them.[58]

The villagers played around with the hospitality custom, inviting Thesiger to lunch at the home of a man in a neighboring village who was known to be stingy and reluctant to expend his provisions in this way; they did this with the victim present, and as he invented excuses, that he would be traveling or working on the mainland, his fellows knocked them down one by one, until he was forced to accept his obligation.[59]

Politics could be played in terms of how lavish was the menu; Thesiger occasionally complained that a householder had been given medical treatment, along with the whole family, and yet provided an inadequate repast when the time came for dinner. A more interesting case was the order in which the visitors were served, and the possibility of protest. Thesiger maintained relations of equality with the young men who paddled his canoes while traveling, and when a sheikh with whom they stopped attempted to feed the master first, before the servants, Thesiger protested verbally but when this failed took political action: he ate one mouthful of food, announced himself satisfied and refused to eat further. When he turned up again, a year later, the sheikh served them all together. It was a miniature case of war and demonstrated a tactic that defied his enemy while keeping within the norms of correct behavior, but also making the desired point.[60]

Everyday customs in the Iraq marshes have been used to exemplify the degree to which human life is political in quality, in situations where people are largely alone and free from outside authorities as they proceed in self organization. One final point can emphasize how private politics can get. Thesiger reported that even urination was inherently political: the men who had some education or had experience off the marshes in the towns urinated in the urban manner, standing, while the local men squatted. Since there is no inherent difference in efficiency or health between the two behaviors, the action of the townsmen was pure insolence, to show that they were, root and branch, better than the stay-at-homes.[61]

THE CONSTRUCTION OF SOCIAL REALITY

Ludwig Wittgenstein opened one of the most famous works in modern philosophy[62] with the words, "The world is all that is the case." This gnomic pronouncement is illustrated in the two small societies included here because of their ability to show concretely how politics inheres in everything people do, in the worlds they create. It is useful to pause very briefly in conclusion to ask what is a world and especially how are worlds created? Political sociology, in a work with the arresting title *The Social*

Construction of Reality, has provided part of the answer to both questions by explaining what is not necessarily obvious amid all the demands life imposes on people, that individuals construct their worlds in interaction with other people.[63]

This social construction of reality occurs not through words but through silent actions, and is literally social because people do not create themselves in some glorious psychological isolation but are created *by others* who observe and react to them. Social psychologists point out the obvious point that we can know others better than we know ourselves because of the unnoticed fact that we can observe them more directly than we can observe ourselves. As Berger and Luckmann point out, the other person is more immediate to us in that he requires no reflection, but we can only know ourselves through others.[64]

The pattern of social construction is so simple it can be hard to grasp firmly, but Berger and Luckmann provide a template: an agent behaves in a particular way, another person notices this behavior, and if the behavior continues, the other person begins to count on it; he forms *expectations*, and on the basis of these expectations chooses a pattern of response. If this response seems appropriate to the first actor, the two actors will repeat those expected behaviors when next they meet, and a small institution will burst into existence, based on this mutual *typification* pattern.[65]

As people and patterns of interaction build up, social structure – a social world – begins to stack up, according to Berger and Luckmann. Certain types of people are expected to act in certain ways, expected to take certain types of roles, and as these worlds grow, the participants build up symbolic justification systems. Certain types of people are treated more kindly than are other types, and reasons are invented to show how and why this is just; other types are dismissed as unworthy, and stories explain this. An overarching story will be invented, which must be "consistent and comprehensive in terms of the institutional order," a "canopy" to cover whatever arrangements have been made.[66]

Social psychology explains that these expectation-response patterns are under constant renegotiation, especially by the profiled groups who are not favored by the existing stories, but this bartering is implicitly hindered by the final stage in the social construction process, the point at which newcomers into the society internalize its norms, thinking them absolute rather than political. Such internalization is partly casual, in that people tend to adopt the institutions in which they find themselves. But at this point "institutions must and do claim authority over the individual," independent of the individual's willingness to shape up.[67]

Institutionalization is also, however, forced by sanctions imposed on dissenters, who are either scorned and ridiculed or, in the extreme case, threatened with expulsion. By this point, the social system seems set in cement, as something natural and normal and therefore right and good. Berger and Luckmann show how this happens between a married couple, where the everyday courtesies and tolerances are worked out quite informally to provide a division of labor in the household and the definition of acceptable activities. At some point there is a qualitative change, however, when children enter the house, because to them the institutions are not negotiable but permanent, something they think of, in their ignorance, as absolute. The world has thickened and hardened, it has become the world, no longer transparent, no longer to be questioned.[68]

Social psychology is not always as attuned as it might be to the political implications of this view of institutions as constituting the world of which Wittgenstein inquired. Institutions will favor some groups in society, fairly or unfairly; and institutions will damage other groups, because institutions are the result not just of civil negotiations, as the sociologists tend to label them, but also of coercion and everyday acts of war. For this reason the inquiry into self organization and into the possibilities of self government needs to be amplified with game theory, which takes a harder edge in considering human political relations of all kinds. This inquiry forms the basis for Chapter 3.

3

The Complexity of Self Organization

THE SEARCH FOR SIMPLICITY

There is a self-serving joke among political scientists that Albert Einstein said he had originally wanted to study politics, but it was too difficult so he switched his interest to physics. The tale is likely untrue in exactly that form (although there is documentary evidence that he said politics was more difficult than physics), but it makes a fair point, that dealing with human beings can be a marvelously challenging endeavor, particularly since the observer is part of the spectacle rather than feeling quite distinct from it. The physicist may naturally feel objective about electrons, but students of politics find themselves in their own microscopes, and this can be scientifically unsettling to the unprepared. That politics is everywhere, from kitchen to classroom to public service, is a difficult lesson for anyone who believes politics is (1) ugly and (2) done by others, usually with unpleasant purposes in mind. This subjectivity adds to the inherent difficulty of finding a coherent framework to begin cutting into the political pie and discovering its contents.

Game theory was intended to serve as this analytical knife for the social sciences,[1] and its entitlement to serve this function is increased by another physicist's use of a game metaphor to define the scientific methods for his introductory class in physics. Richard Feynman defined scientific method as "observation, reason, and experiment" directed to the understanding of the real world.

What do we mean by "understanding" something? We can imagine that this complicated array of moving things which constitutes "the world" is something like a great chess game being played by the gods, and we are observers of the game.

We do not know what the rules of the game are; all we are allowed to do is to *watch* the playing. Of course, if we watch long enough, we may eventually catch on to a few of the rules. *The rules of the game* are what we mean by *fundamental physics.*[2]

The economist Oskar Morganstern attacked the social sciences in much the same terms:

In studying the social world we are in need of rigorous concepts. We must give precision to such terms as utility, information, optimal behavior, strategy, pay-off, equilibrium, bargaining, and many more. The theory of games of strategy develops rigorous notions for all of these and thus enables us to examine the bewildering complexity of society in an entirely new light. Without such precise concepts we could never hope to lift the discussion from a purely verbal state and we would forever be restricted to a very limited understanding if, indeed, we could achieve it at all.[3]

TRIMMING REALITY TO ITS BASICS

Game theory and politics first came into conjunction in the period after the World War II when a series of academic innovations turned up in quite different areas of the political sciences, from public administration to American politics, from public interest groups to constitution writing, all the way up to the international system and war. Anthony Downs was the first to fully catch the political world's attention for rational choice and game theory, but there were a whole generation who took roughly the same approach and made major contributions to the logical analysis of human behavior, working with clearly defined individuals, calculating their choice of strategies under both everyday and exceptional circumstances.

Herbert Simon, a political scientist who later won a Nobel prize for his work in economics, was chronologically the first of these explorers of rational choice and theories of individual decision making, although he did not burn down the barn quite as spectacularly as did Downs.[4] Simon's work illustrated the inherently revolutionary nature of the game-defined method by flipping over its major concept, rationality, by labeling it as "bounded," and therefore depriving it of the aura of universality and really denying its adequacy, in its individual manifestations, to solve problems in a satisfactory manner. He hoped that large organizations might transcend individual limits and achieve rational coherence, but this solution raised further questions he did not answer.

William Riker, another member of this first generation of political game theorists, focused what he called "positive political theory" on

American government subjects and developed the remarkable "size principle," which he hoped would be a scientific principle equivalent to those discovered in physics, the discipline against which he measured political science's achievements.[5] The size principle was defined in terms of many-person zero-sum games, in which whatever is won by one player is lost by the others.

In this narrow context, Riker argued that rational players who had complete information would form only "minimal" winning coalitions rather than seeking as many partners or supporters as possible. The reason for this was obvious if you thought about it in the narrow terms of rational choice theory, because the winning side would have to distribute the payoff among the coalition members, and the fewer those members were, the larger payoff each individual would get; there was no rationality to paying out scarce rewards to superfluous coalition members. While Riker's principle did not explain results in most of the cases against which it was tested, where cautious men tended to favor large coalitions, it had immense heuristic value, explaining such political phenomena as racism and sexism with great simplicity.

FREE RIDING AND KANTIAN ROAD REPAIR

Another member of this first generation of political game theorists is thought to be one of the few academic authors who had a real impact on the daily world. It was believed, before Mancur Olson wrote *The Logic of Collective Action* in 1965, that people contributed money to public causes and public organizations because they supported the ideals or purposes of those causes or organizations. This "traditional" view of group theory, according to Olson, was based on a "fundamental human propensity to form and join associations."[6] Subjecting this naive approach to critical rationality, Olson argued that rational people would not join organizations (and pay the necessary dues) but would "free ride," because the amount of gain they might receive would be so minuscule compared to even the smallest contribution that participation would not be in their self-interest, which rationality requires them to maximize.[7]

The rational person contributes nothing and free rides because the benefit comes to him anyway. So when your favorite organization offers you a sweatshirt in return for your contribution, it may be a case of science making its voice heard in practical affairs. But anyone can do a quick scientific test of the theory by asking five friends whether they would have contributed anyway, without the sweatshirt. If at least some of them say "yes," then the universality of this kind of rationality comes into question.

The rationality postulate also received rigorous exercise with another book in this early political game theory cohort, James Buchanan and Gordon Tullock's *The Calculus of Consent*, which studied the construction of constitutions from the new point of view. The book brought into central focus an issue that had not been fully considered earlier, that there were costs to making decisions and that these costs varied depending on whether you were deciding on which poles to put street lights or on whose human rights were to be abridged. Using the standard variable of "externalities," the economic term for the damage that behavior by one person can inadvertently inflict on another person, as one dimension and the number of required decision makers as the second dimension, Buchanan and Tullock showed how a given decision rule could be optimized so that costs of both sorts were minimized.[8]

In the course of an extended analysis, Buchanan and Tullock used a typical economic technique to make an innovative point, by looking at an artificially small case of three farmers authorized to make road decisions for a neighborhood community. If the farmers were rational in the economic sense, two of them would by majority rule decide to pave only their own roads, and pave them to high standards, leaving the third farmer with nothing but muddy trails. Since common sense suggested this result rarely happens, Buchanan and Tullock invented a new type of actor, the Kantian, who was more ethical than hard-line rational, and paved everyone's roads equally.[9]

On the other hand, there are communities throughout the world, including in the United States, where the roads are paved beautifully on one side of town and hardly paved at all on the other side, and this tends to correlate with the type of people who live in the two different areas. The observer needs to understand that such situations are not the result of oversight or inadvertence, but are deliberately created, in response to a rationality based on ethnic and economic discrimination. Rationality must therefore be given its due, as the later discussion will illustrate.

THE MASTER OF COMPLEXITY

These early proponents of the concept of rationality and the framework of the game showed how revolutionary their ideas could be, explaining racism, free riding, and cynical irregularities in public infrastructure. These early game theorists simultaneously demonstrated that the concepts themselves might tend to break down when rigorously used on political rather than economic issues. Pure self-maximization might not occur, for instance, or coalitions might not be minimal. But the method itself was attractive in its concreteness, and would over the years develop into the approach used in the present work – bottom-up analysis. Rather than abstractions so vague that it was sometimes difficult to know to what they actually referred, the rational choice school provided actual people deciding whether to do actual things. The master of this microscopic brand of analysis was the final member of the early group of political game theorists, a specialist in the Cold War who clarified the theory's foundations, illuminated the degree to which political science must include all of the social sciences if it is to be effective, and who went on to bring complexity theory into the political field.

Thomas C. Schelling, winner of the 2005 Nobel prize in economics for his work on "understanding cooperation and conflict," would seem, from the autobiography he wrote on the occasion of receiving the prize, to be an unexpected contributor to micro theory, since his career had been built on government employment, consultation, and international affairs, particularly arms control; nothing could seem more top-down than such activities. But his concern from the very beginning was bargaining, dating back to the Marshall Plan in Europe after World War II, where he worked in Copenhagen and Paris before joining the White House staff in 1950, responsible for dealings with European governments over the creation of NATO.

This practical bent would combine effectively with the newly emerging game theory in 1957 when Schelling reports he read the classic text, then just published, *Games and Decisions* by Howard Raiffa and R. Duncan Luce. He spent "at least a hundred, maybe two hundred, hours" with the book and would shortly publish *The Strategy of Conflict* (1960), the book that marked the first phase of his seminal contributions to the sociopolitical sciences.[10]

Schelling's relevance for the present argument is nowhere reflected in his Nobel autobiography, in part because of his deep fascination with international crises. Despite thirty-one years at Harvard University and the years since 1990 at the University of Maryland, his writings are far from academic, dealing instead with practical international affairs, military foreign policy, nuclear weapons policy, and now global climate change and terrorism. Yet considered in retrospect, his writings coalesce toward a general political theory that brings out the breadth of the political and suggests strategies for enlarging game theory to fill out areas not yet fully explored in any systematic way. Schelling's work redirects a sometimes abstract economic theory directly into the most concrete questions of self government.

SCHELLING'S MAJOR POINTS

Schelling's general theory includes first his turning of rationality quite on its head, showing that irrationality may under certain circumstances be far more effective than is rationality in ending up on the winning side in one-on-one negotiations. His theory's second major dimension is its emphasis on the importance of understanding one's opponents and collaborators, and the recognition that this task may be much more difficult than we are likely to recognize. If everyone is rational in the idealized economic sense, then our opponents and colleagues can be assumed to be, happily, just like ourselves! If this is not true, but rationality is simply the sauce on a very idiosyncratic spaghetti, then real empirical science cannot be avoided.

The third major contribution is the well-known "Schelling point" in negotiations, already described in Chapter 1, a focal point defined by culture, norms, and personal experience. The vagaries of human cognition have now been popularized by behavioral economics, which demonstrates in laboratory experiments all the shortcuts human beings take in their attempt to think efficiently, and which can work to make behavior predictable again, despite the loss of pure rationality, at least if the observer can achieve insight into this almost invisible layer of social meaning. Schelling is also original in pointing out that much negotiation is tacit rather than explicit; people do not talk the matter over endlessly but may just act with their feet, and leave the opposition to think fast about what to do next in order to restore a status quo that has suddenly been stolen. As Napoleon is said to have remarked on strategy, "one engages and then sees what happens next" (*on s'engage et puis on voit*).

Putting these innovations together within a wider sociopolitical landscape brings Schelling to a fully developed theory of social creation and change that is essential to the present investigation of self organization and self government. Because he argues that whole societies are created as a function of these simple bargaining processes, Schelling encourages the observer to closely study the specific details of human behavior. A particular group of people, some of whom are large, some small, some kindly, some greedy, some fast, some slow, happen to come together at a particular time and a particular place, and depending on the mix of people, the proportions of the group that manifest different types of character and attitude, certain focal points will be found.

These Schelling points represent what the particular members of this particular group find acceptable as rules for joint interaction. This pattern is familiar from the discussion of Berger and Luckmann's *Social Construction of Reality* in Chapter 2, but Schelling adds the sharp economic flavor that sociologists do not always appreciate, that as people find focal points, some members will be dissatisfied or even furious but cannot find a way to swing the decision in a more preferred direction. So a Schelling model, which may appear peaceful, is in fact a boiling political pot, ruled by an ongoing permanent tacit process of negotiation.

NEGOTIATIONS AS ART

Schelling's importance for self organization or complexity theory can be summarized in a slightly long sentence: rationality is not a brick but comes in pieces; negotiations are often tacit and settle naturally on focal points deep in the participants' heads; whole societies are based on this process to which there is no formal end; and everything depends on bringing in the full panoply of contextual detail about both the people and the environment. Schelling brings this argument to life with the use of simple cases to illustrate difficult points. While all economists do this, Schelling's examples seem to have a greater brio than most.

That rationality is not a brick is central to Schelling's whole theory, from specific bargaining ploys to more general principles. The standard game approach to the concept is formal and cognitive, largely placed inside the actor's head, where there must be a coherent and ordered set of values that do not shift about, and from which the individual can make consistent decisions across all the cases presented for action. Schelling takes a wider view where rationality may involve one's hearing aid, and irrationality tells us more than we might expect about rationality.

"Decision-makers are not simply distributed along a one-dimensional scale that stretches from complete rationality at one end to complete irrationality at the other," Schelling argues. "Rationality is a collection of attributes ... Irrationality can imply a disorderly and inconsistent value system, faulty calculation, an inability to receive messages or to communicate efficiently; it can imply random or haphazard influences in the reaching of decisions or the transmission of them, or in the receipt or conveyance of information." Irrationality may turn up, he continues, in "Hitler, the French Parliament, the commander of a bomber, the radar operators at Pearl Harbor, Khrushchev, and the American electorate."[11]

Schelling thus defines rationality as an extended process with separable components: "[t]he value system, the communications system, the information system, the collective decision process," even "a parameter representing the probability of error or loss of control."[12] What is striking about Schelling's attitudes in this matter is that he is more interested in irrationality than in rationality, and indeed overturns the whole apple cart by showing that irrationality can defeat rationality in practice. This counterintuitive conclusion is spiced with a set of illustrations showing just how it works.

- An acquaintance turns up on your front porch early one evening, he explains an emergency has come up and asks you for a substantial loan; you politely decline to make the loan. The same acquaintance returns late that evening with bloodshot eyes, clearly drunk, waving a handgun and threatening to shoot himself unless you make the loan. Since he is clearly out of control, you dig out spare household cash and give it to him, willing to do anything to get this irrational visitor off your porch. Irrationality has triumphed.[13]
- You are arguing with a friend over which restaurant to choose for tonight's dinner. The friend is adamant for Italian cuisine, you are fixed on Chinese, and the argument has hit a stalemate. You are at work, and with a flash of insight you exclaim, 'Here comes the boss, I have to hang up, I'll see you at The Great Wall at 7.' Since you are now unable to argue further (have lost some of your rationality), the debate ends and you have won.[14]
- There are two dynamite trucks meeting on a very narrow mountain road with no shoulder and a steep dropoff on one side. Which truck stops short, hugging the cliff, while the other truck barrels through without stopping? Perhaps deference goes to the truck driven by the driver who has thought to display an open beer can on his dashboard.[15]
- The American president is negotiating a trade deal with foreign governments; if he is a perfectly free agent, it may be difficult to get anyone to agree to the U.S. position; if, however, he is under Congressional constraints and it is too late to convene Congress to change the law before an agreement must be settled, then the president (lacking the flexibility provided by rational adaptation) is in a stronger position.[16]
- Even the officially insane can use irrationality to win points; Schelling reports on mental patients who threaten asylum staff with "I'll cut a

vein in my arm if you don't let me."[17] Schelling also learns from his children, and any adult who is faced with a howling four-year-old will appreciate that in this situation the irrational child wins hands down; the adult will do *anything* necessary to restore calm.

READING THE INVISIBLE MAP

Schelling's second and equally subtle lesson relates to *focal points*, a theme to which he repeatedly returns in both cooperative and conflict-laden situations. Players of these sorts of games must use the infinite question series, "where will he go if he knows that I will go where I think he will go, knowing that he will go where I will think he will go if ...." The answer is simpler than the question, since each will go to the focal point, the unique point both will recognize as unique. What is scientifically interesting about these Schelling points is that they "may depend on imagination more than on logic ... on analogy, precedent, accidental arrangement, symmetry, aesthetic or geometric configuration, casuistic reasoning, and who the parties are and what they know about each other."[18]

Since Schelling shortly after this definition remarks that poets may be better than logicians at finding such focal points, it may seem he has thrown science to the wind; but as is often his practice, he brings the issue down to practical experiments, which he offers to anyone who is willing to consider them. For instance, "You are to divide $100 into two piles, labeled A and B. Your partner is to divide another $100 into two piles labeled A and B. If you allot the same amounts to A and B, respectively, that your partner does, each of you gets $100; if your amounts differ from his, neither of you gets anything."[19] If the conditions are fully understood, it is difficult to believe that there is more than one answer to this experiment; well-socialized Americans will put $50 in each pile. But if you were Henry VIII and your colleague was a courtier? Or if you were Henry VIII and your partner was Anne Boleyn? Perhaps there are many answers, depending on who you are and who exactly is your opponent.

The importance of these Schelling points in bargaining at all levels is that they are tacit, not put into words or official claims but encased in actions, invisible until someone makes a choice and acts on it. This leads to a third major Schelling theme, beyond complex rationality and focal points: the importance of thoroughly knowing the other persons with whom one is involved, in either type of games. "There are undoubtedly special cases in which one can suppose that the other player is like one's self in basic values and can consequently estimate the other's values by the simple application of symmetry. But in too many exciting cases one plays an opponent who is a wholly different kind of person ... It may not be easy for a British or French officer introspectively to guess how terrible a penalty would have to be to deter him if he were a Mau Mau or an Algerian terrorist."[20] This suggestion is not filled out, but does bring the discussion to Schelling's major argument in terms of a general theory of self organization.

Schelling's expressed intention in *The Strategy of Conflict* was to reorient game theory, but despite the reverence in which the book is held by an intense majority of its readers, it is not clear in retrospect that his audience fully appreciated just how far his reorientation extended. Well along in the book, and filled out only in a footnote, Schelling remarks that no clear line can be drawn between the psychology relevant to game theory and social psychology as a whole.[21]

This extension of the territory of game theory leads to the conclusion that whole societies, whole sociopolitical systems of the kind encountered in self organization theories, can be seen to arise from exactly the same processes as those present in smaller, everyday bargaining or negotiating situations. This highlights Schelling's introductory comment that his theory is "a mixture of game theory, organization theory, communication theory, theory of evidence, theory of choice, and theory of collective decision."[22] This leaves an observer of the everyday world wondering how it all looks in actual practice.

POLITICS UNDER THE SURFACE

Self organization is a natural process. It occurs, as shown by Thesiger's account of Iraq's marsh communities, where there are few or no formal institutions. But self-organization also occurs everywhere *within* formal institutions, where it fills empty areas in which there are no official rules or procedures, and indeed sometimes it works against the official rules, in ways quite contradictory to the legal framework. One case of this interesting phenomenon is the battle between outraged congressmen and implacable bureaucrats in innumerable Capitol Hill committee meetings, as they disagree vehemently and not always with civility over just what the laws mean and just what public officials are actually doing, or not doing, in apparent response to those laws.

Outside spectators may think this is a kind of debate between persons trying to find a defensible common solution, but this is a mistake. In fact, these hearings reflect an honest war between people who *prefer different policies* and are self-organized to implement those policies in defiance of other combatants. As George P. Shultz, former secretary of the treasury, once said, "nothing ever gets settled" in Washington. This is not a flaw in the system; rather, these apparently anomalous behaviors are evidence of competitor systems that are either struggling to take power or are established organizations, in power only unofficially but in power nonetheless and seeking more of whatever there is to be distributed.

The reasons for self-organized systems of behavior are sometimes obvious and sometimes not so obvious. One major reason for people to take things into their own hands is that there are no known regulations in existence. Even in what many people feel is an overregulated modern society there are twenty-four hours in the day, and federal, state, and local officials cannot fill all twenty-four of them. At some point, people find themselves facing challenges on which there is no available advice and they rise to the occasion by small acts of social creation, often making alliances with others who faced similar challenges and were drawn to similar solutions. This process will be investigated in more depth in later chapters; here it is useful to observe in a preliminary way how self organization may work out in the everyday world, using a case where it occurs not in an open country like the Iraq marshes, but in a crowded city within a well-established democratic political system.

A CASE IN POINT

The process of self organization can often be seen more clearly if it is caught at the beginning, and for that purpose it is educational to turn to a kind of case study of social behavior in one of the major cities of the world's largest democracy. India is a fully established democratic system, based on institutions and principles inherited from their British colonial experience, but institutions and principles that have been made wholly indigenous to the Indian context.

Their economy, after long slow years under a socialist regime, is now capitalist and prospering; elections are held and voting has brought about major changes in the opportunities for lower castes; the press is free, and the judicial system is developing. Knowing these outline facts, however, gives an interested observer a very thin appreciation of how India works politically. Self organization provides a key to these deeper questions, and a study of the city of Mumbai provides the rich context necessary to show how real people organize themselves. A case study by Suketu Mehta,

Maximum City: Bombay Lost and Found (2004), provides a rich load of data with which to understand this bottom-up organizational process.

The author of the study is a native of the city when it was called Bombay, and was brought to New York at the age of fourteen, was schooled in Jackson Heights, Queens, and did not return to the city for twenty-one years. His inquiry into the city he had known so well, and which had changed so thoroughly during those twenty-one years, combines the wide background of the native with the amazement of the foreigner, and provides ample material for a study of how self organization proceeds both for individuals and for groups.

As a journalist, Suketu Mehta concentrated a large part of his attention on newsworthy events, specifically the Mumbai riots of 1993 caused by the dispute over just which religious group was entitled to the site of a former Hindu temple and Muslim mosque in Ayodhya. But the depth and detail of his social reporting illustrates the exact mechanisms by which the very eccentric processes of self organization actually work themselves out.

The background to the micro-sociological events Mehta describes began with a controversial mosque. The Babri mosque had been constructed in 1527 by India's first Moghul emperor and was demolished by a Hindu mob in December 1992, despite prior Indian government commitments to protect the site. Communal strife increased in January 1993 over the burning of a Hindu family in a Mumbai tenement, and retaliatory Muslim bombing occurred in March of the same year. These are typical headline facts; what Mehta's study provides is a microscopic view of the individuals, entirely self-organized, who took part in the groups at the center of these events, and of the system within which they worked and which they transformed and used, as their games played out on this real-world lattice.

THE COMPLEXITY OF SELF ORGANIZATION

Relations between cultural groups in any society, including India, almost exactly represent the type of situation referred to as complex, too complex perhaps to fully wrap an explanation around, sufficiently complex that whole shelves of libraries are devoted to the history of the matter and the various issues it encapsulates. It is for just this reason that bottom-up analysis becomes so useful; even though it may not settle the matter to anyone's satisfaction, the simplification that results from getting down to real people engaged in real interactive situations does illustrate why complexity *theory* is useful in finding the simplicity at the heart of the matter, or at least some of the simplicity.

In the case of Mumbai, as brought to light by Mehta's challenging case study, the simplicity involves two men and a movement. The two men involved, a local branch leader of Shiv Sena and the citywide Mumbai leader, make an important point, that politics from the bottom up does not mean that everyone is equal; as usual, there will be large and small players. All that bottom-up models insist is that all players, whether in leader, follower, or midway positions, are motivated by their own personal goals and constrained, often severely, by the constraints that other players place on them.

At the self-organized center of the events in Mumbai in 1992–1993 was the organization known as Shiv Sena, or Shivaji's army, a group of Hindu nationalists founded in the 1960s by Bal Thackeray. (Shivaji was the founder of the Maratha kingdom in the seventeenth century.) The background against which the Shiv Sena emerged was demographic. Where once Gujuratis had ruled both economically and politically, with Marathas as their white-collar workers and servants, gradually under democratic India the Marathas came to resent this allocation of roles. As Mehta, himself a Gujarat, says, "The Maharashtrians were people who had been born here and were not consumed by immigrant strivings: a race of clerks. Their ambitions were modest, practical: a not-too-long working day; a good lunch from the tiffin sent from home at midday; one or two trips to the cinema a week; and, for their children, a secure government job and a good marriage."[23]

But times had changed. As Mehta observed it from a personal point of view,

All the time there was a Maharashtrian underclass, emerging, building itself. And now it had gained political power, strength, and a desperate confidence. It was advancing closer and closer to the world I grew up in, the world of the rich and the named. Many of the people on Nepean Sea Road were aghast not so much that the mobs were hunting out Muslims from the tall buildings but that they had dared to come to Nepean Sea Road at all ... The other Bombay now sneaks in through our streets, lives among us, doesn't like us being rude to it, occasionally beats us up.[24]

Shiv Sena organized itself against this background, focused on a hostility to South Indian immigrants who were said to be taking the white-collar jobs away from Marathas. Mehta argues that the organization provided an outlet "for the rage of the young and the poor ... The Sena needs to keep pace with the buildup of their anger," and needs "to corral it, stoke it, absorb it."[25] One generation may succeed and be pacified, but the others keep coming. This demographic background is important in drawing

the dimensions of the Mumbai political lattice, but needs specific people
to become clear, in all the grid's simultaneous complexity and simplicity.

THE INDIVIDUAL IS ALSO COMPLEX

Bal Thackeray is a useful starting point. He was pramukh (party leader)
of Shiv Sena until his death in November 2012, but his route to that
position was almost accidental, unplanned, an unintended consequence
of an eccentric background. According to Mehta's recounting of the tale,
Thackeray was the son of an Indian teacher, writer, and social reformist
who anglicized his name in honor of the author of *Vanity Fair* and who
had five daughters before being blessed with the much desired son; the
son's ego was substantially reinforced by this special status. However, Bal
was a major disappointment to his father who wanted him to become a
musician, for which he had no talent at all. Finally Bal showed an ability
to draw and, after studying front-page cartoons in the *Times of India*,
began to understand the dispute between the Gujaratis and Marathis and
started to contribute political cartoons to local papers.[26]

In 1960 he began a weekly cartoon newspaper of his own, and it became
a spokesman for the local Maharashtrians, who at that point did get state
lines adjusted so they had their own state. But despite this geographic success, the so-called Sons of the Soil still lacked jobs and felt that the available
jobs were being taken by immigrants: Thackeray's role, therefore, became
that of an employment agency. According to Mehta, the Maharashtrians
eventually achieved an 80 percent quota for government jobs, "but they
were always the lowest 80 percent, stenographers and clerks."[27]

This was not considered sufficient, so Thackeray formed the political party, Shiv Sena, although he professed to scorn all political parties,
including his own, as vote-getting machines. Yet self organization is not
done on one's own schedule, but is a continual battle against changing
circumstances. While winning the electoral battle at one point in time,
Thackeray then appeared to be losing the war. He had profited as an
organizer by focusing his group's hostility on, first, Gujaratis, then South
Indians, then Communists, Dalits, and Muslims, in that order. But demog-
raphy was running out on him, as the Maharashtrian population went
down to 42 percent of Bombay's citizens.[28]

Percentages do not explain Thackeray's stature but are only background
to his ingenious use of those percentages to achieve a unique political position. He ruled Bombay with almost absolute power until his death. Famous
politicians and business figures lined up outside his simple bungalow home

to pay their respects and ask for his support before daring to do business in India's financial capital. He governed through riots and mobs and the threat of riots and mobs; he ruled on a small scale, but rule he did.

How exactly is this accomplished? Standard criteria of intellect do not seem to prove relevant; old friends reported he had never read a book, and Mehta noticed that during his interview Thackeray's mind seemed to work either at random or by free association rather than by analytic logic. He did not seem to be clear on the geography of the state of Maharashtra, and was confused on just what the Indian constitution said. He claimed he despised all democratically elected politicians and took a stand above politics and yet was a quintessentially political figure.[29]

His talent was to understand Bombay itself. What did he understand? The answer was unexpected, at least to people who do not think like Bal Thackeray. Bombay is attractive, he says in the interview with Mehta, because in Bombay "crime has a good scope"; there is opportunity for pickpocketing, especially in the railroad system. Extortion is also a growth industry in Bombay. You simply telephone someone and make your demand, saying you will send your man to pick up the money; "out of sheer fear they will pay up." Thackeray notes that crime is good business in Bombay because the police-to-criminals ratio is low; you can commit crimes, even up to murder, and just fade back into the slums, the *zopadpatti*. Crime provides good opportunities: "You can earn without doing anything."[30]

Bal Thackeray's own explanation of his success is that he "gets things done," which means in part that he can adjudicate interpersonal conflicts that are too byzantine for the law courts. He analyzes during the Mehta interview a famous film star then under indictment and scorns the government for prosecuting the star with insufficient evidence; but if the verdict is guilty, then "hang him." As Mehta comments: "This leader doesn't waste time on theory or process; he advocates direct immediate action: Hang them. [This is the sort of] leader whom a young man, with little education but a lot of anger, can understand, can worship. [His] strongest support has at all times in his career come from sixteen- to thirty-year-olds. 'Young blood, young men, youngsters without jobs are like dry gunpowder. It will explode any day'."[31]

KEEPING SELF ORGANIZATION IN MOTION

Explosions must be controlled, but there must be sufficient occasions for violent activity. Thackeray's major strategy is to continually designate new enemies to keep his Shiv Sena "boys" busy, according to Mehta's account. Thackeray is opposed to artists who may portray Hindu gods inappropriately, he bans Pakistani concerts from Bombay, his mobs force theaters to shut down rather than show a Canadian-Indian film about love between two unhappy Indian women on grounds such affairs allow wives to escape dependence on husbands. Thackeray hates Valentine's Day as a Western gimmick, and his thugs trash shops that sell cards or restaurants that feature Valentine dinner specials.[32] This contrasts with his enthusiasm for Michael Jackson.

The proliferation of enemies is central to Thackeray's role in Shiv Sena. As Mehta summarizes it, Thackeray's young followers work twelve hours a day, are humiliated by the upper classes, are treated like sheep in crowded commuter trains, and are badgered by their families for every rupee that supports the extended family.

Such a man lives with a constant sense of his own powerlessness, except when he is part of a mob, part of a contingent of seventy patriots fighting for the country's honor, walking unmolested into movie theaters, posh apartments, and the offices of the cricket lords of the country, smashing trophies, beating up important people who drive fine cars. All the accumulated insults, rebukes, and disappointments of life in a decaying megalopolis come out in a cathartic release of anger ... The crowd feeds on your anger, digests it, nourishes your rage as your rage nourishes it.... It is not their city anymore, it is your city. You own this city by right of your anger.[33]

What is interesting about this description, in the present context both of complexity theory and the theory of self government, is the way in which it adds new dimensions to the rather abstract lattices constructed by mathematicians. Self organization may sound, to the uninitiated, like a rather civic enterprise in which people tidily settle their amicable lives in harmony. Mehta's account of the patterns of explanation that inform a cycle of murderous violence between communities is a description based on the full range of real human complexity, not in a sterile computer environment but in the real world, where all the most violent human emotions are engaged and on the critical edge of going out of control.

Bal Thackeray's behavior as leader of Shivaji's army illustrates a central theme in the analysis of self organization – that every participant, leader or non-leader, is in the same everyday quandary. Like the metaphorical cells in the lattice of the Game of Life, the individual actors react to their neighboring environments with a small array of choices made available to the particular field; and like those cells, their understanding of their environment is restricted to the surrounding conditions (Bombay is good for crime), and their choices for action (I get things done). It does not follow that leaders are in possession of any full understanding of their followers as rounded political actors. In other words, complexity theory dissolves unrealistic ideals about leadership and leaves observers with the facts, undisguised by illusion.

The theory of war as presented by figures such as Clausewitz assumed that the great general has an intuitive but perfect grasp of the strategic situation, as well as the genius to rally troops to achieve the higher goals implicit in the war. Complexity theory suggests that such an estimate of leaders is romantic and illusory. Shiv Sena cannot be explained by Thackeray or any other leader; it is necessary to work elsewhere on the bottom, and to become acquainted with the other people underneath. It would not be correct, as Mehta's experience made clear, to call these men followers. They do not so much "follow" as they play their own games, rigorously individualistic despite the organizations with which they interact.

SELF ORGANIZATION OFFERS OPPORTUNITY

The Shiv Sena figure to which Mehta's study most frequently turns is Sunil, a young man who at the beginning of the inquiry was deputy head of the organization's local branch in Jogeshwari, a Mumbai slum. "He was in his late twenties, a short, stocky, mustached young man with a certain flair in dress and manner." Over the next several years Sunil becomes a solid member of the middle class: "His cable [television] business is expanding, and he has also started a small factory making pens, a mango-trading operation, and, with the purchase of a van, a tourist business."[34]

The police use Sunil's good offices to put an end to minor disputes, and the government has issued him a Special Executive Officer card, which gives him "almost no power" but a great deal of legitimacy. "[W]hen he flashes it around, few people think to ask him what it means, since it bears the seal of the government of Maharashtra."[35] Sunil is also a murderer, which is what brought him to Mehta's attention in the beginning, when he was studying the 1993 riots. Sunil is quite willing to discuss the murders, which he feels were done during "war" and can be justified by the trigger event that set off the riots, the burning of a Hindu family when a bomb was tossed into a locked tenement room by unknown persons.

A member of the family was a young handicapped woman, and the battle cry of the Hindu mobs was that she had been gang raped, a claim for which there was no evidence either in the press or in police reports but which was sufficient to outrage the Shiv Sena troops and create a riot in which hundreds died, mostly Muslims. This triggering phenomenon is a major interest of complexity theory, where it seems to be a mathematical affair and is frequently illustrated with the bandwagon pattern of people joining a presidential campaign; the Mumbai riots were more perplexing.

According to Sunil's account, the interrelationships between the two communities were difficult to untangle. He reported to Mehta that once when his young daughter was ill and no Hindu doctors could help, he took her to a Muslim holy man in a nearby neighborhood and she was cured. "'He didn't ask for money,' said Sunil of the exorcist. 'Even if you go to their *dargah*' – shrine – they won't ask for money. They are unselfish in that way'." Sunil also had a Muslim friend whom he escorted back to her own neighborhood during the riots to protect her; but once there, the local Muslim men threatened him until the friend's grandmother talked them down and took Sunil safely out of the neighborhood under her burka.[36] Mere acquaintances were fair game, however; even people who had known each other as children or done business together in more peaceful time were murdered without pity.

ORGANIZATION, PUBLIC AND PRIVATE

How do people end up in mobs that engage in this sort of bottom-up war? Sunil illustrates one possible pattern; he himself can be seen as a self-organized system, a particular person with particular talents, hopes, and bitter memories, who more or less consciously puts these together in the person he becomes. As Marx neatly summarized it, men make their own history but not just as they please. Sunil was born in the slums of Bombay, the son of a poor factory worker. When Sunil was eight, both his parents were hospitalized, and because hospital food was so bad, Sunil would race home from school, pick up the food his sister had prepared, and run to the hospital; if he arrived after visiting hours, the doorkeeper would refuse him access, while happily accepting bribes from other visitors to be allowed into the hospital. Sunil drew a logical lesson: "If I can't do this, take my father his tiffin, then I can't live. If one has to live, one should live in a proper way. Then I realized that a man has to make money anyhow in Bombay – through the underworld or anything – and that even murder is all right."[37]

As a teenager, Sunil started hanging around with gangs, running errands for them, "watching and learning how men make money in Bombay." He passed the tenth standard academic exams on the second try, and for the twelfth standard he took the more direct route: he hired a stand-in to take the exams for him and was awarded a first-class degree.

After this he joined Shiv Sena and it became his family, almost in a literal sense, since the boys gave blood when he needed transfusions. This affiliation formed the basis for his further development. Not only can he now pay for his family's care at the best Bombay hospitals; if anything displeases him, he can call on Bal Thackeray, who "will phone the hospital, and they will fear him."[38]

Sunil provides Mehta with one graphic example of how self organization works in the economic sector in Mumbai, and how the different organizations and politicians around the city interface with each other. Sunil and two of his Shiv Sena colleagues are in the process of "capturing" land in the slums of the city. The first step is to find a vacant plot of land – any property that is not presently built upon will serve the purpose; the men's choice is a parcel of land owned by the railway company and intended as a dumping ground. On one side of the muddy lot is a factory, against which Sunil has built "shacks" that he has given free to laborers to live in temporarily.

The shacks are literally that: "two sticks of bamboo in front support sheets of cardboard, and lots of black tarpaulin is draped over the whole structure"; it takes about an hour to build these housing units. City officials have demolished the huts three times; Sunil waits until they leave and puts them up again; if there is a fourth demolition, he will replace them with brick shacks.[39] The right of the laborers to live, free, in these huts is enforced by Sunil and Shiv Sena; when Sunil decides to build permanent structures, the inhabitants will be paid and will vacate. If Sena elects a representative to the legislative council, the illegal slum will be made legal and Sunil will have acquired valuable property.

Self organization, however, leads Sunil to prefer not to wait for a Sena representative to be elected. Tired of the demolitions of these properties and others in his slum area, Sunil visits the daughter of the local member of parliament, "to tell her father to get the police to stop demolishing the shacks." The daughter keeps him waiting outside the door and questions his authority to make such a demand. He suggests to her that at the next election, a street riot could stop voting in the district for perhaps four hours; and since that particular district voted heavily for her father, the loss of those votes would be devastating, and his troops would only go to jail for a few months. "'There was a silence,' Sunil recalls. 'She said, "Come inside"'" and the decision was made, no need to wait for official institutions to act.[40]

The whole family can engage in this creative self organization of authority in a flexible environment such as Mumbai. Sunil's wife is not, he reports, beautiful, but she appears to share his interest in politics, and with a little encouragement will exercise it. She ran as an independent for the city council and lost by a small margin to a candidate supported by Shiv Sena and the Bharatiya Janata Party (Indian People's Party), its ally at the time. At the next election, the opposition will put her on the ticket or pay her to withdraw. In the meantime she uses the election to increase her level of political legitimacy.

When she observes, at a stand near her home, a rickshaw driver refuse to take a pregnant lady to a dangerous neighborhood, she asks a constable for help and is ignored. Sunil tells her to tell the constable she won 870 votes in the elections and to demand action. His wife follows this advice, and the lady is ultimately given rickshaw service, and the policeman is reported to higher officials for his initial failure to act. "'I made my wife realize what kind of power she has,' Sunil says." Mehta sees Sunil as "an exemplar of the capitalist success story."[41]

MANY ARE CALLED, SOME ARE CHOSEN

Shiv Sena as a self-organized process has a third role available to its members, beyond the leader and the entrepreneur; the local term is *tapori*, or street punk, as Mehta translates it. The major exemplar of this position is Amol, a slum resident, who Mehta introduces as the leader of a provocative march past a local mosque. Amol is a man "of impressive size" and one who has "the reputation of an uncontrollable hothead" and is "unmanageable when drunk"; he has murdered Muslims but, with the inconsistency so prevalent in Mehta's Bombay, regularly makes a two-day trip to the shrine of a Muslim saint whom he worships. Amol and all those like him prosper, according to Mehta, on strife. "They owe their positions, the respect they are accorded, and the living they make to strife."[42]

"Alliances must shift constantly to ensure that strife continues, so the definitions of friend, enemy, and human being are relative terms." The roles are allocated by the participants themselves, as each man evaluates each other man on his character and nature. Amol is a foot soldier or street punk because he is "too passionate to be a shooter, too undiplomatic to be a *neta* [politician], too stupid to be a *bhai* [don]." When a man's evaluation of himself fails to fit that of his companions, they cut him down; Amol once got annoyed and ran against Sunil in a local election, and Sunil got Amol's campaign workers so drunk that they did not properly campaign, and as a result Amol lost.[43] This is the hard edge of self organization as an informal process; decisions are not made by a single individual alone, but are controlled by the preferences of neighbors on the living lattice, and neighbors can cut down individuals without mercy.

Self organization falls apart if not constantly stimulated. Amol is reported as having lost faith in Thackeray, whom he feels is sitting around idly and in too much luxury while the foot soldiers are getting beaten up and jailed while obeying his orders. When word gets around that Mehta is going for his interview with Thackeray, the troops give him a message to pass along, that they are still "ready to die" for Thackeray; they remind him of those "who laid their lives down on a word" from him. But Mehta thought that there was "a hint of reproach in their questions, as if they felt their Saheb had been neglecting them, these people who had died for his love."[44]

DANCING ON THE LATTICE

There are two eccentric but helpful concepts available to capture the central themes of complexity theory while working one's way through the sometimes impenetrable thickets of everyday politics in the everyday world. The first of these terms, which has already been encountered, is the *cellular automaton*, which should bring to mind, as a model for describing real events, an endless lattice in which each of the cells is carefully watching its near neighbors and reacting through its small repertoire of available gestures to the circumstances it perceives. As the picture presented by the "market" guides economists in thinking about the world, the picture presented by the cellular automaton serves as a guide for students of bottom-up politics.

The usefulness of the cellular automaton as a metaphor for bottom-up analysis is that it infallibly directs attention to the infrastructure of events rather than to a superficial label pasted over and perhaps hiding real events. The label of "riot," when seen as a cellular automaton, disappears and is replaced by a collection of recognizable people with different and perhaps opposing complaints about the status quo. "Water shortage" similarly disappears when viewed as a cellular automaton, and is replaced by a mixed landscape of water customers who are using the scarce resource for diverse and perhaps questionable purposes. "Failing schools," when looked at from the cellular automaton viewpoint, are transformed into real students, some of whom are making great progress and others who are not succeeding, mixed with a variety of teachers, all of whom have different motives and purposes in the classroom. "Deadlocked democracy" in turn disappears, as a cellular automaton, into the world of particular men fighting continually for money and its hoped-for impact on their reelection. In each case, the observer is left to ask whether the solution is not more obvious than it at first might have seemed, when it is viewed from an individualistic perspective rather than from behind a top-down label.

The second of these unfamiliar but essential terms comes not from this lattice, but from biology – it is the *autocatalytic set*. As used by complexity theorists, the idea goes even behind biology, to chemistry or physics. If the question is how life got started, back in the very, very beginning, the autocatalytic set suggests an answer. Catalysis is the process by which a chemical reaction is speeded up by some component element. In the primordial soup, with many elements washing about in a random way, it might take a long time for the appropriate elements to find one another, to fuse, and to begin to grow; but if there were elements whose interaction was catalytic, the change could speed up and new forms be created.

In the human sociopolitical systems considered here, the autocatalytic idea takes observers beyond the simple cellular matrix, where everyone is the same and follows the same rules, to a more varied field where different events are occurring in different areas of the lattice and where, sometimes, these separate conditions and actors recognize that they complement and supplement one another, and self organization occurs. This may occur in an empty field, but most frequently autocatalytic organization occurs within existing institutions, to which its relation may be positive, negative, or simply independent.

As seen in the preceding discussion of Shiv Sena, a particular group of people may find that in the social game they have played for several generations, the payoffs are no longer as high as they used to be, and there is general discontent. In another section of the social lattice, a man seeking his proper place in society accidentally comes to prominence, and because his ideas are attractive to the discontented men in his vicinity, a bond between them is formed. The field also contains another group of people who have some but not all ideas different from the first group. These different elements act on and react to each other, endlessly, as the process evolves.

As Schelling argued, it is not possible to "solve" such games in the abstract, but at least some of the possibilities resulting from such convergence can be traced in the empirical world. The autocatalytic set is an important mid-level concept that provides guidance in understanding human behavior in context, as shown in the Mumbai case described. The next step in complexity analysis is to further follow Schelling's guidance, that the choice of practical strategy depends on a full understanding of the other people in the lattice, with and against whom the games are being played. This is the subject of Chapter 4.

4

The Social Complexity of Games

The understanding of a self-organized world and the basis for a better appreciation of self government both depend, as Schelling argues, on the ability to put oneself into the other players' points of view, to understand their reality from their particular position in the lattice and the story they tell themselves about how things work and where those other players stand in the larger picture of things.

It is generally difficult to understand other people, for two reasons. First, one may not *want* to understand them; second, one may lack the necessary tools to proceed on the inquiry, assuming one is willing to undertake it. Not wanting to understand other people is easy to explain; frequently we disagree with them, and our first imperative is to "bring them around" to our own point of view. If instead we tried fully to appreciate their position, we might be forced to sympathize with them, and this might be personally inconvenient. Nature encourages everyone, for this reason, to prefer mystery.

For the heroic minority of people who prevail upon themselves to be curious about the other folks they meet in the ongoing ubiquitous politics of daily life, the problem is the scarcity of useful tools for the analysis. Psychology should help, but B. F. Skinner's effort to make psychology scientific through the use of the mathematically defined adaptation model was almost counterproductive for many purposes. The T-maze as a metaphor describing human learning from experience, as mice, pigeons, or men make choices and learn from the rewards they receive or fail to receive, is remarkable in its ability to explain behavior in all corners of the natural and social world, and this chapter will return to adaptive learning in its conclusion. But to even partially understand the particular Peter or Paul currently confronting oneself across the social game field, it would be necessary, according to Skinner, to know all the actions and responses that made up their life history.[1] Since this is not feasible, it is easy to claim individual people cannot be explained.

Despair, however, is too easy a solution. While every human being, like every snowflake, is unique, they are not unique in every dimension, but are created in many ways by the societies into which they are born and within which they conduct their lives. Societies, as already suggested, are self-organized and coherent in the values they manifest. While particular parents or life experiences can be idiosyncratic, overall the larger society and its sub-societies seep through the irregularities and impose some stable patterns on the ideas and behavior of the people who live within them. Untangling the social influences that guide the behavior of specific individuals in recognizable ways is a major step toward the ancient goal of self government.

THE POLITICS OF SOCIAL GAMES

Sociology is a subtle science because its aim is to describe the bag we live in, and to describe it from the inside. It is Plato's problem of the prisoners in the cave, studying the shadows on the walls but without any way to escape, as did Plato, into an outside world of perfect objectivity. Two innovative sociologists have been particularly sensitive to this difficulty, which might be called bottom-up epistemology to emphasize its philosophical importance in the study of self government.

Erving Goffman and Harold Garfinkel attacked the problems at different though complementary levels of analysis, and each man was in some sense appalled at the ethical and social significance of the hidden worlds they discovered.[2] Hidden is not quite the right word, because as social beings, everyone participates in the behavior Goffman and Garfinkel described; but it is just that fact, that people do it every day, that makes such behavior difficult to see, to notice. Goffman's basic method was simply paying close attention to what went on around him; Garfinkel found it more interesting to disrupt daily events, in order to get beneath them; but in both cases the method was uncomplicated, easily available to the naked eye.

Taking sociology abroad, into countries and worlds other than our own, is educational for the reason that the study of people quite unlike oneself makes plain how much of what we do not understand about the other people with whom we engage, in games of self organization, derives from the principles of social life created by different cultures. Garfinkel called this by the curious name of the "invisible visible," that which is so familiar that it disappears. After a brief review of the sometimes surprising viewpoints of these revolutionary micro-sociologists, their methods are applied to two foreign countries that outsiders rarely penetrate – Iran and China, both cases particularly challenging to Americans – in order to test the sociological concepts and explore the logic of modern life in them.

Erving Goffman is a paradoxical guide to the complexities of social reality. His work was, on the one hand, unusually accessible to nonacademic readers; he published widely in the popular book market with works that read often like a neighborhood gossip session, revealing everyone's fallibilities. Many readers today react immediately to his work, feeling that he has exactly expressed how they see the world, although they had not previously seen it so thoroughly spelled out.

But on the other hand, aside from the anecdotes and the trivia, Goffman's work is profoundly philosophic, dancing back and forth across the frontier between illusion and reality. A graduate student at the University of Chicago, Goffman worked with major figures in sociology there and elsewhere, including a year at Harvard University with Thomas Schelling in 1967, and taught at the University of California, Berkeley and the University of Pennsylvania.

The major insight behind his sociological method came from his dissertation fieldwork in the Shetland Islands, where he was supposed to study social structure but was instead fascinated by the interplay between local people with each other and with the visitors, and the way everyone's conduct was, in a bottom-up sense, *theatrical*. People were not just living their lives; they were putting on acts for each other, dramatic presentations the purpose of which was to control the conduct of other people, especially the response of those other people to themselves.[3] In other words, Goffman grasped the ubiquitous politics around which this study of self government is built.

What Goffman saw on his Shetland island were rich folks tramping around town in fishing boots, seeking to convince the working fisherman that they were "one of them"; he saw crofters (tenant farmers) offering luxurious meals to impress their guests while eating very plainly when alone; he saw householders carefully selecting which alcohol (or tea) to offer visitors according to the perceived eminence of those visitors; and in a largely treeless landscape he saw people arranging their faces in appropriate expressions to match the house they were about to enter.[4]

DRAMA IN THE LATTICE

To anyone who has followed the present discussion of the complexity of self government to this point, Goffman's approach may not seem entirely new; is he not just bringing the analytical lattice to the Shetlands and showing what games are being played there? At the time he wrote, however, game theory was hardly a gleam in anyone's eye, and so Goffman worked out his ideas in compatible but distinctly different terms, adding the glow of the footlights and the roar of the crowd to an essentially spartan game framework. His first and major work, *The Presentation of Self in Everyday Life,* added immeasurably to the understanding of the politics of daily life and of self government.

What he did was to illustrate, ranging throughout the small and the large spaces of society, the many interactive situations that make up the structure and texture of the sociopolitical world and that, for this reason, give different groups different definitions of reality and of themselves as part of that reality. The fundamental dialectic underlying all social interaction is that "when one individual enters the presence of others," he will want to know the facts of the situation so that "he could know, and make allowances for, what will come to happen. And he could give the others present as much of their due as is consistent with his enlightened self interest."[5]

The basic Goffman framework is deceptively simple: it is first *theatrical* and can be applied "to any concrete social establishment," domestic, industrial, or commercial; this definition accords with the ubiquitous politics argument, summarized as haecceity in Chapter 2, that the same patterns occur everywhere, not just in official locations but anywhere people meet.[6] It is important to notice a slight, characteristically sociological shift in Goffman's thinking here, since while game theory starts with individual players, Goffman's dramaturgical world begins with *interactions*, any case where individuals exert *reciprocal influence* on one another. Where economists see people as stand-alone individuals, for sociologists the web of relationships wraps individuals closely together, constituting each other's reality.

In such interactions people enact *performances*, which entail co-participants, audience members, and observers. An established pattern of action will have *parts* or roles or routines for individual people. When any part is played on different occasions, it establishes a *social relationship*, and to such relationships are attached certain *rights and duties*.[7]

Goffman's examples center on medical institutions, where patients and doctors engage one another; restaurants, where waiters and waitresses and customers negotiate over rights and duties; lawyers and clients; sports figures. It seems a relatively benign social world.

What is terrifying about Goffman's model is not this simple structure but the underlying logic it invokes. If everything is performance, then it follows that we do not *know* anything about each other; our knowledge of all persons, including ourselves, is inferential. We take clues from people's appearance and conduct, according to Goffman, and from stereotypes about how certain kinds of people act in certain situations, but a particular interaction will conceal, will hide, the performer's real beliefs, attitudes, and emotions.[8]

Individuals in interactive situations need information for practical reasons; information helps define a situation, indicate to all players what is expected of them, and indicate how each should best act "in order to call forth a desired response." The individual wants to control the conduct of others and express himself in such a way that others will get the impression he desires them to have. Much of this interaction is tacit: Goffman's actors are defined not just by what they say but by what they are, or more accurately by what they appear to be. As noted in Scotland, even the expression on one's face can be decisive. In summary, the self "is a *product* of a scene that comes off, and is not a *cause* of it."[9]

PERFORMANCE AS POLITICS

Such behavior seems political perhaps first in the individual sense; Goffman's larger educational contribution is his explanation of how ignorance interacts with ignorance to produce sociopolitical self-organized groups. When participants to an interaction express their definition of its meaning, frequently these interpretations will be so indeterminate that there is no open contradiction between the different participants. Goffman warns we should not take this to mean consensus; it is rather that each person suppresses their own deepest feelings and projects a definition of the situation that they think the others will be able to find acceptable, at least temporarily.[10]

This produces a veneer, a surface agreement in which everyone participates and to which they subsequently feel obligated, and which includes a division of labor where each participant chooses, or is chosen for, certain roles and a reciprocal modus vivendi is established on the basis of this arrangement. This agreement includes the claims that are to be honored, and thus is moral in intent, placing values on individual persons that are settled but may (or may not) be open to further negotiation.[11] Goffman here amplifies Schelling's concept of a focal point in a curious way, since it becomes not a specific solution to a problem, but a bottomless foundation on which a group erects itself. Since the origin is indeterminate in this way, interest focuses not on the moment of formation, but on subsequent development within the group as its unprepared members are forced through history to find out exactly what they have created and what is their place within it.

One final aspect of Goffman's model needs to be emphasized because of its particular relevance to the sophisticated observer of governments of all kinds. Many of Goffman's examples of theatrical interaction come from a more literal use of the dramaturgical metaphor, so that there is a stage, an audience seated separately, and so on, not just two people facing off in improvised settings. When using the full metaphor, Goffman defines a *front* as containing standard elements of setting (furniture, scenery) and persons (appearance and manner), which are used by a *team* of performers for specific audiences who are excluded from back regions and only allowed to see the official routine.[12] This is much of what ordinary political campaigns enact, and they should be interpreted consciously in these terms.

In restaurants, medical establishments, and other group organizations, the entire team is dedicated to the correct performance of the show, according to Goffman's metaphor. The team is characterized by familiarity and solidarity; the team holds in secret any facts "that could give the show away," and works to achieve general impression management. The audience too has a major role in the show, since the performers must, if they are to be judged successful, give the audience what it expects to receive from the performance. This is a picture that should be seriously pondered by anyone who complains about the government they live under, or the politicians whom they support. Caveat emptor indeed.

THE INVISIBLE VISIBLE

Goffman's micro-sociology is a classic example of the ideas of people who worked toward a complexity theory long before the social sciences had even a premonition that something interesting at this level of analysis was coming over the horizon (a critic accused him of trying to computerize society, which is of course part of what complexity theory involves). Yet Goffman had a friend and colleague who took the inquiry even a step closer to the bottom.

Harold Garfinkel, who did his doctoral work at Harvard and spent his academic career at UCLA, went so far down in his analyses of human social behavior that he coined a new term, *ethnomethodology*, to emphasize that at the very foundations of our eminently political lives are frantically creative human beings faced with the appalling fact that the social rules are incomplete, that the rules do not tell members all they need to know to get through the day, and that if participants are to be successful in completing required tasks and fulfilling required functions, they will have to invent new processes. To make up for these missing instructions, the individual draws on tacit knowledge lodged in the world around him, patterns he is almost unaware of but feels to be natural and appropriate to the necessary challenges he faces.

What made Garfinkel famous at the time he wrote were his notorious "breaching" experiments, where he sent his students off with instructions to go home and act like a boarder, formal and polite as one would be in an essentially business relationship, following all the official rules of their society. Families were not grateful for this unexpected courtesy and dignity, but were outraged by these inexplicable performances, driven to distraction by this hitherto son or daughter who had now become a stranger and intruder in their midst. Other students were asked to answer the everyday greeting of 'Hello, how are you?' with follow-up responses like 'How am I in what way, please?' Garfinkel's purpose, amply borne out, was to illustrate how much of what people do is held together by unexamined group knowledge, and how ordinary exchanges between people depend on this underlying substructure. Only by "making trouble" in everyday life, Garfinkel argued, could we begin to become aware of the Platonic caves in which we all live.

From this point of view, "the objective reality of social facts [is] an ongoing accomplishment of the concerted activities of daily life, with the ordinary, artful ways of that accomplishment being by members known, used, and taken for granted." For meaning to exist, the event's participants must assume "that each will have furnished whatever unstated understandings are required" to support things. This may not be obvious or easy; members must soak up the silent social structure "from fragments, from proverbs, from passing remarks, from rumors, from partial descriptions, from 'codified' but essentially vague catalogues of experience and the like." [13]

THE INVENTION OF MEANING

Garfinkel went to great efforts to present this new view of the world in compact form, for instance the following sentence: "Socially-sanctioned facts-of-life-in-society-that-any-bona-fide-member-of-the-society-knows depict such matters as the conduct of family life, market organization, distributions of honor, competence, responsibility, goodwill, income, motives among members, frequency, causes of, and remedies for trouble, and the presence of good and evil purposes behind the apparent workings of things."[14] Normal people may have to read such a sentence several times in order to dredge up its full implications, but its meaning is perfectly clear: everything in life depends on things that are determinate but not at all clear. The challenges inherent in self government could not be better stated.

For Garfinkel, finally, this background knowledge is never complete, ambiguity is never entirely removed, nothing will ever be "accurate, distinct, or clear enough." This fluidity means that it is possible for a person not to know what she has said until she discerns how her auditors react; they may take the words and fill in a different background than that used by the original speaker.[15] One striking example of human creativity described by Garfinkel was the student response to a computerized "psychiatric advisor": the students typed in their questions, received answers, and heroically "made sense" of the answers as meaningful responses to their individual psychological problems. In fact, the computer simply generated random comments that had no connection with the questions, and the students' ability to find sense in nonsense was perhaps slightly discouraging for those with a belief in human communication. Garfinkel also studied juror decisions and concluded that the outcome came before the decision; in other words, that the official decision was defined retrospectively, as the jurors justified actions that were really based on their gut reactions.[16]

Garfinkel's ethnomethodological perspective is perplexing only for persons who have never been abroad or never gotten outside their own comfort group, because when people are interacting with familiar companions, in ongoing situations, it is more than likely that everyone is doing what is expected of them so no "breaching" occurs and everyone's illusions about the right and natural way to run a society remain intact. Anyone who is exposed to other groups or countries, however, finds long-established assumptions immediately breached on all sides.

The complexity approach, supplemented by such analysts of the human condition as Goffman and Garfinkel, provides leverage on getting to the bottom of these other kinds of political lives, clarifying the games they play and the terrain or lattice on which they work. Two quite different societies abroad will help in appreciating this process. Both Iran and China tend to breach American expectations in all directions, and are therefore particularly useful in understanding how different worlds are put together, and how open-minded visitors might learn to understand these worlds in the terms of those who live in them.

To begin the study of other peoples from the bottom up, sympathetic travelers are useful; they combine a preliminary appreciation of the culture and daily life of the country they chose to visit with the irritation encountered by meeting the demands of the local folk and their sometimes inexplicable preferences. Such visitors are not the last word, but they are a natural place to start. Elaine Sciolino was a correspondent in Iran for *Newsweek* and *The New York Times,* was on the plane that took Ayatollah Khomenei back to Tehran in 1979, and covered the country through the reformist presidency of Mohammad Khatami that began in 1997. Journalists are sometimes captivated by the countries they cover, and when this is the case, their reporting can qualify as both historical and social scientific in quality.[17]

Sciolino's first point of opposition when it came to Iranian customs was defined by her gender, a Western woman in a society where local women were condemned to wear the chador, the tentlike garment that shrouds the wearer from head to toe in black obscurity. As a visiting journalist Sciolino was rarely required to adopt the total outfit, perhaps only when interviewing clerics, but her human sympathies were completely engaged by the custom. The chador, like all clothing, is straight out of the Erving Goffman's playbook; it is an example of 7-day, 24-hour politics designed to keep women in a subordinate social position, The costume is deliberately inconvenient to wear, lacking sleeves or fastenings so it must be held in place with hands or, if one were also trying to carry a child, held in place with the teeth.[18]

The custom leaves women open to constant criticism, by officials and even by strangers in the street who feel entitled to proclaim that someone has failed in observing *hejab*, appropriate covering. Oddly, the chador was introduced by women, upper-class women who used it to proclaim their superiority in virtue; but the women Sciolino meets who wear the chador particularly resent this vulnerability to criticism from any stray passerby.[19] Sciolino devotes a full chapter to the varieties of female dress in Iran, emphasizing the variety of options women have devised to meet or escape the mandate, and she is personally infuriated by the custom, yet she is generally somewhat perplexed that the women themselves do not consider abolition of the chador a fight worth pursuing.

Such an unexpected discovery brings the observer directly to the central question in the complexity of self government: Can we understand people who are entirely different from ourselves? Looking past Iran, the seemingly minor issue of what women wear on their heads or bodies has provoked bitter controversy not only in traditional societies but across the developed world as immigrant communities grow up and seek only partly to assimilate. In Iran there are two different schools among women themselves; according to Sciolino's inquiry, there are those who willingly practice *hejab* and those who do it out of convenience. The reason behind these choices is different in each case, and students should note the underlying point that how a person behaves may not be a direct indication of a single underlying attitude.

THE DIFFERENT DIFFERENCES

The Goffman perspective is most effective for the type of women who wear the chador by deliberate choice; as he would understand, they do it as a performance. Wearing the chador signifies these women's full membership in a community, *and* because they can claim this full membership in the community, proved by their full adherence to its rules, they are entitled to the respect that is accorded such full members. People's need for social respect varies for many reasons, but for those for whom it is vitally important, adherence to the rules is an almost guaranteed recipe for success. Explaining the women who dislike the custom but have learned reluctantly to live with it is more difficult, because the outsider expects a little more willingness to stand up for their rights.[20]

To begin to appreciate their lack of gumption, Garfinkel's attention to the invisible norms of different societies is diagnostic. In Persian society, unlike many groups in the Middle East, when Iranian men seek recreation, it is usually to have a night out with their families, their wives and children. This is quite different from societies where the men alone gather outside the home, leaving their wives restricted to the household. What does this difference imply at the Garfinkel level? It strongly suggests that women are seen in Persian society as more important than they are in other regional societies; among Iranian men, women seem to be defined as unequal but important participants in a rich and frequently romantic tradition. This difference shows also in what goes on in society where the chador is worn: by being covered, women are allowed to get good educations, allowed to undertake careers, and are in general able to pursue their own interests in the home, whether these interests are artistic, aesthetic, or as entrepreneurs.[21]

Under the chador are frequently found women who are entirely modern, and who think there are more important battles for them to fight. In addition, those who attack upper-class Iranians with Western lifestyles frequently do it not for moral reasons, but for economic ones; religious norms give poor Iranians, who have no power in their own lives, the right to attack the rich.[22] The game is not sincere, therefore, and the lines between what can and cannot be done in Iranian society are fluid and open to constant negotiation.

Sciolino recounts a revealing one-on-one negotiation that illustrates the bottom-up nature of these apparently universal social constraints. During an interview with an ayatollah shortly after the revolution, Sciolino was wearing a chador while her Iranian translator was wearing "a sweater, jeans, and a head scarf." The ayatollah inquired sharply of the translator about her lack of a chador. "'I respect you and so I am covering my hair,' she replied. 'But there is nothing in the Koran that requires me to wear the chador.' At first, he looked at her quizzically. But Shariat-Madari was an easygoing sort of ayatollah. 'Okay,' he replied, smiling. 'You made your point.'"[23] The young woman's point was casual but classic; self government requires "a decent respect for the opinions of mankind," but not an abject submission that would violate the individual's life, or fortune, or their sacred honor.

GETTING BENEATH FOREIGN POLICY

If the attitudes toward women are a first barrier against understanding other societies, in Iran the second barrier is the difficult foreign-policy issues between Iran and the United States. As Sciolino remarks, for Americans Iran is nothing but veils and terrorists, and the dramatic impact of having American diplomats held prisoner from November 1979 to January 1981 has not entirely faded from communal memory.[24] The hostility seems mutual, and if congressional hostility to the country is endemically high, anti-Americanism seems to prevail equally in Iran. The situation is of course more interesting than such stereotypes suggest, and both Goffman's and Garfinkel's ideas give immediate guidance.

Foreign policy is inherently theatrical, and is played primarily at a top-down level. Individual persons in either country, as they attack the other country root and branch, are doing what they are expected to do; if they are leaders, they have been hired and are kept on in the current administration just so long as they toe the line (or stay "on message" as current usage puts it); citizens similarly uphold their native patriotism by sticking with the approved emotions. "Death to America Day" and the Fourth of July are similar in this sense; they are patriotic holidays and no more.

Bottom up, the situation in Iran is quite different from the stereotypes. Sciolino encountered the theatrical aspect of anti-Americanism when she was visiting Tehran's Behesht-e-Zahra cemetery for the war dead. The director, a disabled survivor of the Iran-Iraq war, gives her an enthusiastic tour of the vast area, which has playgrounds, benches, a convenience store, and a restaurant to accommodate the patrons. Hamid's pride in the many martyrs of various conflicts in the nation's history is deep and sincere. Later, when she asks for a ladies' room, he leads her to a sign that reads: "This way to the American and Israeli embassies," which is what the toilets at the cemetery are called; but her host is horrified to discover belatedly that Sciolino is an American rather than French as he had thought, and he apologizes, tearing up the sign.[25]

After they have discussed their families and personal experiences, Hamid suddenly suggests he would perhaps have time to learn English and to visit America, and asks, "Can you help me to get a passport and a visa?"[26] She is so surprised she challenges the likelihood of this, and Hamid backs down. But it is an interesting Garfinkel-level indicator of just how superficial his conventional social attitudes may be.

Among the Garfinkel-relevant dimensions of Iranian attitudes toward the West is the history of American and/or Western involvement in Iran's history, most of which is completely unknown to men and women in the American street. Sciolino lists a series of historical events, which, while invisible to Americans, are sharply present in the living memory of Iranians, starting with the overthrow of Mohammad Mossadegh, the democratically elected prime minister of Iran from 1951 to 1953, whose government was ended by a coup engineered by American and British intelligence agencies because of his nationalization of the oil industry.

Also on the Iranian list of negative background experiences with America are the U.S. role during the Iraq-Iran war from 1980 to 1988, where the United States "tilted toward" Iraq, and the USS *Vincennes* downing an Iranian civilian airliner, claiming it was an accident and paying compensation to victims' families, while the commander was later awarded for "meritorious conduct." Everyday Iranians also blame the United States for economic sanctions, for problems over Caspian Sea oil and gas lines that will negatively affect Iran's industry, and of course the enduring issue of Israel and Palestine.[27]

GAMES PILED ON GAMES

Micro-sociological tools help the observer work past obvious stereotypes about other people, but escaping obvious misinterpretations does not necessarily lead any closer to the more serious goal of understanding strangers, at home or abroad, in greater depth, as they perhaps understand themselves. Sciolino's primary role is that of a reporter for news media, and her chapters cover the usual topics, in addition to veils and terrorists: the security services, the state of the media, the economy, discontented youth, and so on.

The real contribution of her analysis, however, goes beyond the standard topics, none of which evoke the individuality of the country but merely run down the standard checklist of usually critical elements that lead citizens of one country to disparage the customs of other countries. Taking a more sympathetic strategy, Sciolino found herself fascinated not by foreign policy or religion, but by human nature; she saw Iran as an "exciting, daring laboratory" where experiments were proceeding in both public and private venues, "a contradiction, a traditional society wrestling to reconcile itself with the present."[28]

Her metaphor for the country, and the source of her title *Persian Mirrors*, was the palace with walls covered by tiny mirror fragments in a mosaic that has no putty connecting the pieces but exists solely because the pieces have been so closely fitted to one another that there are no gaps. Nothing better "captures the complexity of the country" than these mirrors, according to Sciolino's analysis, because they "symbolize purity and the light of God" and yet "distort images at the same time." "Iran can be dazzling and light filled, a reflection of its complexities, but it can also be cold, confusing, and impenetrable."[29]

Despite her appreciation of Iran's complexity, Sciolino brings to it a logical analysis that fits directly into the present inquiry: "It was as if an entire country was playing a game of chess in which the rules had been turned inside out. The game started once the king was off the board and the bishop and his pawns had taken over. Both sides were trapped in the memory that the clerics' revolution had begun as a popular one."[30] This "democratic" aspect of the revolution constrains the rulers, who despite their enthusiasm for establishing theocratic control of the whole society are nonetheless constrained by their past as leaders of a movement that overthrew a genuinely unpopular ruler and replaced it with a regime supported by the people. So control must be exercised gently, Sciolino argues, and is a kind of a cat-and-mouse game among all players.

Sciolino emphasizes several simplicities within Iran's societies that help explain its ongoing self organization. The first is difficult to translate, so Sciolino leaves it in Persian, *taarof* – it means "exaggerated good manners" between people, "politeness that when translated literally diminish[es] the self in front of others": "It says 'I am your slave' or most graphically 'step on my eyes'."[31] Strangers are often led astray by this code because Iranians follow it religiously. Sciolino's example is a Canadian who tried to purchase a hat, but the shopkeeper, deep in *taarof*, persistently refused to take money, insisting it was a gift. Shortly after the man gives up trying to pay and leaves the shop, he is arrested. The shopkeeper had turned him in as a thief. Both Goffman and Garfinkel emphasize the point: one must know the roles in the drama thoroughly, and proceed very, very carefully.

The purpose of *taarof* is obvious and all societies do it; people lie in order to keep the social fabric reasonably intact. The Persians, however, have adopted it as a general principle, perhaps as a result of their long and troubled history of invasions and changing political regimes. Sciolino listens to and reports the explanations given by experienced Iranians. "There's a hidden reality, a hypocrisy that keeps the peace ... It protects the dignity of the other. Architects don't build glass houses in Iran. If you don't speak of everything so openly, it's better. Being able to keep a secret even if you have to mislead is considered a sign of maturity."[32]

The principle could be inconvenient to Western journalists who simple-mindedly believed in straight facts. Sciolino wrote a feature story on Azeri cave people who lived interestingly in whitewashed caves with bookshelves carved into the walls, woven carpets, electricity tapped from below, and so on. Where Sciolino found the whole community charming, her official friends were unhappy with the story, which they felt made the country look not interesting but backward. A related problem arose over a story Sciolino wrote on a government official who willingly agreed to the interview and seemed pleased it would be published; but the next day he was furious and denied everything. When reminded that the interview had been tape-recorded, he responded, "Even if I said those things I deny them now."[33] Such a level of personal freedom should be educational, especially to people, like Americans, who claim to believe in freedom but have never considered taking it to such devastating extremes.

THE POLITICS OF REALITY

The principle of concealment permeates many areas of Iranian life. Emphasizing the idea that everything people do is political, Sciolino remarks on the politics of front porches, which are not usually suspected of political significance. American front porches, she notes, "face out to the street" and entitle the homeowners "to watch the world go by." Iranian homes, conversely, have "front gardens hidden behind high walls" and "no connection to the street life outside." Architecture reflects socio-psychological differences: "America's heroes are plainspoken, lay-it-on-the-line truth-tellers who love relating their life stories. For Iranians ... self-revelation often is seen as a sign of weakness, or at least self-indulgence," since no one but the family can be trusted.[34]

Sciolino gives a footnote to this pattern in describing an Iranian wedding. At some point in the ceremony the person who is officiating asks the bride if she agrees to marry the groom; the bride does not answer but the guests do it for her, with the ritual phrase, "the bride has gone to pick flowers." Only on the third try will the bride finally answer the question and agree to the marriage. The general lesson is that, in Iranian society, one does not ask direct questions, or if one has the temerity to do so, there may be no answer. As one Iranian told Sciolino, in many cases events are "an open-ended process and we don't know the answer. Even if we know the answer it is unwise to tell you ... [it is better to] keep things in the shadows. Improvise."[35]

This attitude of what can almost be called ontological delicacy in Iranians' attitudes toward one another, an insistence on everyone's individual privacy and on their right to maintain inviolate their thoughts and purposes, has ramifications in several important areas of Iranian society, from religion to civil liberties. While Iran is a theocracy, it is not a police state, according to Sciolino's personal estimate, and in an odd way there is a strong flavor of democracy, including brash electoral campaigns, rambunctious debate among members of an only loosely organized clergy, and an ongoing political scramble between press, government, and the public about just what the rules are, where the lines are drawn, and how firmly set are either the rules or the lines.

This is creativity at an ethnomethodological level, emphasizing Garfinkel's lesson, that even the smallest decision may call into play the society's whole sense of itself, a barely conscious set of intentions that in Iran is working itself out especially in the younger generations that have largely forgotten the revolution but are aware of its aftermath and the constraints it imposes.

THEOCRACY FROM THE BOTTOM UP

To describe Iran as a theocratic state, as is commonly done, is a typical top-down error in that it implies an orderly government based on a neat religious hierarchy, and as Sciolino reports, such a description is not a good fit for the country she describes. "Unlike catholic Christianity, in which priests are ordained by higher-ranking clergy, Muslim clerics [in Iran] rise through a democratic process – the consensus of their peers. A cleric can't call himself an ayatollah; other people give him the title, based ostensibly on the depth of his learning and the sagacity of his writings."[36]

Clerics are largely self-selected religious scholars who attend religious seminars in Qom or Mashad and follow a course of study that may take twenty years. "Contrary to the perception outside Iran that religious truth is monolithic and that dissent is not tolerated, one of the defining traits of Shiism is its emphasis on argument. Clerics are encouraged and expected to challenge interpretations of the Koran, even those of the most learned ayatollahs, in the hope that new and better interpretations may emerge."[37]

The Goffman-Garfinkel interactions this background provokes are illustrated in the case of Ayatollah Hosein-Ali Montazeri, from his student days a close confidant of Ayatollah Khomeini, who made the 1980 revolution. The tie was so close and enduring that Montazeri was to be Khomeini's successor, but over the years, while Montazeri remained orthodox on Iranian foreign affairs (the United States was the Great Satan), he began to be critical on domestic policy, openly chastising the regime for failures in the economy, injustices in society, and excessive violence in suppressing dissent.

From 1989 onward, therefore, Montazeri was cast out of the government and became a non-person, living under partial house arrest in his modest home in Qom. Despite his sequestration, however, Montazeri was not silenced, in 1997 openly criticizing the current leader. By 1999 he was considered so dangerous that newspapers were not allowed to print his picture or mention his name.[38] Yet his messages continued to circulate, up to his death in 2009, at home, of natural causes. It seemed, in some sense, a distinct separation of church and state, and provided support for the present argument, that events look different when taken from the bottom rather than the top.

BE CAREFUL WHAT YOU WORK FOR

The degree to which relations between the Iranian government and the Iranian people are dynamically political rather than autocratic is also shown in two other areas of daily life: the battles waged over the news media and over the rights and demands of students and other young people. In each case Sciolino links behavior patterns to her earlier point about the fluidity of rules in Iran, based on the culture's Garfinkel-like appreciation of the hidden dimensions of social understanding between people. In general, she argues, Iranians expect to have their privacy respected and, in general, the regime honors this expectation; the issue is just where the line between private and public is drawn at any given point in time. While the Islamic Republic was initially supposed to abolish censorship, this opening was frequently closed by conservative forces in the society, but the debate was closely argued and the winners varied.

Early on in the revolutionary period, a newspaper leaked the report of a top secret security meeting, quoting a general of the Revolutionary Guard in some incautious remarks about clerics; in the ensuing uproar, the state claimed this had violated the general's freedom of speech – "a position rich in irony and portending even more daring challenges to the official line. Unwittingly, it conceded a point most important to any journalist, namely that there is a right to free speech in the first place."[39] Most helpful to protesters of all sorts was the absence of central control, shown in the way a court could shut down a newspaper one day and have the Ministry of Islamic Guidance issue it a new license to open under a different name on the following day.

Iranian students and young people are also deeply engaged in a politics that is interactive rather than confrontational, although it is the public battles that get attention from the international media. Sciolino's report on Iran concluded with the period under the reformist president Mohammad Khatami (1997–2005), so her expectations were perhaps higher than they would be today, but she found little real resistance against the basic Iranian constitution and the rule of the clerics it enforces; the young people's concern was rather with economics, their inability to get jobs and the resulting barrier this created to marriage because they could not afford to set up households independent of their parents.[40] The problem may be irresolvable because it is so tied to the stranglehold of the conservative clerics and bazaari merchants on the economic system, which benefits them by protecting them from the competition of the international market.

Given this, the young are creative, finding niches within the existing system. Others simply vote with their feet; even children of the ruling clerics have fled to the United States. That even harsh, rigorously applied punishment to keep the young safe from Western influences may fail and even be counterproductive is suggested by Sciolino's theory that the clerics' ban on public dating drives the young into private spaces and "encourages young people who might have dated casually to have sexual intercourse because an active sexual life is one way young people can rebel against the system."[41] Such a course of action cheerfully makes the game theorists' point, of course, that the outcome of one's act cannot be calculated without full study of the persons against whom one tries to prevail.

GRASSROOTS POLITICS IN CHINA

A second exercise in the understanding of people quite unlike ourselves, aided by some classic masters of social theory, involves China. Again top-down concepts are worse than useless, since the handy label of "communism" simply suggests Stalin, Khrushchev, and other Cold War stereotypes that are barriers to understanding actual events. The participant observer who provides raw data for this study is a Peace Corps volunteer who was assigned to a teachers' college in a small city in Sichuan Province, in the west of the country, far from major coastal cities. Data from such a source over a period of two years of service there allows study of the more private lives of the people involved, but much of the larger picture as well.[42]

Peter Hessler and his Peace Corps colleague turn up in Fuling on the sixtieth anniversary of the Long March, the trek the communist revolutionary leaders made in 1936 to escape their enemies in the civil war. The celebration of this event is pure Goffman, students bravely attempting the thousand-mile journey, with only sixteen young survivors successfully completing the challenge and being welcomed by communist officials with as many bells and whistles as possible.[43] The implicit politics is of course present: women students were not allowed to participate, ostensibly to protect their more fragile selves but more strategically to protect the men students, who would be embarrassed if they failed while a woman succeeded.

The two Peace Corps volunteers, who would teach English at the school, began their stay with various confrontations with the Party officials. They were given the best apartments in the building, along with telephones, their own washing machines, and other luxuries. They had to fight off the Party's attempt to "give" them tennis also, since it would have evicted players from a neighborhood bowling green. The apparent generosity of the Party officials at the college was again not to be taken at its surface value but was a form of bragging: we can give

you anything that a capitalist might wish for, so do not dare to feel superior! This cynical interpretation was buttressed by the officials' other
behavior, which was to forbid the English-speaking Chinese faculty
at the school to have any communication at all with the Peace Corps
teachers; once when an invitation to dinner was actually extended,
officials shut down the road leading to the host's home so that the visit
never took place.[44]

As Hessler wrote of their arrival, "politics was everywhere you
looked." The welcoming banquets were also political drinking matches
among the men, and although the Peace Corps warned volunteers to
stay out of these events, Hessler and his colleague could not resist joining and ultimately gained considerable respect for being able to drink
their Chinese colleagues under the table, the Chinese apparently having
a genetic intolerance for alcohol, which gave the Americans an easy win.
Chinese participants who failed to drink up to the local standard were
bullied, scorned as no better than women, and mocked viciously and
repeatedly.[45]

The theatrical aspect of interpersonal behavior emphasized by
Goffman's writings was evident also in the students' behavior, at least
at the beginning. Hong Kong was returned to Chinese control during
Hessler's time in Fuling, and this triumph turned up in student essays
on topics such as "the happiest day of my life." The Opium Wars of the
nineteenth century were also a sensitive topic because they represented a
humiliation of the Chinese nation that did not just rankle as an historical
issue but was painfully felt as a contemporary, lively injustice.[46]

In the other direction, Chinese students were wont to criticize
American race relations and comment about immoral American women.
During English classes the characters usually characterized as buffoons
in Shakespeare's plays were redefined as noble peasants; but when they
came to Rosencranz and Guildenstern, the students understood the situation instantly because they were familiar with tropes of betrayal.[47]

A painful difference in the structure of teaching struck Hessler during
his two-year lessons in Chinese, when any mistake he made with the language was cut down with "*budui*" meaning "wrong," even if some parts
of the answer were correct. Hessler found this bitter. "It was the Chinese
way. Success was expected and failure criticized and promptly corrected.
You were right or you were *budui*; there was no middle ground." As an
American, however, he longed for the American way: "I was accustomed
to having my ego soothed; I wanted to be praised for my effort." His students had the reverse problem; when he praised them for making "a good

effort," they found it meaningless; if a student was wrong, he believed he or she needed to be corrected, without softening it with irrelevant praise.[48]

THE CLASH OF CIVILIZATIONS

Beyond the theatrical aspects of social interaction the two Peace Corps volunteers encountered in their two years in Fuling was their own Garfinkel role: they "created trouble" everywhere just by being utterly unfamiliar to everyone. First of all they learned what it felt like to be stared at constantly, even when they were not doing anything that seemed to them unusual. At the ceremony celebrating the Long March they stopped by in shorts and t-shirts on the way to a hike, but everyone could not stop looking at them, so the mayor put them on stage, in their informal dress, among everyone else dressed formally. Along with this, people who stared did not necessarily see them. A student commented on Hessler's blue eyes; the interesting point was that he had hazel eyes – but he was a Westerner and don't they all have blue eyes, unlike us?

On the street, local toughs screamed *waiguoren* (stinking foreigners) when they saw the Americans, but more respectable Chinese gave the volunteers no sympathy for this lack of decency; they should understand the men were ignorant. Outside the college, however, most ordinary Chinese were interested in talking with Hessler and often had opinions untouched by Party discipline. One former student, who had been dismissed from school because he participated in demonstrations instead went into business for himself and made an excellent living as an entrepreneur.[49] Other ordinary citizens commented that Hong Kong was rich only because mainland China had no opportunity to interfere with its rapid development, illustrating the difficulty, even in Communist China, of getting people to see things correctly.

Hessler's real contribution to understanding Chinese life from the bottom up, however, is his close relations with the students in his college classes. Getting to know them was a slow process, since they were unfamiliar with Westerners and tended to rely on formal rules in dealing with him and his classes. They were treated rigorously by the college, being fined for minor infractions and being required to do nonacademic work like cleaning the classrooms. And while tuition was free, if the students did not go into government schools to teach upon graduation, they would have to pay back their tuition.

The students followed these rules willingly and worked hard because, as Hessler noted, it was better than life outside school; if they had not passed the entrance examinations and been accepted, they would have been mere peasants, living miles from any city or even any transportation, working the muddy countryside for a hazardous level of subsistence. The students were accustomed to rote learning, but Hessler liked them because of their honesty, their ability to study poetry and drama for its beauty, as contrasted with American students he had encountered, who seemed jaded and cynical.

Since he was teaching an English class, it was natural for the students to be assigned essays. Sometime his assignments went amusingly wrong; one time, in a moment of impatience, Hessler told them to write "anything you want," and in return got lists of clothes, appliances, and other things on a young person's wish list. But more importantly, these essays gave him direct access to the visible but invisible areas of their past, areas that defined their present. One set of essays, written late in his tenure at the college, detailed the students' parents and grandparents and the brutal and bitter lives they had led, during famine, Cultural Revolution, and changes in Beijing leadership; family members starved to death, a grandfather was shot by Communists because he owned some small piece of land, people survived by eating pine needles.

He could not grade such papers, Hessler said, because they were too sad, nor did he have the heart to return the papers with the usual critical comments. Such personal political histories made plain much about China that might be mysterious to those without access to this past. The Chinese call the common people Old Hundred Names, and one acquaintance told him: "Many Americans think there are problems with human rights here. In fact, Old Hundred Names doesn't care about that. Old Hundred Names worries about eating, about having enough clothes," certainly not about democracy.[50]

OLD HUNDRED NAMES

The college people in Fuling did not care much about democracy either; peasants, they felt, were too ignorant to vote; and anyway the common people had learned, throughout past history, to go along with the higher authorities, whomever those authorities were. At the time Hessler was in Fuling, the Three Gorges dam was scheduled to be completed in the near future and would flood much of the city, but there were no protests. People had been told it was beneficial and they trusted that this was true, although there would be major changes to cultural artifacts and to the environment. Debate had been encouraged in the 1980s, Hessler reported, but the leaders grew "tired of" this kind of democracy and just went ahead with the project on their own.[51]

Hessler was befriended by a representative Chinese family who ran a local noodle shop just outside the college campus, and who prospered in a moderate but regular way by minding their own business, literally. When changes occurred above them in the social hierarchy, they adapted, reducing other expenses when faced with being charged a higher rent; when opportunities offered themselves they seized them, getting a driver's licence in hopes of someday opening a taxi business; and in respect to their existing business, they worked hard and long and carefully. Hessler remarked: "Their world is small, but they take good care of it."[52]

Hessler met only one dissident among his students, and while he had imagined, before going to Fuling "that they were noble characters – charismatic, intelligent, farsighted, brave," in fact this did not prove true. His "best students … were the ones who had been recruited long ago as Party Members … [it] was good for your career, and in any case all of the students seemed to think that it was good to be patriotic in the narrow way that they were told to be." His only dissident "was a loser. He was a bad student, and he was socially awkward. He had no friends" and it "was hard to imagine" any big changes being made by such people.[53]

By his second year at the college, Hessler's Chinese language skills had improved to the point where he could engage in discussion with his students, and their relations tended to change radically because of this difference. Anything sensitive could be said in Chinese but not in English because it was constrained by its classroom flavor. The students proved quite capable of criticizing the Party for breaking Goffman-type rules while putting up with official ones. When Hessler's Peace Corps associate was visited by his parents, the officials were rude, refusing quite arbitrarily to allow the father to lecture on agriculture before the class. Since respect for parents is a major rule in Chinese culture, the students felt badly about this.

A more general problem emerged at the end of Hessler's tenure when the students put together a drama for presentation to other classes. His friend's Spanish class put together a skit based on Don Quixote, which featured a student playing Lei Feng, a worker-martyr with selfless devotion to Chairman Mao, who charged off across the staged countryside fighting injustice and attacking various windmills and tigers; he recruits a Sancho Panza by offering him Taiwan as a reward. This raucous parody leaves the audience laughing helplessly, while the Party chairman only smiles and next day vetoes presentation of the skit at the general competition.

The students, who thoroughly enjoyed their creativity, were sufficiently cross at the Party decision to complain, a very unusual course of action among students who were constantly trained in following the official rules. After a week's negotiation the Party decided that the skit could be presented, but only to the English department and with expurgations. The students accepted the compromise, but at the end dedicated the whole exercise to their two American teachers, speaking so quickly that the party cadres did not catch what they were saying.[54] It forms an interesting example of the Garfinkel creativity that will bubble up, notwithstanding communist discipline, even in a small city in a distant province.

LIFE AND DEATH IN THE T-MAZE

Thinking about the ways in which the members of different societies interact in the process of *becoming members* of those societies, it is clear that rational choice theory, so dear to the hearts of game theorists, needs to be broadened to fit cases of simple learning. Where game theory tends to focus on situations that are reasonably clear and relatively important, much sociopolitical behavior is smaller and fuzzier, as Schelling, Goffman, and Garfinkel have all emphasized. Behavior at this level is certainly rational but the circumstances are different. Where rational choice assumes a supermarket model with each of the options laid out, carefully labeled as to cost, and with a cashier available to gladly trade the chosen good for the labeled price, in the bottom-up world it is not always clear (1) what the options are, (2) what their cost is, and (3) whether you are an acceptable buyer.

The alternate model of rationality is built on the T-maze used by experimental psychologists to torment mice and pigeons and thereby increase human beings' understanding of themselves and their learning behavior. The T-maze typically consists of one runway leading to another at right angles to the first; at the end of each arm of the cross-piece are moveable doors that are designed to hide whatever is outside that door. The exploring traveler in this maze must then make its choice without any immediate information on whether one or the other arm of the T leads to a reward, a punishment, or nothing at all. This environmental structure is of course very similar to everyday reality, where it is difficult to know just what the results of behavior will be, sometimes even when the situation is familiar.[55]

Most people instinctively recoil from the idea that their individual behavior can be explained mathematically, but the behavioral psychologists who study animals have made a strong case for this argument, and it directly simplifies the issue of just how people make the decisions that comprise their self government. As is now familiar from complexity theory, the individuals described by the adaptation model can be described with great economy, using one probability and two coefficients. The basic probability that describes an inmate of the psychologists' T-maze is the one describing whether the creature is more likely to turn right or left, depending on the results of past turns and the rewards found there. The two coefficients relate to the speed of the subject's learning, which is different depending on whether it succeeds or fails.

Since the subject cannot see what rewards are present outside the doors, the probability of going right or left in the T-maze, or of making choices in everyday matters, is based on past experience, so that if earlier trials in the maze tended to produce rewards for turning right, the subject will have, at any point along the way, perhaps a 0.75 probability of continuing to go right. Along with this probability, two coefficients complete the job: the rate of learning from success and the rate of learning from failure. In everyday terms, if someone learns slowly from success, they are pessimists; whatever the reward, *this time* they don't think it will continue. If someone learns slowly from failure, they are optimists; things are not going well this time but they are bound to get better.

THE ECCENTRICITIES OF SELF-EDUCATION

The T-maze is everywhere in politics because people are always wanting to do something with which they have no experience and perhaps no predecessors. John F. Kennedy had no clear examples on how to handle his religious difference from all preceding presidents; George H. W. Bush had no prior examples that would tell him what to do when the Soviet Union was in the process of collapsing. In ordinary human affairs the same pattern occurs daily; two old friends may run into a new situation and neither is quite clear which side the other is on; each would like to salvage the friendship but is uncertain just what is the proper thing to say. In most cases of this sort almost everyone falls back on their instincts, more technically known as their personal probabilities, in order to move ahead into the unclear future. People send up trial balloons and wait to see what happens, as Goffman postulated.

The reason the adaptation model is important here in reference to self government is that men's choices in the games they play may be guided by an adaptation process, and it is educational to notice how subtle the process can be. First, in terms of the interdependent decision process so emphasized by Thomas Schelling, it turns out that slow learners tend to prevail over fast learners, which seems somewhat counterintuitive, until the model is inspected closely. A person makes a choice and then notes whether it was successful or not, whether or not he was rewarded. When two individuals interact and the results are not satisfactory, the fast learner changes more quickly than does the slow one. As Lave and March point out, therefore, smart parents spoil their children because smart parents adapt to children's actions faster than their children react to their parents; conversely, smart children will spoil their parents.[56]

What is crucial in the learning process is the type of environment in which an individual lives. A benign environment, where everything the individual does is rewarded, both right and left turns, falsely teaches people that their specific behavior is causing the happy results.[57] People therefore become addicted to behavior that may have nothing to do with the results and insist that they cannot change their behavior without the sky falling. Or the individual learner may live in a malevolent world, where there is no reward at either branch of the T-maze and the unhappy mouse searches hopelessly back and forth, first learning that there is no reward on the right so that he must next time go left, only to be taught that the left does not work either. A surer road to social tension can hardly be imagined.[58]

The adaptation process can be a very personal one and have very immediate human impacts. One hypothetical case illustrates this: a second-grader is observed to be "dangerously withdrawn" and the school authorities worry about him; an observer is sent to the class and notices that when the child is seen to be alone, the teacher tries to be supportive by paying attention to him, praising his work. When the child is with the group, the teacher does not show any favoritism to him but interacts with all the students equally. All this sounds quite correct: extra help when a child seems to need it, but no favoritism between students generally. Only the adaptation-oriented psychologist notices the causal impact: the child is "rewarded" for solitary activity and "not rewarded" for social behavior. Curing the child entailed a change in the teacher's behavior, giving the child attention when he played with the group and ignoring him when alone.[59]

In studying other people, or indeed one's own behavior, it is easy to assume that behavior coefficients are innate; people are born cheerful or mean or public spirited. This is to jump too quickly to conclusions. Self government requires a broader focus on the whole landscape, to search out the reinforcements that are being accidentally or deliberately given to members of the group, so that behavior is unobtrusively but thoroughly controlled. Disorderly societies are not accidental, nor are orderly ones. Frequently a group gratifies some members with excessive rewards and punishes other members with inadequate rewards; the difference between self-organized communities and self-governed ones depends on how clearly these patterns are recognized. Chapter 5 inquires into this distinction in a dramatic case on the European landscape, where a revolution changed everything and nothing simultaneously.

5

The Complexity of Change

Time has always fascinated philosophers, and change is perhaps the one constant factor in the universe, a paradox in itself. Change is a difficult topic to study: even physicists must deal with the inconvenient fact that a particle's speed or location cannot be determined without changing it. And the physical sciences are well ahead of the social sciences, which are not even clear on just what should be measured. Various early political scientists cheerfully called the social world a "blooming, buzzing confusion" and left the whole question alone. Complexity theory is one of the few available methods in the social sciences that is fully at home with change, not just isolated cases of change but as an ongoing, universal, unstoppable, sometimes amazing process.

To develop living, dynamic models of change, complexity theorists strategically simplify their realms so that each cell in the lattice or each actor in the grid has a limited array of choices and is given a limited array of predisposing attitudes in respect to those choices. One famous computer model, developed by Robert Axelrod, involved the maintenance of social norms: the grid was filled with two types of agents, first those who were designated as *bold* and likely to break norms, and second by those who were *vengeful* and punished those who broke norms. When the players tended to be bold, vengeance had a field day and boldness fell because there was so much vengeance in the field that it was costly to be bold; but then when boldness fell, vengeance fell because it was no longer called for. When vengeance dropped, boldness increased dramatically because there was nothing to hinder it. In this computer case the fluctuations went on and on endlessly, rather like the real world.[1]

Change cannot always be so radically simplified, and the sciences of self organization must necessarily deal with human behavior in multidimensional lumps, where everything and everyone seems to be interwoven with everything else. Both sociologists and anthropologists tried to overcome this size problem by focusing on the norms people lived by, but without the leverage provided by complexity tools, there was a tendency to assume stability; people Garfinkel would critique as "sociological dopes" were expected to follow a society's fixed, traditional rules without modification or question.[2] This made it nearly impossible to explain where change came from.

THE CREATIVE PLAYING OF CARDS

A French anthropologist, Pierre Bourdieu, reacted against this static bias by a creative use of game theory, taking it from the level of life and death on the chessboard to the landscapes of the real world, showing how lives were irrevocably changed by the choices the players made.[3] Bourdieu defined "social capital" or personal status as the payoff from this sociopolitical gamesmanship, and provided an unexpected metaphor to show exactly how it might work. Say you are a parent in one of the North African tribal areas where Bourdieu did much of his field research. At some point your children reach marriageable age, and it becomes appropriate to make choices about whom they will marry. Strict anthropologists think the choice is predetermined by kinship and custom; Bourdieu sees it as poker. The parents seek to make the best possible use of the "hand" they have been dealt, with the children as the cards.[4]

As a poker hand has greater or less value depending on the particular patterns of aces, pairs, or flushes, it is possible to see one's children as having different values in the kinship market. Some may be smart, others hardworking, some handsome, others dutiful; and the overall combination of these children matters as outsiders observe and evaluate the social capital of the whole family – a brigand among the children may devalue the rest (or raise their value, depending on the culture). The children are like cards, any of which may be a winning hand, depending on who else in the neighborhood is trying to play other sets of children.

If one has a strong elder son, this may be attractive to another family with a higher social standing; if such a marriage is made, it then has the effect of increasing the values of the other children, because the family status has risen. In this case, a handsome or virtuous daughter may be played off to an equally good or better marriage in the next round. The important point is that the rules are being used, are being followed; but change is occurring because there are people with their own agendas, working creatively with those rules, playing serious games.

STRUCTURING STRUCTURES?

Pierre Bourdieu, similar to theorists such as Goffman (whom he knew personally) and Schelling, summarized this process with the recursive model of *habitus*.[5] The invention of new terms is not always a good intellectual strategy because it clutters up the syntactical landscape with words more mysterious than useful, but "habitus" is one of those rare cases where a new word is necessary because none of the old words exactly fit what he wanted to say. Bourdieu's definition of habitus is thick and packs a lot of human and sociological intelligence into a reasonably compact package.

Habitus is defined by Bourdieu as "systems of durable, transposable dispositions, *structured* structures predisposed to function as *structuring* structures, that is, as principles which generate and organize practices and representations that can be objectively adapted to their outcomes without presupposing a conscious aiming at ends or an express mastery of the operations necessary in order to attain them" – in short, orchestrations without a conductor.[6]

This anthropological vision is complexity theory's concept of self organization presented in large territorial dimensions, trying to capture the way in which individuals work within existing conditions to achieve their goals, and by those activities change some of the original conditions so that nothing looks quite the same and nothing looks quite different. Bourdieu's "structuring" structures and "structured" structures combine a society's explicit guidelines with the individual person's tacit strategies to capture the way active participants can rearrange the web within which they are entangled.

The point of introducing Bourdieu here is to tie together the principles represented in the several theories discussed earlier: that there are in any society structures (Goffman's performance criteria) that can and must be used creatively (Garfinkel's innovativeness in the face of ambiguity) in whatever human interactions in which one participates (Schelling's interdependent game theory) to bring about support or modification of the existing order of things.[7]

Nothing is ever entirely new because each individual has some existing background in a given society, but nothing is ever quite the same because at least someone is always encountering new problems and inventing new responses. If change continues long enough, people begin to call it a revolution, but each revolution is different because each revolution begins in a different state of affairs. It was long believed, rather casually, that the British, American, and French revolutions were similar. With hindsight, scholars are recognizing how false this conclusion was. The principle is even more true in informal social revolutions, as demonstrated by the one to be discussed here.

To illustrate the complexity of change, a picture is worth many abstractions, and the focus of the present chapter here turns to a specific country that beautifully illustrates what change is, how it occurs, and how the past clings to the present and constrains the future. The case is Italy, and it is edifying for several reasons: first as a critique of the thoughtless way many people arbitrarily make judgments about other countries' political systems; and second as an illustration that bottom-up analysis does not mean one can only deal with the man in the street – it only means that actual people are present, and those actual people may be leaders as well as ordinary folk.

Two bottom-up empirical case studies provide the data for this discussion of self-organized change, one covering the traditional Italian system and the other documenting the rise and the reign of Silvio Berlusconi.[8] The examination of this transition illustrates how the past and the present interact, in the hands of individual people. It should act as either an incitement or a warning to all observers of politics in high and low places.

ITALY'S NONPOLITICAL PAST?

Italy has a peculiar history within mainstream political science because it was one of the five countries included in one of the first "scientific" studies initiated after World War II, a survey research study of democratic citizens in a book titled *The Civic Culture*, by Gabriel Almond and Sidney Verba.[9] The authors took public opinion surveys, then an entirely new method, into Britain, Germany, the United States, Italy, and Mexico in order to probe the nature of the participant culture they presumed lay behind democratic institutions, a culture that was thought to oil the wheels of democracy by providing norms of trust, activism, and cooperation.

The survey was rich in results, many of them negative, since it found that even British and American citizens were unlikely to be participants in their governments; this led to development of the concept of "subjective" efficacy: people *thought* they would be listened to if they contacted an official, although they had never done so. This unexpected discovery of apathetic citizens even in the fully developed democracies caused the authors to change the title of their study from one emphasizing participation to one emphasizing a more balanced "civic" attitude, where people's loyalty was emphasized rather than the activism that top-down preconceptions had suggested. This was an early lesson in the fallacies created by top-down preconceptions about how the world should work.

There was a curious sidebar to this famous study, that Italy in a sense flunked the exam. The results of the Italian polls proved, according to the methodology used, that Italians were not political – a conclusion that was largely a result of the questions posed by the American research program, which presupposed that "proper" democratic citizens would, above all other things, be proud of their political systems. The Italians, with a rich culture and a long European tradition behind them, were proud of their opera houses, their ancient architecture, their monuments, their art, and so on. This sort of response found no resonance with the American analysts, and the Italians were therefore considered low in political competence.[10]

Years later, Joseph LaPalombara returned to the study of the country that had been originally analyzed in conventional political science terms as a failure, and used an entirely different approach in trying to explain the nature of Italian government.[11] His method was not standard in academic circles – some reviewers referred to it as "journalistic" rather than scientific – but today it can be recognized as an early case of bottom-up analysis, long before computers or complexity theory were available. LaPalombara developed his analytic method simply by ignoring all the American stereotypes about the Italian political system and trying to see it as a unique living system that was invented by the Italian people and their leaders to solve a particular set of problems – in other words, a tacit Schelling negotiation between players with mixed motives, under very challenging circumstances.

The stereotype of Italian politics after World War II was that the country was a joke; governments succeeded one another in rapid succession, sometimes lasting only a few months; Ronald Reagan greeted visiting Italian prime ministers by asking, "How's your crisis?"[12] This apparent disorderliness was amusing but not a serious concern, because, after all, Italy conducted regular elections and a democratic facade was in place, but LaPalombara seems finally to have decided that the nation deserved a more sympathetic interpretation. It serves as a starting point for the study of change, by describing what Italy was like *before* the Berlusconi revolution.

BETWEEN CONSENTING ADULTS

LaPalombara's basic premise was that Italy, like any country, put itself together after World War II in exactly the way complexity theory defines the process of self-organization; by taking into account the important groups present on the relevant lattice of the country and seeing what arrangements could be made that would be satisfactory to the most powerful of these groups. This set of decisions, about how to organize the country as a European democracy, was not made in isolation from social, economic, and political facts on the ground, but incorporated them into the contract – a social contract that was not some idealized model derived from Hobbes or Locke, but a *practical* arrangement.[13]

The basic facts were that the industrial north and the agricultural south of the country were roughly equal in strength and roughly equal in aggressiveness; neither would back down, so they simply set up the country around that difference, according to LaPalombara's interpretation. It was important that the arrangement be considered a democracy, because the United States, as a major world power, considered that criterion to be essential. LaPalombara argues that the Italians therefore wrote a constitution that covered the international requirements and then hardly ever looked at it again, ceding all power to political parties that operated independently, and outside, of the formal structure.[14]

There was an associated compact made between the government and the citizens, in LaPalombara's analysis: that the citizens would be allowed great freedom of action by the government in return for the citizens' toleration of the government's behavior, which was based on soaking the state for the benefit of elites. Lawmakers would, for instance, pass regulations about housing codes and the like, but would provide that such codes would come into effect in a few years' time rather than immediately. If a citizen therefore wished to build something on his property that was going to become illegal, the law gave him plenty of time to complete the project before the law went into effect. The government was also reticent about enforcing tax laws.[15]

Such arrangements, indeed such an attitude, could not of course be stated publically without scandalizing outside observers, so the Italian elite employed a method of *sfumato*, the practice of talking in public endlessly without saying anything. Politics became what LaPalombara defined as *spettacolo*, pure spectacle that served to hide the underlying reality of the arrangements. The ambiguity of government was amplified by the electoral process itself. While Italians voted in large numbers, and voted consistently for either the Church, labor, or communism, the outcome of the elections had little relation to the actual government that was formed. Coalitions came and went, policies came and went, everyone received a proportionate slice of the pie, and indeed everyone tended to prosper. The Italian economy, under this peculiar arrangement, flourished for many years.[16]

LaPalombara's investigation of the Italian people did not stop, as did most political science research, with citizenship rights and obligations, but went deep into the people's underlying cultural attitudes. Italians make a fetish of appearing different from each others, he noted, with local towns and regions priding themselves on their cultural superiority over others. Observers have seen this individualism as amoral familism,[17] but LaPalombara argued that Italians are actually artists and philosophers, that they pride themselves on their ability to cope with imponderable truths, that they create an impression of chaos in order to be admired for their ability to transcend it, and that their demand that each man be allowed to follow his own passions means that their tolerance of other people's individuality is almost total. Prisoners in jail are allowed to vote, LaPalombara notes – an example of toleration rare in other so-called democratic states.[18]

At bottom, according to this analysis, Italians are purely political, believing that all life is lived in the disputed arena between sovereign individuals, and that, as Machiavelli taught, it is important to know exactly who has what power and to deal with that knowledge as rationally as possible. Conflict is moderated because Italians do not expect to be treated fairly and therefore make arrangements to survive by other means; and anyone who seriously expects to be treated fairly is *fesso* or foolish. Drivers are skilled because they expect other drivers to be not only dangerous but perverse.[19] The wise Italian, in other words, does not expect to be protected by government; he is quite ready to defend himself.

The informal governing system of Italy was made up of three groups, according to LaPalombara: *la class dirigente* or ruling class, containing the recognized leaders of major sectors in society – the industrialists, landowners, bankers, educators, trade unionists, lawyers, architects, engineers, and so on; *the political class*, a specific subset of the ruling class, the occupants of key positions in political parties and in the bureaucracy; and behind it all, *la razza padrona*, the master race, the country's leading capitalists.[20] Recruitment into the political class was individual rather than ideological; opponents or critics were absorbed as conditions suggested, taking in anyone who was politically useful in the immediate context. While criticism of these political classes appears venomous among the Italian public, LaPalombara argues the criticism is largely theatrical, without any real alienation attached.

Tax evasion is widespread and forms a payoff to the citizenry, the result of the tacit pact of "live and let live" in the Italian culture. There are no informers, according to LaPalombara, and this fact demonstrates the acceptability of the informal rules that govern the country. If any political action is needed, it is handled through personal contacts, and through intermediating patrons and organizations; but Italians do not ask much from democracy, understanding its limits. Under the existing system, LaPalombara concluded, it is very difficult to know actually who is responsible for anything; four-fifths of the laws pass in legislative committees, where collaboration is the rule, and these sessions are not open to the public, with only minimal records kept. To the question of whether anyone is actually in charge of "this interesting country," LaPalombara answers for Italians of the time – that they believe nobody is in charge and that they are grateful for this.[21]

THE INVISIBLE VISIBLE

When Alexander Stille, the writer who would chronicle the changes brought about in Italy by Silvio Berlusconi, remembered the old era of Italian life, it was a world "relatively poor and shabby." People took their relaxation sitting outside their homes in chairs on sidewalks, chatting with neighbors; the more prosperous vacationed in Yugoslavia to avoid capitalist tourist centers. Stille lived without a phone for two years because it seemed impossible to get one. "There was a shortage of metal coins and so shopkeepers would give you handfuls of candy instead." Stores closed entirely in August "because people believed in rest and vacation, even though there was a lot of money to be made" from tourists. There were kidnaping and kneecapping and a Mafia war in Palermo.[22]

Yet for rich and poor alike, it was a "remarkably pleasant place to live"; while strikes were widespread, life was good and the people were passionate about politics. He found old men in Milan, in "hats and mustaches and suspenders and gray suits, dress of an earlier era," who were anarchists, old-style liberals, monarchists, Fascists, who stood in the plaza for hours, arguing politics; "getting out of the house and talking politics was a form of entertainment and sociability."[23]

Although Stille's book's title, *The Sack of Rome,* contains an obvious commentary on his feelings about the changes wrought by the rise of the Berlusconi empire, the book is of necessity objective and carefully written; in Italy one can be sued even if the facts are correct. The tale is also remarkably rich in its factual base; in Italy everything seems to be known to somebody, and eventually to everyone. What is interesting about the Italian story in respect to the approach defined by complexity theory is that it illustrates all the sociopolitical frameworks discussed in earlier chapters. The present chapter works these perspectives out, in detail, following a necessarily partial review of Stille's amazing mother lode of facts on recent Italian political history.

GETTING STARTED

Little is known about Berlusconi's childhood and youth except what he chose to include in a campaign biography, where his purpose was to show that he was exactly like every nice Italian boy with a saintly mother and a kindly father who passed on a love of soccer. As a young man he was a popular performer, playing bass and singing with a band; when the band leader's jealousy got him thrown out, his personal, partly sexual attractions forced his reinstatement. He graduated from the University of Milan with a prize-winning thesis on advertising contracts and went almost directly into real estate and building in the 1960s. Soon he went out on his own, with a large housing complex in a bad location, amid chemical plants and no nearby shopping areas.[24]

When the construction market slowed and the project came to a halt, Berlusconi demonstrated the pattern of behavior that would make him famous. In trying to prove to potential investors that there was real public interest in the housing project, he invited all his relatives to come by and pretend to be buyers; but they kept greeting each other so cordially that the potential financial investors saw through the ruse and backed out, furious.

Not to be deterred, Berlusconi developed a personal relation with one investor's secretary, was tipped off that the investor would be taking a certain train, joined him and captured his affection with stories of sexual exploits, and arrived at the end of the journey with a promise of funds from the now-converted supporter. He also added three stories to the apartment complex where only five had been officially approved, a profitable gimmick that escaped negative attention because he had hired the city's town planner as his project manager.[25]

In his next, even larger building project Berlusconi demonstrated another quality that would distinguish him in many fields over the years – he turned in an American direction. "Milano 2 was more than a housing development; it was a cultural statement." This second project would provide housing for 14,000 residents in American-style luxury with all the amenities, conspicuous consumption protected from the riotous street culture of Milan on a large formerly aristocratic estate. "Milano 2 was a place where a man could wear a Rolex watch and a woman a fur coat without fear or shame." While it was not where the true aristocracy lived, Milano 2 gave a home to the new bourgeoisie of "upwardly mobile corporate managers, middle- or upper level executives, stockbrokers and admen." Berlusconi in this way found himself attracted to the anti-counterculture movement, and bought into the new conservative newspaper, *Il Giornale*, that "rebelled against the cultural domination of the left."[26]

REARRANGING THE WORLD

The reason Berlusconi got the land for Milano 2 so cheap was that it was right under the flight paths of the local airport, so there was "deafening noise of jet planes landing and taking off," and this made it difficult to sell the apartments. Berlusconi's strategy was a triumph of gaming skills, using the underlying values of the culture along with aggressive salesmanship to get his way. He did not simply depend on political allies among the Christian Democrats, but set up the scene so that his preferred course seemed to be the obvious, natural choice for the authorities to make. First he designated a portion of the Milano 2 project for a hospital, then had his lobbyists claim that changing the air routes would ease the suffering of the hospital patients, although the hospital was not yet built.[27]

Residents whose quiet neighborhoods would be destroyed by the change in flight paths protested vehemently; airplane pilots objected to the new routes because they claimed they would force takeoff and landing maneuvers that they considered "dangerous." Berlusconi then paid the local Polytechnic University to report the change was "optimal," although they later recanted under pressure when his role in commissioning the report became public. Finally the change was made, and the per-square-foot value of the Berlusconi apartments doubled. He was becoming one of Italy's richest men.[28]

The full quality of the life Berlusconi was organizing around himself cannot be fully appreciated simply by studying his entrepreneurial successes. Much of the news today about Berlusconi involves his estate at Arcore, acquired in the 1970s after the deaths of the owners, leaving the villa, which had been in the Casati Stampa family for centuries, to a teenage daughter. The villa, built on the foundations of a Renaissance-era convent, had "145 rooms, vast grounds, a hunting reserve, stables, a rich library with ten thousand antique volumes, an art collection deep in paintings of the Venetian school from Tintoretto to Guardi."[29]

As Stille describes the transaction, Berlusconi acquired the estate at an unreasonably low price because his attorney had become the attorney of the young *marchesa,* who had left the country to escape the tragedy of her parents' deaths; when she decided to sell in order to pay estate taxes, the lawyer was given broad authority over arrangements and sold the vast property to Berlusconi at the price, in 1973 dollars, of about $850,000; included in the sale, against the heiress's wishes, were the library, the paintings, and the surrounding land.

Berlusconi deferred payment for several years, taking possession in 1974 but not completing the sale until 1980; and during that time, the young woman was required to pay all the taxes. Stille also notes that a further property of the Casati Stampa family was acquired some years later, an 800-acre estate including a medieval castle, much of the town of Cusago, and sixty farmhouses and agricultural land. Berlusconi paid nothing for this but exchanged stock in one of his companies, which in fact had no value and could not be sold on the open market. On this land, which was officially designated as "green" or environmentally protected, Berlusconi convinced the town council to allow him to build a condominium development. "Land that was bought at 345 lire (about 41 cents) a square meter was then sold for 3 to 4 million lire a square meter, an increase of about 10,000 fold."[30]

People who are introduced to Berlusconi's history as exemplified in the Arcore and similar stories are tempted to mutter something unprintable that might be translated as "scoundrel." The analyst of political society from the bottom up has a more subtle task: first to notice how effective such behavior is – Berlusconi was rich and on his way to becoming the richest man in the country, and this was quite early in his career. The second task is to see if there is a simplifying rule to be extracted from his behavior, as complexity theory calls for, some brief summary statement that would define the strategy that was in play, as each Italian day followed upon the one before.

Perhaps Berlusconi does in fact bring out the philosopher that is supposed to inhere in Italians, according to LaPalombara, because one of his best friends stated the principle clearly and simply: "Anything that is not specifically forbidden is allowed."[31] It is interesting to notice how such a principle opens the world to opportunities that are not obvious to people who think in more conventional terms. The Berlusconi rule is exactly the kind of creativity that Garfinkel envisioned, but at a much wider scale than that in which most people work, and in a society where the rules were not regularly enforced anyway, as noted in LaPalombara's thesis about the contract between government and people that neither would interfere with the other any more than seemed necessary.

IF IT'S NOT ON TELEVISION, THEN IT DIDN'T HAPPEN

Berlusconi himself presented the world with one of his more charming rules; it referred to women but applied universally. "Think of how many women there are out there who would like to go to bed with me, but don't know it. Life is a problem of communication."[32] This rule was central to his revolutionary impact on Italy: Berlusconi had the genius to see that the Italian people wanted something but did not yet know it, and he was (1) smart enough to know what it was they wanted and (2) energetic enough to give it to them. Being rich is pleasant but it does not change the world; seeing into the future and acting on that vision very frequently does change the world. But how does this happen, in detail and from the bottom up?

The change began with a collateral discovery that occurred during the construction of Milano 2, when Berlusconi was wiring the development for cable television, planning to create a private station for the condominium. As a result of a Supreme Court decision legalizing commercial television only at a local level, it occurred to him to create a normal broadcast station rather than a restricted one. His station became one of several hundred small stations that sprang up overnight after the court decision, all of them prohibited from becoming nationwide because the court wished to ensure that the official government station, RAI, would continue as a monopoly.

The government's RAI television network was operated within a particular cultural world, according to Stille's history: it featured the pope's mass on Sundays and much high-minded programming including the history of science and philosophy, great world literature, and programs giving advice to farmers on fertilizers and irrigation; the station ended programming at 10 PM when it felt all good Italians should be in bed. There was very little advertizing on RAI because it was run by people who believed in programs of cultural value, and when anyone turned up at the advertising division they had to wait in line and were just handed a list of prices. When one of the early directors of RAI ended his career, he took holy vows and entered a Trappist monastery outside of Rome for the rest of his life. It was the antithesis of capitalism, but it was supported by a society and a culture in which the church and the Communists, both popular institutions, vigorously disapproved of exuberant consumerism.[33]

Berlusconi's assault on the elite-centered culture in which television was thought to be a public service devoted to education and noble purposes proceeded at several levels, but the result was comparable, as Stille vividly puts it, to Lincoln's freeing the slaves. The first step for Berlusconi was largely practical, to acquire a *national* network despite the court's attempt to leave that monopoly to RAI. To escape the court's restriction, Berlusconi bought local stations all across the country and by 1981 had what was in effect a national network, although all the stations were local. His direct political ally in this was the new Socialist Party under Bettino Craxi, which supported his maneuvers, while socialist-controlled banks were a major source of the funds Berlusconi used to buy the stations. Berlusconi's television revolution was to see that the new medium was not an educational vehicle but designed for rampant entertainment and the advertising revenues that could be attached to that entertainment.[34]

This change of course deposed the Italian elites who sought to keep cultural standards high, but Berlusconi baldly proclaimed, to anyone who doubted this shift in program content, that most members of the audience had an eighth-grade education and even then were not at the top of the class. He bought up "as much American programming as fast as he could borrow money ... entire film libraries at record prices, using a seemingly limitless supply of money."[35] The result was "lowest common denominator" television: game shows where the participants were reduced step-by-step to nudity, soap operas with opulent lifestyles, shows that would make housewives feel the world was a brighter place.

THE LINCOLN COMPARISON

This new programming style opened the advertising floodgates for Berlusconi's second revolution, the recognition that Italian businessmen had been stifled by the old elite culture and now must be brought forth to full participation in his newly defined television world. Advertising costs money, so it was not easy to convert men schooled in the old regime to put forth their money on this shockingly new approach. At the beginning Berlusconi did not ask for payment unless the company's sales went up, or he took payment in their products, which he then redistributed to other clients as goodwill gifts; he was selling not just a product but a better world, as Stille describes it.[36]

Added to this whirlwind of personal activity were Berlusconi's salesmen, whom he turned into a new class of people different from old stereotypes. He was himself rather austere in personal regime, did not drink or smoke, jogged regularly to keep fit, and rarely attended others' parties; he tended to work eighteen-hour days. Berlusconi brought the same style to his employees, emphasizing physical fitness, no smoking, no beards, fresh breath, no sweaty palms, radiant self-confidence. Stille emphasizes that personal strategies were the most important elements of the regime; Berlusconi passed on his vivid mantras as guides for his salesmen, summarized by the picture of *il sole in tasca*, the sun in your pocket, bringing joy into a room just by entering it.[37]

Berlusconi taught that it was important, amid this consumer-oriented joy, Stille notes, for salesmen to play on human vanity and credulity; to make a convincing argument, invent an anecdote and attach it to someone famous, preferably an American. In contrast to the older Italian practice of speaking in deliberately obscure terms, Berlusconi urged his employees to use images rather than abstract concepts, because images stick in others' memories better and make a stronger sales pitch. Be especially nice to unpleasant people, who will be eternally grateful just because no one else treats them well.[38] His salesmen made their clients into their friends, as Berlusconi made his salesmen into his friends; it was a new and egalitarian world.

With all his advertising revenues, Berlusconi could afford losses elsewhere in his many businesses, according to Stille, who argues that Berlusconi was a better salesman than he was an actual manager. But he was well supported by his political friends; when Berlusconi took office, a socialist was appointed to head RAI, so there was a kind of truce between the networks. And Berlusconi paid back in important ways, using his media to help friends and harry enemies. He expanded into France after charming Francois Mitterand with an impromptu piano performance, but then did not do as well as he did at home; while the nude game shows were popular with the French, they were more strict than Italians were about people obeying the law and they fined him for excess advertising. Things went better in Spain where audiences loved the programming and the socialist Gonzalez was in power longer to provide support in getting around antitrust laws.[39]

Eventually, Stille records, Berlusconi went into sports as a sidelight, buying AC Milan, which was bankrupt at the time, and acting on his usual pattern, spending money extravagantly to purchase top players. He bought fans with spectacular theatrical events such as having the players deposited in the soccer stadium from three helicopters while the public address system played Richard Wagner's *Die Walküre*.[40] He micromanaged the team and won the national championship in 1988 and European championships in 1989 and 1990.

What Berlusconi realized, according to Stille, was "that soccer and television could be mixed together into an explosive synergy. While owning a soccer team might not be lucrative, televising soccer certainly was and is so popular it became a genuine cultural force." With soccer so popular, Berlusconi's name rose to the top of the national polls, and while he "almost certainly didn't get into soccer with politics in mind," at some point "he realized that through soccer he had stirred up emotions that had political weight."[41]

LIFE AT THE CREST OF COMPLEXITY

How does self organization occur in the real political world? Up to this point the very simplified view of Berlusconi's career that has been gleaned from Stille's far more detailed biographical history may make it seem that men make their own history, and largely as they please. Berlusconi has seemed to rise from nowhere into a field that was largely empty, or perhaps has seemed to recognize an empty field beyond the usual Italian piazza where his talents could unfold without hindrance. While it remains true that Berlusconi, with his talent for spending vast amounts of money in creative ways, tends to batter down all opposition, this is only true in retrospect and from an outsider's serene viewpoint.

A closer view of the Italian political scene during Berlusconi's rise shows that from *his* point of view it was dangerous, quirky, harrowing, and insecure. His television empire was at the mercy of political leaders and could be taken away at any unexpected moment; his political supporters were widely charged with various sorts of corruption and might be driven from power at any time; reformers were attacking malfeasance in all corners of the Italian political system, and Berlusconi was either on their target list or would shortly be there. Observers note that he paid his employees exceptionally well and raised their salaries amply without being asked; some thought this was the result of generosity, others thought he was buying their silence and loyalty against his enemies.[42]

In addition to all this entrepreneurial activity, Italian politics was also changed forever by the end of the Cold War, under which the Italian Communist Party changed its name and the Christian Democrats, who had lost the Communists as their favorite opponent, no longer dominated the electoral process. Many new parties sprouted, and the demands on politicians, facing an electoral field that was largely unknown, were extreme. If the left won the election in 1994, Berlusconi feared they would take away his networks and their banks would call in his loans; his anguish grew extreme; he is reported as saying, "I'm exhausted, on the point of a nervous breakdown ... Sometimes I even find myself weeping in the shower."[43]

Berlusconi's friends and allies were strongly against his entering politics, Stille reports, since they felt that anyone as rich as he should not be in politics because of the automatic conflicts of interest it would generate. But as the *mani pulite* (clean hands) judicial investigations got closer and closer to Berlusconi's political protectors and his own business corporations, the situation shifted and everyone recognized the impending peril. If an electoral win by the left would be a disaster for everyone, then the point was to run a rightist campaign that would win; and this was made possible by a new electoral law that favored broad coalition parties rather than narrow ideological groups. Berlusconi's allies tried to find alternative candidates, but anyone who was suitable refused to run, either because they could not tolerate the odd coalitions needed to get the votes or because they refused to be sold like soap.[44]

There was a demand without a supply, as Stille notes, and Berlusconi felt this was just his territory. He looked at past politics in Italy and found the politicians gray and boring and their speeches incomprehensible; he then translated his whole business organization, root and branch, into the political realm. His major company became a political machine; the employees became campaign workers; his television stations became candidate oriented; clubs were set up in every parish in Italy. The political party was named after the soccer chant, Go Italy! While *Forza Italia*! meant nothing, it was cheerful and attractive. The party was anticommunist because Berlusconi believed, according to Stille, that communists do not appreciate individuals, but in general the new party was not political in the usual sense; it did not propose specific policies but focused on "hopes," "dreams," and "the new Italian miracle."[45]

His electoral alliance was contradictory, between the separatist Northern League of industrialists and the post-fascist parties of Rome and the south, but Berlusconi's personal style made them seem respectable, his well-cut suits and overwhelming smile in the place of other politicians who were sometimes surly, or ill-dressed, with their speeches rarely crisp and clear.[46] Stille's account concludes that with the addition of modern campaign technology, including full access to his television network for complete speeches – something that was never done before – Forza Italia won 46.3 percent of the vote to the center left's 34.3 percent. The first government with Berlusconi as prime minister would last only seven months, but it confirmed the revolution. Society, politics, culture, even Italian psychology would never again be quite the same.

SELF-INTERESTED GOVERNMENT

What happened after electoral success? Italian politics can be endless, but there is space here only to summarize Berlusconi's official tenure as it relates to the study of habitus, of change, and of the individual behavior that drives self organization from the bottom up. Berlusconi was in power overall for a total of nine years, from 1994 to 1995, 2001 to 2006, and 2008 to 2011. To describe his time in office, the term "corruption" is inappropriate, hardly doing justice to the scope of the self-centered political world he invented and sustained.

The most massive manifestation of this worldview was Berlusconi's attitude toward the law and the institutions that made the law; here he simply rearranged the legal system, first to protect himself and his friends from prosecution, and second to benefit himself and anyone who would join him.[47] In terms of self-protection, Berlusconi's primary need was to escape the *mani pulite* judicial prosecutors who were vigorously pursuing corruption among public officials, a corruption involving massive payoffs to politicians in return for lucrative arrangements for businessmen. Bribery had ruled traditionally in Italy and had worsened substantially under Berlusconi's new Socialist Party patron, Bettino Craxi. As the prosecutors got closer to Berlusconi's associates, his companies, and himself, holding elected public positions provided legal immunity from prosecution. To be officially elected was to be safe.

Perhaps more striking in respect to his attitude to the law was the way Berlusconi ran his government: his corporate lawyer became party leader in the senate and worked for tax breaks that would benefit Berlusconi's company. According to Stille's account, there was amnesty for tax evasion and building code violation; public works contracts were opened to corrupt firms; reforms that had made it possible to fire bureaucratic workers were abolished (because those workers tended to vote for Berlusconi). Berlusconi's private lawyer, who defended him in court cases, was put in charge of the agencies that conducted the investigations of corruption. When his real estate company faced mass arrests for corrupt practices, a law was passed that made it illegal to prosecute a long list of white-collar crimes, including those involving his employees.[48]

Laws were passed to make conditions in prison more pleasant, so Mafia dons who had been isolated on island prisons were brought onto the mainland to accommodations where they could more conveniently conduct business. Most broadly there was the Cirami law that allowed criminal defendants "to get rid of their prosecutors on grounds of 'legitimate suspicion' that the entire prosecutor's office might have a bias against them." As Stille quietly comments, the idea that prosecutors should be neutral was somewhat unexpected. One opposition politician suggested it was a case of "destroying the whole Italian penal code" to protect one man. Berlusconi went even further when, about to become the rotating president of the European Union, he argued it would be unseemly to indict such a person, and the legislature duly passed a law to this effect.[49]

EVERYBODY DOES IT

Berlusconi almost single-handedly killed the *mani pulite* reform movement, at least in part by deliberately destroying the reputation of its leading prosecutor, according to Stille's detailed account. Antonio Di Pietro was, at the time Berlusconi entered politics officially, one of the most popular men in Italy. Like many reformers, Di Pietro seemed to believe that virtue was its own reward, and for a while this was true; but as Thomas Schelling has pointed out, there are no purely cooperative games, and one's opponents may be more virulent if not smarter than oneself.

Operation Clean Hands began in Milan in early 1992 when traditional parties had been severely weakened by the end of communism and businessmen were encouraged to complain about the constant bribes they had been forced to pay to those parties to get anything done. The Milan prosecutors worked upward from these businessmen, through members of parliament and finally top party officials, uncovering a whole architecture of corruption. Stille comments that the system of bribery "was so pervasive, so rapacious and so scientific in its application that it was shocking to even the most cynical Italian observers."[50] The public was outraged: Craxi was pelted with coins when he dared to appear in public, as a sign of public scorn, and the system seemed well on its way to reform.

Berlusconi initially seemed to support the prosecutors because he too had been required to pay bribes, but on the other hand the prosecution threatened the gains bribery had brought him. In practical terms, for his first election Berlusconi benefited from his late announcement of his candidacy, which left little time to investigate his record. After his victory he publically asked Di Pietro to become interior minister, but the latter declined. Soon Berlusconi began to fear Di Pietro's popularity, anticipating he might even become head of Forza Italia. Stille describes how, to prevent this threat, Berlusconi launched a smear campaign to destroy Di Pietro's reputation through a series of false charges. Nothing could be proven, and eventually apologies were issued, but the damage was done. Instead of a battle of good against evil, the dirtying of the reformers told the public that everyone was on the wrong side of virtue. The old saying fit the new circumstances: "*Tutti colpevoli, tutti innocenti* (If everyone is guilty, then everyone is innocent)."[51]

Finally Stille's tracing of Berlusconi's impact on the Italian economic system needs to be mentioned. When launching his first campaign, he had promised to dispose of his various companies to avoid conflicts of interest, but this was pure rhetoric. His media network was the center of his political and economic and social power, and he defended and expanded it in all directions, fighting off judicial attempts to limit it as a monopoly. In one illustrative case, an entrepreneur tried to develop the phone system into a new independent television network beside Berlusconi's and the state's networks. Early public response was positive, until a new company bought the telephone company and canceled the new network; the reason was, as the new owner told friends, "that as long as the government set the telephone rates, it was impossible for him to risk displeasing Berlusconi." In apparent appreciation for this courtesy, the government aided the telephone company some time later when it was having difficulty entering Turkey's system; Berlusconi went personally to Ankara and facilitated the deal.[52]

The overall result of this tightly knit economy was that there was no open market in Italy; the telephone collaboration gave two areas of the economy monopoly control, phones and television; other ties were made at the time between Fiat and the state chemicals industry, Benetton, and the national highway system. Profits were good – 5.8 percent for government property versus 1.3 percent for private firms, according to Stile's figures – but innovation died. When Berlusconi's own backers tried to move in a pro-business direction, he cut them down.[53]

The result was to increase the national deficit, lower the country's credit rating, and cripple the economy by one man's domination of so many markets. The same thing happened to press freedom, where Berlusconi complained so bitterly about any objective news, news that did not bias the story in his favor, that editors finally gave up, sometimes just running wire reports to avoid any possible harassment from Berlusconi's agents. And interestingly, he has degraded Italy's political system, getting his own employees and dependents elected to parliament, instructing them how to vote, and firing any who disobey, making public power so useless that the members no longer bothered to attend; at which point he started offering prizes to those who were willing to attend parliamentary sessions.[54]

PLUS ÇA CHANGE ...

Even this brief sketch of Berlusconi's career makes it plausible to suggest that a revolution occurred in Italy during the period recounted in *The Sack of Rome* and that Berlusconi played a major role in that revolution. In terms of Bourdieu's *habitus*, Berlusconi was both a structured and a structuring event. What specifically did he adopt from existing Italian culture and society? First his family values, including the traditional family, ruled firmly but kindly by his parents, and who were always honored by their adult son; his mother was reported to be present at every Arcore dinner to the very end. Berlusconi also always presented his wealth as something done for his children, following a norm that Italians respect. His sexual exploits, a traditional mark of European manhood, kept him perpetually interesting and did not seem to offend either Italian men or women, although the courts occasionally objected.

Soccer is a traditional structure, and Berlusconi simply absorbed it. Corruption had always been a comfortable sin in Italian politics; if his exercise of the prerogative had been more vigorous than any of his predecessors, it nonetheless left the public feeling that he would not interfere in any of their more modest but also questionable pursuits. Berlusconi had also left the mafia intact; he showed no antipathy to the group over the years, and when attacked by it, he responded appropriately. When one mafia group threatened the lives of his children, he responded with perfect taste by hiring a chauffeur from a stronger mafia family to drive the children safely to school. Stille reports that Berlusconi's party, Forza Italia, welcomed mob candidates and mob support in southern Italy.[55]

If in these ways Berlusconi worked within traditional structures, and was formed by them, what kind of changes did his career bring about? There is some debate over what a "revolution" entails, but Berlusconi's impact fully fits the major definition provided by Theda Skocpol, that a revolution is a complete inversion of the socioeconomic system of a country. Berlusconi's impact was slightly idiosyncratic because the inversion was partial: he inverted the class structure, overthrowing an old aristocratic elite and replacing it with a consumer-oriented working-class egalitarianism, but the capitalist culture he allowed to flourish did not have a free market base on which to rest, nor could Italy quite be called state capitalism, since Berlusconi personally owned or controlled a remarkably large percentage of the economy. But the conversion to capitalist cultural values cut across the intellectual, artistic, and political practices of Italy.

Where the old Italian media had emphasized educational and high artistic values, the new norms on Berlusconi television were pure entertainment, pleasures for the lower classes, especially women. Consumerism enlivened the economy, advertising manipulated the market, advertising revenues were the backbone of Berlusconi's personal prosperity. He also changed the political system in multiple ways. Berlusconi destroyed what had been a powerful reform movement among Italian citizens who supported the *mani pulite* prosecutors; whether the citizens lost hope, given Berlusconi's defamation of the movement's leaders, or whether prosecutors feared to challenge a man who held the entire Italian media system as a personal weapon is not clear, but the reform era seemed to have ended.

THE QUESTION IS THE DETAILS

If Italy has changed in some ways while remaining the same in other respects, the complexity-theory question is how it happened, how Berlusconi achieved what he did. The question is so large and perhaps so imponderable that it is convenient to break it up into sections, using the theorists discussed in earlier chapters to guide the inquiry. First the theatrical approach of Erving Goffman will show how much simple drama was present in every stage of Berlusconi's career; second the ethnomethodological framework of Harold Garfinkel will explain what were the remarkable skills that Berlusconi brought to bear on his private problem of how to be rich and famous and powerful. Finally game theory, as used so flexibly by Thomas Schelling, will come under the complexity umbrella to explain what battles Berlusconi fought and what strategies he used. The imaginative artistry of Berlusconi's transformation is illustrated by the fact that, in individual acts, he sometimes managed to combine all these approaches in a single ingenious package.

Berlusconi's effectiveness, from a dramaturgical viewpoint, seems to originate in his boyhood, a natural physical appeal that along with a *simpatico* manner made him the center of attention. The sexual theatrics, along with his obsessive concern that television never show the wrinkles of aging or a bald spot about which he was very sensitive, support this aspect of his presentation. But under the surface was a formidable intelligence, which must be acknowledged: he rose to wealth and then fame by thinking through every detail of an endeavor and providing every service himself if there was no one else available; he rewrote television scripts, managed stage sets, invented program formats, developed sales slogans and promotion campaigns; he predicted audience shares and keyed programs to the audience; he encouraged employees to call him directly, ignoring their bosses, it they had problems.[56] He was, in short, the master of every detail that might make a difference for or against his performance ratings.

The Berlusconi political act was as well programmed as his business performance was: the man himself was always well dressed, always smiling, speaking in simple, clear images that everyone could understand, and always completely convinced what he was saying was the absolute truth. Stille is careful with this issue, noting that most politicians behave this way; the difference he found between Berlusconi and other politicians, however, was that other politicians seemed to understand the difference between truth and untruth, whereas Berlusconi did not.[57]

Berlusconi in fact reveled in this aspect of his own thinking, distributing Erasmus's *In Praise of Folly* to clients and arguing that the most important decisions in life are not based on reason but on visionary folly, where miracles are created by ignoring negative circumstances. He included untrue facts in his widely distributed autobiography, which says, incorrectly, that he studied at the Sorbonne and, also incorrectly, that he toured Lebanon with his youthful music group. Both points, while untrue, seemed to add luster to his self-painted portrait, and the Italian phrase seems to justify this strategy: *Se non è vero, è ben trovato*; if it is not true, still it is well said. This fit with Berlusconi's own philosophy, that "If something isn't on television, it doesn't exist."[58]

Berlusconi carried this thesis through in his carefully wrought political campaigns, setting up his official announcement in an Oval Office–type setting, providing detailed media training for campaigning party members, televising whole speeches when they were made by himself, while the opposition got scant minutes on his network. Even the Arcore estate was a part of this performance, showing him as master of a unique cultural landmark, but carefully mixed with down-home television interviews where he talked about his children because people are bored with politics anyway. This passion for appearance also occurs just before polling days, when Berlusconi claims the party will get an overwhelming mandate, so that opposition voters will feel voting against him is fruitless and will stay home.[59]

IN PRAISE OF VISION

The performance tactics to which Berlusconi devoted such close attention can be effective even when employed by mediocre politicians; carefully wrought campaigns will usually beat amateur efforts even without other political virtues. Berlusconi, however, was unusual in the way he himself identified his particular intellectual talent and that has been investigated earlier here in terms of Garfinkel's emphasis on the visible invisible, those things that everyone *could* see if they looked but that most people miss entirely. What Berlusconi saw is now clear: he saw people who were counseled to moderate lifestyles by Church and communists alike, but who would prefer more flavorful lives, based on their own mundane pleasures rather than the high-minded amusements of the rich. He saw also that Italian politics had grown sufficiently uncouth that people were finally fed up, and he saw that television was a new power in these circumstances. And he gradually learned that all this could fit into a single package surrounding himself.

The revolution was in the cultural class structure but went beyond that. Berlusconi's media consistently emphasized the importance of brightening the lives of Italian housewives, which *per contra* suggests that traditional norms may weigh rather heavily on that group. But rather than emancipating women, let us brighten their lives where they are. As such a captive audience, women were a major support of Berlusconi's television programming, and also of his political ambitions. The middle classes similarly were to be encouraged, without criticism from the left of the political spectrum, in the full enjoyment of their consumer-oriented ambitions. The old elites continue to pursue their usual pursuits in Italy, but they govern only sporadically, when the economic system needs to be put back into respectable order; however, short of such serious economic crisis, postmodernism prevails.

Finally it is interesting to consider Berlusconi as a gamesman, recalling Thomas Schelling's important insight that there is no competition so severe that there are not some grounds for cooperation, and that there is no liaison so close that there is not latent quarrel somewhere in it. Berlusconi's entire game strategy manifested a recognition of this principle, whether it was in economic, political, or social matters. Stille reports an unexpected characteristic of Berlusconi's gaming behavior, that he disliked conflict and would go out of his way to avoid it; rather than fighting people, he would try to buy them. If there was a zoning inspector who might object to extra floors being added to a building under construction, he would be hired as project manager. If a journalist wrote critical articles about Berlusconi's various empires, he would be put on the payroll. If a political opponent looked dangerous, he would be invited to join ranks and rewarded handsomely for doing so.

People who cooperated were richly repaid: journalists could keep their old jobs and be paid extra as special contributors to Berlusconi publications; business executives who bowed to Berlusconi's authority and dropped any form of competition with his industries would be rewarded by help with international expansion of their markets; politicians in office who were willing to serve Berlusconi's financial and business needs were coddled, entertained lavishly at Arcore, and supported against their enemies by Berlusconi's television networks. The executives that filled the ranks of Berlusconi's many companies were, as long as they had no original ideas of their own, beautifully compensated.[60]

The other side of this coin was that anyone who refused to sign up with Berlusconi was outlawed and vulnerable to the most vicious of personal attacks, particularly those carried out by his television and media networks. There were no constraints in this war: detectives were hired to dredge up any behavior that could possibly seem incriminating, false stories were purchased from mercenary observers where no useful facts had been found, court cases were invented, compromising offers were made and publicized. After these defamation campaigns had extended sometimes for years, the facts might be refuted and an apology issued, but the impact could never be erased. Enemies could be destroyed by a media attack even without any visible culpability if they failed to follow Berlusconi's line.[61]

Italy was not, of course, an easy playing field, and Berlusconi was in turn attacked from many directions over the course of his extended periods in economic and/or political power. His favorite countertactic was, according to Stille, to muddy the waters by inventing plausible alternative explanations. When prosecuting magistrates began to investigate one of his company's offshore accounts, used to get around Italian regulations, and also to direct bribes to friendly politicians, there was a real problem because he had sworn to resign if such behavior could be proven. Suddenly on one of Berlusconi's more respectable television newscasts appeared an interview with a "mysterious Tunisian lawyer" who claimed to own the accounts. This "alternate story" served to confuse things sufficiently that it took a long time to prove Berlusconi guilty, and by that time the statute of limitations had expired.[62] As suggested earlier, his sincerity was complete; he believed himself, and this carried weight.

Complexity theory tends to overturn old ideas, and among the oldest of ideas about change is that it occurs with some regularity and in certain identifiable directions. The pattern of change documented in the present chapter shows how illusory such common theories may be. It is very difficult to determine just what Berlusconi's revolution accomplished, but it is impossible to deny that it accomplished real change. Old theories sought equilibria, where all forces attained balance and stability was assured; old theories predicted progress, where things grew slowly but steadily better for at least some of the participants. Complexity theory, working from the bottom up, accommodates the grittiness of history shown in the story of Italy's recent sociopolitical explorations. It invites analysis and speculation.

6

The Complexity of Political Intelligence

UNDERSTANDING OTHER PLAYERS

In the investigation of self government as a new focus for political attention, the role of intelligence takes an important place, both as the means by which the present is understood and also by which the future may be considered. It was easier to deal with political intelligence in an earlier era when people assumed "statesmen" would arise and contribute their wisdom to the solution of political problems. In modern times, intelligence is sometimes thought to have moved into the scientific disciplines, but there is also widespread distrust of science and the supposed elites who practice it.[1]

So intelligence has become a more controversial question, and the modern reformulation of the issue is to ask *whose* intelligence. From this direction, complexity theory offers the well-known and ambiguous science known as Artificial Intelligence, which began as an attempt to computerize the solution to problems that had solutions, such as proving theorems in mathematics, or making medical diagnoses, or playing perfect chess, but is most useful to students of politics in a slightly more empirical form, the study of the specific ways specific people think, how they arrive at their sometimes surprising conclusions, and how this process of conceptual construction affects interactions with them in the various games that can be played in the course of self government.

This question is particularly central to the use of the game model and its possible uses in influencing the understanding of the everyday political world, because, as Schelling encouraged everyone to recognize, there can be no effective strategies unless players *understand* their opponent or partner with a reasonable degree of depth and logic, having accepted the perhaps bitter fact that the opponent's or the partner's way of thought is entirely different from their own ways of thought, as are the other people's goals entirely distinct from their own goals.[2]

The economists' axiom of rational behavior was intended to overcome this problem of human difference by assuming that all people, when they were consciously and carefully attending to their business, thought in the same way. When this was recognized as too idealistic, economists compromised by arguing that *most* people, *most* of the time, were rational, so the idea could be used to make analysis and prediction possible.[3] When Artificial Intelligence tried to pin this down, however, it became clear that what people are able to do swiftly and intuitively could only be accomplished by computers through the writing of a great deal of inconvenient computer code. Chess games could sometimes be won, but the game of real-time thinking in the everyday, everywhere political world, was more subtle.[4]

Over the years, some social scientists did take on the challenge of exploring the political thought process and cleared some trails in the intellectual thickets. The present chapter uses this social scientific background to analyze one of the contemporary world leaders with whom it is the most difficult for outside observers to sympathize – Robert Mugabe of Zimbabwe. President of the country since its first free elections in 1980, Mugabe, at the age of ninety-one today and still in office, has violated every precept in the civic rule-book, and his career shows how theater, breaching activity, games, and self organization can combine in a political system that is simultaneously simple and complex, a fitting summary of how bottom-up politics sprouts, flourishes, and bears unexpected fruit in a ruggedly empirical world.

THE LOSS OF RATIONALITY

The beauty of saying things clearly, even if they are wrong, was illustrated by two psychologists who took the economists' concept of rationality to heart and went out and tested it rigorously on everyday as well as statistical reasoning problems. The economists' defining contribution was to establish rationality as a formal model, defined as self-interest, maximization of gains, transitivity of preferences, and consistency of choices every time the same alternatives were presented.[5] This seemed straightforward, especially when it was qualified, as by Milton Friedman's argument, that even if *everyone* did not act rationally, *most* people did so, *most* of the time. Furthermore, rationality applied only to means, not to goals, so it tended to seem practically useful while leaving open larger questions about what ultimate purposes people pursued. Downs argues, for instance, that a monk who purges his mind of all logical thoughts to achieve a state of mystical contemplation is rational in the economic sense; given the goals he pursues, the means he employs are appropriate.[6]

Rationality frequently slipped onto a purely monetary scale, which was useful because it made actual calculations possible, using numbers rather than imprecise words. This was, however, exactly where the *behavioral* economists, who investigated rationality in laboratories using their students as subjects, found the first fundamental flaw: Could it be possible that a dollar was not in fact a dollar?[7]

Experiments showed that most people would drive an extra twenty minutes to save $5 on a cheap $10 calculator, getting it at half price, but would not bother to go elsewhere to save $5 on an expensive $125 electronic device.[8] That meant that the two $5 bills were different – they swelled or shrank depending on how the consumer thought about them. But a dollar is supposed to equal a dollar, in any reasonable economist's mind, so this peculiar finding represented a definite problem, not so much a pothole as a massive sinkhole in the road to rationality.

Game theorists had already found that normal people do not seem to think in strategic terms when playing games – they do not, for instance, recognize that the payoffs in the matrix need to be evaluated so as to minimize one's losses rather than unrealistically hoping for gains – but Amos Tversky and Daniel Kahneman took the question directly into the experimental laboratory and compiled inescapable evidence that very few people, even trained statisticians, are rational in the exact sense.[9]

The explanation of the problem came in two stages. First, Tversky and Kahneman showed that as a means of simplifying decisions, people used *heuristics*, rules of thumb that seemed to facilitate decision making but frequently led people astray from a larger perspective. Second, Tversky and Kahneman argued that people *frame* choices in different ways in order to understand how to resolve them, and that people may make inaccurate and inconsistent choices depending, very often, on arbitrary frames that influence their thought processes; this was the source of the $5 problem.

Where rational choice assumes objective decisions based on real facts, Tversky and Kahneman used simple experiments on their university students to investigate how decisions were made in cases where uncertain events were involved, where people were trying to figure out their

environments under the kinds of ambiguous circumstances already considered by Schelling, Goffman, Garfinkel, and Bourdieu. The beliefs in
question related to evaluations of the real world, the very foundations
on which people constructed their lives. The beliefs were in probability
form – the likelihood that object A belongs to class B, or originates from
class B, or can be generated by class B.

How, for instance, do people figure out the probable profession of
a man described in the following terms: "Steve is very shy and withdrawn, invariably helpful, but with little interest in people ... A meek
and tidy soul, he has a need for order and structure, and a passion for
detail."[10] The most statistically correct way to identify Steve's profession
is by base-rate frequency, according to Tversky and Kahneman, so a "reasonable estimate" of his profession might be that of trades that include
substantial numbers of workers, such as that of farmers, lawyers, or engineers. Yet when most people are presented with Steve's description, they
immediately pick "librarian" because the term fits the personal stereotype
so neatly. In the abstract, this may seem a harmless habit, yet in more
recent years the pattern shows its pathological side with the prominence
of ethnic and other forms of social profiling.

THE HAZARDS OF JUDGMENT

This pattern of jumping to conclusions illustrates Tversky and Kahneman's heuristic principle of "representativeness," which people use to
make quick guesses. Because the process is personal and informal, the
guesses are sometimes useful but frequently biased. Stereotypes replaced
base-rates even when the descriptive material was meaningless, and were
used even when the subjects were told what the base rates were. Along
with this dangerous shortcut, experimental subjects showed a real talent
for making long-term predictions, and making them inaccurately, on the
basis of very short-term experience. Given a description of a good student
teacher performance, for one particular day, people blithely predicted
that the teacher would be successful five years later on after a remarkable
and brilliant academic career.[11]

This indifference to the principles of statistical reasoning was widespread, and surprised the two psychologists because they found it even
among trained research scientists. Everyone was insensitive to the
Law of Large Numbers, which states that the true average of a given
event will emerge only gradually over many repeated trials. But instead
of looking for large samples, people were quite confident in making

predictions based on very small samples. Asked for instance if a large or a small hospital would be more likely to have more or less than the average of 50 percent male children born in a year, the majority said there would be no difference, where in fact the smaller institution would show more irregularity than the larger, because the large hospital provides more cases and a better estimate of the population average.[12]

The Gambler's Fallacy was also found to be popular, the belief that after a long run of red on the roulette wheel, black "must" come up because it will result in a more representative sequence. The interesting point is that when subjects are told this is not true, and the reasons are explained, they still continue to believe it. Yet as the authors point out, a roulette wheel has no memory, and the probability of red or a black result is 0.5 every time, assuming the equipment is fair.[13]

Another well-established law that no one appreciates is the law of regression, applied in 1885 by Francis Galton in comparing the heights of fathers and sons; measurements showed that tall fathers did not have tall sons, nor short fathers short sons, but that there was a movement toward the mean. In general, high results tend to drop when repeated, low results tend to rise. This can sometimes lead to wholesale misinterpretations of daily events.

In one case, the study involved aviators who were praised at the conclusion of successful runs and punished for poor ones. The misleading results occurred on succeeding flights because those who had been praised on the first trial did worse on the second, and those who had been punished on the first trial fared better on the second trial. The untutored conclusion would be "give more punishment, less praise"; but the pattern is actually explained differently, by the law of regression, which says that every extreme result tends to "regress" toward the mean. The airmen who had done well naturally did less well the next time around; and those who had done badly naturally did better. So the result had nothing to do with punishment or praise, but "the human condition is such that, by chance alone, one is most often rewarded for punishing others."[14]

The heuristic of "availability" also ruins the consistency of rational thinking and provides further insights into how people actually think. People's attention and their resultant decision depends on recent experiences (a neighbor's house has just burned, so they become more prone to buy insurance), notoriety (famous cases are not representative but are easier to recall), and imaginability (in planning a trip, imaginable hazards are overrepresented and unimaginable ones underestimated).[15]

Related to this phenomenon was illusory correlation, where people found relationships that were actually contradicted by the data. Tversky and Kahneman argued that people "systematically violate" the criteria of consistency and coherence that are the basis of rationality, and there is a double bias in the framing, "controlled partly by the formulation of the problem and partly by the norms, habits, and personal characteristics of the decision-maker."[16] This conclusion is of course just like the sociology of Goffman and Garfinkel, which emphasized the major role played by personal customs and individual creativity in daily affairs, but it is now integrated with rigorously economic models of rationality.

WORKING WITH IRRATIONALITY

The school of behavior economists took considerable delight in carrying these experiments out into the more everyday world where irrationality seemed to blossom everywhere one looked. Lawyers refused to lower their hourly prices to $30 in order to assist poor retired people, but were quite willing to do it pro bono, for free – a clear case where social norms replaced economic norms. Similarly, credit companies asked that the difference between a cash and a credit transaction be called a "cash discount" rather than a "credit surcharge."[17] In both cases there is a massive, and invisible, superstructure that entirely encloses a particular bit of behavior and gives that particular element a quite different significance depending on the observer's view of the world.

When a day-care center tried to encourage parents to pick up their children promptly by charging a fine for being late, more parents chose to be late. What is the explanation for this classic example of the complexity principle of "unintended consequences"? It seems that under the earlier *social* norm that encouraged parents to community courtesy, the parents had tried to live up to the stated ideals and to act responsibly; however, when the rules were changed and the system became more legalistic, the harried parents were glad to pay the fine and escape the rules. The importance of sheer gullibility in the response to outside forces was shown in medical research, which has repeatedly demonstrated that placebos work as well as drugs in making people feel better, and that the more a medication costs, the better people feel after taking it.[18]

Behavioral economists put the conclusion starkly: "[P]eople are susceptible to irrelevant influences from their immediate environment ... irrelevant emotions, shortsightedness, and other forms of irrationality." Ariely concludes: "[W]e are pawns in a game whose forces we largely fail to comprehend" and we think we are in control but vastly underrate the degree to which other things influence us, "experts as well as novices."[19]

These cases and experiments are useful because they highlight the oddities in the reasoning process, but the conclusions drawn by the authors are much wider: that individuals frame their cognitive lives in terms of states to which they have adapted and which are "sometimes set by social norms and expectations" as well as their "level of aspiration, which may or may not be realistic."[20]

Particularly in the social world under study here as related to self government, there is an "absence of objective standards" and this relates to self-control, in that one may consciously impose on one's self a controlling frame that makes it possible to ignore reality entirely. The benign example of this is often Ulysses plugging his ears not to hear the song of the sirens and be lured from his planned course. But there are malign cases as well, such as ignoring social injustices in the interest of protecting a pretty picture of group harmony.

Underlying the analysis of socially skewed reasoning are many of the materials discussed earlier, such as Erving Goffman's emphasis on the dramas people stage for the other people in their lives, and Harold Garfinkel's study of the almost invisible lessons we inherit from our social groups and then impose upon the present, as well as the social origins of the reality in which people live. In all cases the conclusion is the same, that human cognition has an ethical dimension; people can sometimes choose the games they play, and they should choose consciously and carefully; but sometimes the choice can be made accidentally, or for perverse reasons by circumstances outside their control. Influence can be as ephemeral as the mist but nonetheless can chill to the bone.

While it is instructive to be shown exactly how badly everyone exercises their sovereign task of decision making, the present inquiry must go further to inquire into the specific biases of specific people so that their behavior can become more understandable. If game theory requires the intelligent player to understand how his partners and his opponents think, then some sort of cognitive mapping strategy is necessary, and some early Artificial Intelligence work on political leaders shows how this might be done.

THE GOLDWATER MACHINE

At its heights the discipline of artificial intelligence (AI) can be on the very frontiers of the cognitive sciences, dealing with such questions as whether a vector composed of random o's and 1's can learn how to survive in a digital environment, but AI's utility in helping people understand each other, as behavioral game theory requires, is more mundane. Perhaps the first direct attack on the problem was designed in reference to Alan Turing's original criterion for deciding whether or not artificial intelligence was really intelligent, whether someone interacting with a computerized interlocutor could tell whether they were dealing with a real human being or a computer program.[21]

Because the Turing test was whether an observer could determine who or what they were dealing with, the emphasis was on dialogue. The computer would be asked questions and would have to produce plausible responses; a requirement that involved many scientific disciplines from linguistics to cognitive psychology, psychoanalysis, ethnography, and sociology of interpersonal relations. Because of the question-and-answer format, the interest was not simply in cognitive structure itself but in the processes by which the artificial belief system created its reactions to the real-world facts with which it was presented, where events might or might not fit the initial belief system.

The sort of exercise was first brought into the political realm and made famous by Robert Abelson, a professor of psychology at Yale University, who chose a well-known conservative politician as the subject for a study of belief and cognition focusing on foreign policy attitudes; the model was known informally as the Goldwater machine, after Senator Barry Goldwater of Arizona.[22] The underlying assumption was that conservatives would be easier to model because they had fairly complete belief systems and adhered to them with a relatively high level of consistency. Once the belief system was written into computer code, the user should be able to feed in new pieces of information and test the system's intelligence by seeing how it reacted, expressing joy or regret at the news items, or incredulity, or confusion when told, for instance, that a person it considered bad had done a good thing, in which case it might deny or rationalize the news item so that the belief system could survive without making major changes.[23]

The superstructure invented for the Goldwater model illustrates the kind of information that may be needed to appreciate the thought processes of other human beings from the bottom up, as game theory requires. Abelson and Carroll started with an individual belief system defined as "an interrelated set of affect-laden cognitions" about the person's world, and the point of the computer model was that it could "maximize the explicitness" of these beliefs and how their interrelations played out, rather than relying on vague generalizations. Rejecting the old distinction between rationality and irrationality, the Abelson-Carroll approach used *subjective* rationality, "rationality within the constraints of [the person's] own experience and motivation."[24]

Subjectivity was not absolute. "It is far too glib to assume that 'people believe what they want to believe,' since unpleasant realities must often be accepted in some form, and pleasant absurdities must often be rejected." The Goldwater model had two strategies for dealing with the real-world facts with which it was presented: the *credibility* test and *rationalization*. Credibility was evaluated on whether the fact was already stored in the system, as a belief, or whether the opposite fact was stored, or whether by logical inference a match could be found. Rationalization was used where a clear inconsistency was found; it involved "explaining away" the fact by inventing other reasons the event might have happened.[25]

MAPPING THE NEIGHBORS

The substance of the cognitive model, the actual beliefs Goldwater was thought to hold, was predictable and the form was simple: a sentence composed of a concept and predicate, the predicate usually a verb followed by a concept ("subject-verb-object"); for instance, "Cuba subverts Latin America." These basic units could be combined at a horizontal level, as in "Russia controls Cuba's subversion of Latin America," so that there could be organized storage of concepts of "responsibility, causation, and impact."[26]

In addition to this horizontal layout of beliefs, the model included a vertical dimension where some concepts were instances of, or kinds of, other, more general concepts; Brazil, for instance, was an example of the concept of a Latin American nation, or India an example of a left-leaning neutral nation. In the other direction, some concepts were higher-level qualities of lower-level concepts, so there was a logical hierarchy of concepts. The thought process could then, for instance, travel up and down throughout the system, looking for variations on the central concepts and determining how well they fit together.[27]

The Credibility Test was used in two ways: to screen incoming sentences for their plausibility in terms of the existing beliefs, and to evaluate the "reasonableness" of self-produced sentences the system would "like to believe." The result would be any of three possible results: the facts contained in the sentence might be credible, incredible, or dubious. The first step in processing incoming information to untangle these different possibilities would be to see if the sentence were already stored in the mental model, or if the opposite were stored.

If neither of those strategies succeeded, Abelson's model would conjugate the entered sentence to search for evidence or counterevidence. If the statement was "Liberals support anticolonial policies," and if this could not be found anywhere in the system, then the system would search for "instances" of liberals – Adlai Stevenson, for example – and would check all predicates connected to him – for instance, "Stevenson makes flowery speeches," or "Stevenson ran for president" – to see if any might be an instance of "anticolonial policies." If Stevenson were found to "oppose Portugal on Angola," then that would give some support to the original statement.[28]

In other words, in the Abelson and Carroll model, the "chain of inductive reasoning" starts from liberals, drops down to examples of liberals, finds behaviors attached to those specific people, and moves back up to see if their behavior fits into the original statement. One case would not be enough, so the system would check out Earl Warren, but perhaps find that the Supreme Court justice was not documented on anticolonial policies. A rough rule was that half the cases found had to support the statement for it to be credible in the Goldwater machine.[29]

Failing to solve the credibility problems with these procedures would lead to a second attack on the "liberals support anticolonial policies" statement, this time with the use of a deductive approach rather than the inductive one used first. In this case the system would work upward from the basic sentence to a higher-level generalization. If one of the qualities attached to Liberals was "left-winger," and one of the meanings attached to "support anticolonial policies" was "mistreat U.S. friends abroad," then this proposition would allow deduction of the original sentence.

In some cases the Credibility Test will simply fail without coming to a conclusion, but there are two further mechanisms in the Goldwater model for a more interesting outcome. The *Denial* mechanism is invoked when a sentence is "credible but upsetting," and the process is just the opposite of the Credibility Test; the system negates the sentence and tries to prove that negation by searching the system's beliefs from this opposite point of view. Under certain circumstances Abelson's machine would take a final step, "Attempt Rationalization," designed to explain away sentences where there is an inconsistency between the subject and the predicate: either a favored person does a terrible thing, or a disfavored person does something praiseworthy. The system's strategy is to "deny the psychological responsibility of the actor" either by crediting major responsibility for the act to someone manipulating the actor, or defining the action as unintended and accidental, or by hoping that the act will eventually lead to desirable ends.

Solving this set of problems involves a higher, executive level of the model, with statements indicating which specified actors control which other actors, and perhaps also how the world works, for instance that "Q can accidentally cause P," or "P may lead to R." For example, if the problem is that "Cambodia rejects U.S. advice," the explanation may be that China controls Cambodia and therefore is the source behind Cambodia's rejection.[30]

ROUNDING OUT THE MACHINE

Abelson and Carroll postulate that an executive function might be developed to act independently rather than just responding to one sentence at a time that the researchers enter into the system. Such an executive might have a "worries list" that would allow it to think through various problems on its own if nothing else was happening. Other colorful abilities include an "incredulity reaction" when the subject and the predicate are inconsistent. The machine can also add the input sentences to its basic memory and so learn from its experiences.[31]

The Abelson approach was conceptually simple, based on the assumption that people organize the social world around them on the lattice in terms of what kinds of people are prominent in various parts of the field, what are the important issues for this group of participants, and how the different participants feel about the important issues. What slowed the inquiry was the technical difficulty of getting a computer, which has very stringent requirements for the storage of data, to map a complete world. As Abelson noted, tautologies clutter up the memory structure and yet cannot be excluded; the computer does not know that "colonial powers oppose anticolonial policies" unless it is explicitly included, even though the statement does not "enrich" the system in any way.[32]

Abelson, who taught statistics at Yale, was deeply concerned with scientific results, and hoped empirical use might be made of the approach. He suggested three methods for developing models like the one he described. The first method he suggests is the most elegant, and computer specialists have begun to work on it; it begins with random digits and allows the system to learn from the environment in which it is virtually situated.[33] The results are technically interesting but too advanced for use in studying *political* intelligence.

A second approach suggested by Abelson is the interviewing of a real person to collect the dimensions of his belief structure; at least, however, this requires a subject who is "articulate and cooperative" and willing to answer questions that attempt to elicit his whole semantic architecture. As shown in the Goldwater machine case, this involves listing concepts and predicates at several levels of abstraction and tying them together for inductive and deductive intellectual activity.

A third method suggested by Abelson is used later in this chapter: the analysis of a well-known individual by paraphrasing central principles of his belief system so that they can be fitted into a reasonably coherent system. This cannot be done, Abelson notes, using some neutral method like content analysis of speeches because the "prose of public figures ordinarily omits many obvious facts and definitions presumably taken for granted both by him and by his audience."[34] In the present context micro-sociology and behavioral game methods allow the observer to get beneath the surface. Cognitive political models become possible, that is, when Garfinkel's ethnomethodology is used to fill in the unspoken surrounding details.

THE KAISER AND THE TSAR

Another study in early artificial intelligence models takes the Goldwater lesson further by showing how two decision makers, facing exactly the same set of contingencies, can live in different worlds. This emphasizes a basic axiom of behavioral game theory, that no player can automatically assume that his colleague or opponent thinks about the world in the way that he does himself. The case chosen to illustrate this not-always-obvious truth was the outbreak of World War I, which mapped the decision processes of the German Kaiser and the Russian Tsar in the week during which the crisis burst upon the international scene.[35]

As with the Abelson model, the emphasis in the Kaiser/Tsar model was on psychological mechanisms as they influenced decisions and behavior, but the cognitive systems were composed of messages that represented *interpersonal* attitudes in a more direct way, not just as part of the general picture of the world but involving actual *persons* who were behaviorally relevant to an emerging crisis. The presence of the two decision makers was also important in showing how the background ideas related directly to behavioral choices made by the participants.

Pool and Kessler's decision makers' memories were made up of actual behavior, stored in the form "Actor 1 has engaged in a Relationship X with Actor 2"; for instance, the king of Ethiopia conferred with the president of Egypt. Toward these facts there were two possible attitudes: the first was *affect*, referring to the attitude or feelings which one actor had toward another actor, or toward an interpersonal relationship between two actors; the second relationship was *salience*, describing the importance of an actor or of an interpersonal relation between two actors.[36]

Since the total field of information is always too vast for the individual decision maker to notice or to remember every item, psychological mechanisms restrict "and distort" the input, so that the decision maker "has an incomplete and imperfect picture" of the total set of relationships. In the Pool and Kessler simulation, while both the Kaiser and the Tsar were given exactly the same messages, by the end of the week their worldviews were almost entirely different.[37]

These different views of the world developed because of five filtering principles used: the study hypothesized that people "pay more attention to news that deals with them" and "pay less attention to facts that contradict their previous views"; people also pay more attention to news from trusted sources, to news events that other actors think are important, and to actions they are committed to. Gaming is central to this approach, the authors correctly note, because it forces each player to revise his attention to take the other player into account, rather than thinking in a purely solitary hypothetical world.[38]

Using historical data from newspapers and historical documents, Pool and Kessler provided a computer simulation that basically fit the events of the week prior to the war. The two leaders, the Kaiser and the Tsar, paid attention to events particularly salient to themselves (and not each other), and missed several cues that might have prevented the war. Especially revealing was the discovery that each of the leaders perceived the other leader's actions "unmitigated by [that other leader's] moderating intents, while remaining conscious of his own moderate intentions that he must have (wrongly) assumed equally obvious to the other."[39]

The actual computer simulation ran the seven days from July 25 through July 31, 1914. The authors fed approximately 200 messages into the systems of the Kaiser and the Tsar for every day of the week, for a total of 1,400 messages, and watched as each decision maker picked and chose his way among them to fill the space designated as "attention." The determinant seemed to be "an unconscious pleasure-maximizing calculation" of the two leaders, based on the consequences that might result from inattention: "an unpleasant story that has no action consequences for the hearer may be disregarded because that way pain is minimized," but a "danger" message will get immediate attention in order to avoid the consequences.[40]

On Day One of the crisis, for instance, both men gave primary attention to Austria's ultimatum to Serbia, but for the Kaiser, almost equally important were German mobs rallying for war, while the Tsar emphasized Serbia's response to the ultimatum. A simple algorithm compactly shows how the decision process proceeds, since the process repeats itself for each of the messages that is received and then cycles back to the beginning to pick up the next.

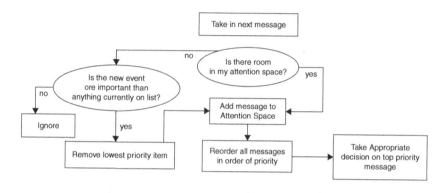

THE VIRTUAL MIND AT WORK

Working from the George Miller hypothesis that the mind can attend to seven, plus or minus two, items at a time, the Pool-Kessler model emphasizes the capacity of the decision space and makes available that number of items to each *event space*. If an event is very important, the decision maker will seek as many messages as possible; if it is unimportant, then fewer messages will be collected. The decision maker tries to keep the attention space as full and as up-to-date as possible, but there is an inertia factor, to reflect the difficulty of moving from one current problem to another, even if that seems necessary. Anything over two days old is removed from attention and placed in memory and is eventually forgotten entirely.

The decision maker's "mind" (the quotation marks are provided by Pool and Kessler) consists of two major sections: "one representing the kind of stable backlog of experience that each person carries with him into any new situation; the other representing the flow of new messages and information which the decision maker processes."[41] The background area is stored in the computer as an "affect" matrix, indicating how each actor feels about each other country in the field, in other words a lattice composed of interrelationships.

The other section of the model's mind has a hierarchical set of structures stored as lists. At the top of the hierarchy is the attention space, followed by a list of pressing problems. Below this is the "put aside" list, which serves as a buffer for the memory, and finally the deep memory, within which events gradually sink to the bottom and are lost. The daily decision process works on the attention space, while the put-aside list is for problems that are important but impossible to deal with immediately; if the attention space thins out, then the decision maker can pull these delayed items into activity.

Through this simple but complex process the Kaiser and the Tsar developed their two worlds that looked quite different, even though based on the same events. The Kaiser "attempted to localize the Serbian conflict ... and concerned himself with Belgian neutrality," along with attention to a domestic bank crisis. The Tsar, on the other hand, was concerned with Russia's relationship with France, and the visit of the French president to Russia; he also worried about England's commitment to what would later become the Allied cause in the war.

By the end of the seven days, the two international leaders "are not looking at the same world although reality impinges itself on each. Three events, Russia's mobilization, Germany's mobilization and the secret treaties, are in the attention space of both men. But two events, the collapse of Europe's stock markets and Germany's military precautions, are also in the attention of the Kaiser, while two other events, Serbia's Balkan allies and the Russian press, are in the attention of the Tsar."[42]

In the digital world of computer models, the conclusion that the Kaiser and the Tsar, as well as a large number of other European players in 1914, lived in seriously different landscapes is not implausible, yet the lesson is easily ignored in thinking about government and attempting to understand the very diverse ways in which different people engage in it. The problem has perhaps become more obvious with the explosion in personal media in the twenty-first century, because people are for perhaps the first time in history able to talk only to people who agree with them.

But all dimensions of complexity theory, from games to social organization, depend on a broader understanding of the serious differences in life worlds. To explore one example of one very different such world, the discussion turns to a case study of a man too easily dismissed as a pathological tyrant but who, after thirty-five years in office, seems to have outlasted his opponents.

THE MILD-MANNERED SCHOOLTEACHER

Robert Mugabe, president of the African nation of Zimbabwe, is an especially challenging subject for an exercise in understanding the full cognitive range of agents represented on the global political grid, because his behavior is so outrageous that it seems to defy explanation, especially analysis sensitive to the role of any kind of rationality in political matters. Mugabe harasses international visitors, including inspectors from the UN, speaks up for the thugs who attack the Zimbabwean opposition and seize white-owned farms, builds grandiose national monuments with money that might better be spent elsewhere, and gives speeches that defy all civility.[43]

It can also be noted that he has remained in power continually for thirty-five years, and when he remarried in 1996, the ceremony was attended by many African national leaders, including Nelson Mandela; he has, therefore, considerable staying power, as illustrated by the European Union, which recently lifted its sanctions on the country. While the West has clear grounds for designating Mugabe, in the usual top-down labels, as an autocrat, tyrant, or dictator, from the complexity theory's perspective the conclusion is more difficult to discover. History allows the curious observer to begin an attempt at tracing the cognitive architecture that carried Mugabe through a challenging life.

Mugabe was born in 1924 in colonial Rhodesia, carved out of the veldt by Cecil Rhodes and ruled as a white colony primarily by English settlers. Robert was one of six children born into a mission family, which the father deserted when his son was ten; the boy was intelligent and slightly solitary, was educated by the Jesuits, and began teaching in 1945. Later a university scholarship introduced him to Gandhi and Marx, but he was not politicized until a stint teaching in Ghana, where politics were more active.[44]

In 1960, Mugabe returned to Rhodesia where Joshua Nkomo had founded a moderate nationalist party, and after its repression, Mugabe formed the Zimbabwe African National Union; in 1964, he was arrested and spent eleven years in prison while Ian Smith, leader of the new Rhodesian Front, declared independence from the British in 1965. A three-way contest between Britain, the black nationalists, and Smith, including guerilla war from neighboring states, ended in 1979 with the Lancaster House agreement imposing democratic elections. "He impressed people who met him with his soft-spoken demeanour, his broad intellect, and his articulate manner," according to one observer, "but all this disguised a hardened and single-minded ambition."[45]

Although Mugabe was considered to be a terrorist because of his activity during the war, the British allowed his candidacy in the first independence elections in 1980, and he won 70 percent of the black seats in parliament. Elections were not his first preference; he would rather have fought the war to its end, completely defeating his opponents, but his outside supporters had refused to continue their backing and he had no choice. This represented a major division in the black community: whereas an older generation headed by Joshua Nkomo wanted reconciliation with white society, Mugabe instead wanted "to bring down not just white rule but Rhodesia's capitalist society with it."[46]

The neighboring states and their leaders were a major influence on Mugabe when he first took office as prime minister. Do not, they said, throw out the whites because if you do, your economy will collapse. Heeding their advice and slightly chastened by the need to actually govern the country now that he was actually in charge, Mugabe began his tenure in the prime minister's office as a model of generous civility. Whites had already begun to leave the country, horrified by the prospect of black rule, but Mugabe assured them of his goodwill so cordially that the flood stopped.

Mugabe met with Ian Smith and worked collegially with Christopher Soames, the British minister seconded to him to ease the transition, even urging him to stay on longer to help guide the novice state. Smith remarked on Mugabe's "maturity, reasonableness and sense of fair play," after early meetings; a former Rhodesian official who had engaged during the war in plotting Mugabe's assassination was pleasantly received by the new prime minister and concluded that Mugabe "was emerging as someone with a greater capacity and determination to shape the country's destiny for the benefit of all its people than any of his four [white] predecessors." Mugabe also appointed white ministers to his cabinet.[47]

AFTER THE REVOLUTION

To some extent the white exodus continued, but many farmers were delighted that the wars were over and they could return to their high life as wealthy settlers; there were no more military call-ups, no economic sanctions, no gasoline rationing, and they could take up their former leisure pursuits: trips to the eastern highlands, cruising on Lake Kariba, and game viewing. They also continued to dominate commercial farmland, commerce, industry, banking, and education. Migrants, usually to South Africa, included retired civil servants, soldiers and police from the previous regime, skilled artisans, and all the professions – doctors, accountants, teachers, nurses.[48] There was general fear in the white community that jobs would be Africanized and the settlers' children would not fare well.

For a while the new government in Zimbabwe under Mugabe was a definite honeymoon, but it was very short. One early shock came when a white general was refused promotion by the government. Although earlier white governments had also denied this general his desired promotion, the general this time resigned and struck back by announcing publically that he had asked Margaret Thatcher, then prime minister of Britain, to annul the election after the blacks won. Ian Smith's government had also refused to promote the general, but that was of course a different matter. Such defiance seriously threatened the cooperative myth Mugabe had tried to institute. But the damage came from both sides; an old, reckless friend of Mugabe offended whites by criticizing the church, calling Anglican churchmen instruments of oppression, then was involved in the death of a white farmer, and claimed immunity under the same law Smith had used to protect whites accused of killing blacks. The Indemnity and Compensation Act had granted immunity to those who acted to suppress terrorism; now the definition of terrorism had been inverted.[49]

The dynamics took on a life of their own, as complexity theory would predict: one side made critical speeches, the other side upped the ante with venomous and scathing media attacks. Smith's party in parliament said their black colleagues should go back to the bush; Smith himself said black Zimbabweans should be grateful to whites for all they had done to develop the country.[50] From that point it rapidly became clear that there was no going back. A major principle in everyone's cognitive map seemed to be the statement: "this country is ours and we deserve the top spot." Clearly it had become a zero-sum game.

In December 1981, the ZANU party headquarters was bombed at a time Mugabe had been scheduled to meet at a conference there, but was delayed; 7 people were killed and 142 injured. Mugabe attributed the blast to reactionary forces in both Zimbabwe and South Africa and complained that his government could have had counterrevolutionary forces "put before a firing squad" because of their past treason but instead forgave them, and yet those forces had failed to repent but were instead working to harm racial relations, sabotage the economy, and overthrow the officially elected government.[51]

This was a critical juncture in the development of Mugabe's political thought: he had tried moderation, allowing the old colonial elite to maintain its economic pursuits and its frequently lavish lifestyle, and the response had been vicious, in effect taking his effort at cooperation as not a positive gesture but as an admission of weakness and an opportunity if not an invitation to reassert their dominance in its full grandeur, despite the new democratic regime's expectation that since it had fairly won the election, it deserved a greater degree of political respect and consideration than it seemed to be receiving from the white participants.

The pattern is often typical when a new, formerly subordinate but newly empowered group treats the former rulers gently. Instead of being rewarded with gratitude from those former rulers, the new leaders find themselves scorned and dismissed as inadequate to their new position. This situation represents a classic game theory theme that is central to its analytic power: the fact that one player cannot really know what he has done in making a particular move until he sees how the opposition reacts. This is what makes politics so educational. It is also what makes self government so subtle.

THE VIRTUAL MUGABE MACHINE

To understand where these crucial events left Mugabe, it is appropriate to begin work on a cognitive map that will lay out the landscape he might have constructed as he looked around him, using the approaches discussed earlier in terms of the Goldwater machine and the Kaiser and the Tzar model. First and most indignantly, Mugabe would have seen a former ruling class determined to retain its favored position in society and to keep the former lower class at the very bottom level of society, not just impoverished but scorned as well. The second feature in Mugabe's cognitive map would be less obvious to an outside observer and would require a deliberate effort to recognize: Mugabe's friends were frequently his worst enemies; it was his own people who were almost as troublesome to him as were the white colonials.

One black group was the opposing political party run by Nkomo and prone to wanting compromise with the whites. Another group was Mugabe's own activist friends who were furious at the white elite, who rejoiced in the black electoral victory, and who were both very greedy and uncontrollably impatient; they wanted their reward and they were not willing to wait. They had also been taught by the former rulers, not explicitly but by watching their behavior, that there were no holds barred when one achieved political power; one took what one wanted.

Mugabe therefore was not a sovereign ruler, presiding with full control over a quiet government, but a political man facing an explosive social mixture, invisible to people who think elections solve all problems and that in their wake everyone will start anew, discounting inequalities and resentments from the past. In studying Mugabe's cognition, history is particularly important, because his solution to nation building in Zimbabwe was effectively to turn the white regime's political architecture, as well as its culture, upside down. Where the white colonials had ruled arbitrarily, he would rule arbitrarily; where the white colonials took all the country's resources for themselves, Mugabe would work to see that everything of value went to his friends. This served not only his ideological preferences; it acceded to the demands of his followers and was therefore doubly useful.

The underlying Garfinkel dimension, that array of attitudes almost invisible in a society but widespread because they exist in everyone's social memory, is important in explaining the rage over which Mugabe reigned. It was a not too distant past, in 1890, when outsiders arrived in Mashonaland looking for gold or, if that failed, for land. Cecil Rhodes distributed large tracts; others took land on their own, including missionaries and land speculation companies. The newcomers took the best land, causing uprisings in 1896 that killed 10 percent of the settlers.[52]

After that, Africans were restricted to special areas, and overcrowding grew. A 1931 land apportionment act extended the white areas and banned blacks from holding land outside their restricted areas. After World War II, more settlers arrived and, needing more land, simply went ahead and took it. All institutions in the colonial society supported these practices; when the courts found in favor of the indigenous people who were displaced from their traditional lands, the government simply overrode the courts.[53]

The local people fought guerilla wars through the 1970s with land grievances the major theme, and resentment was raw. After the 1980 elections the government was supposed to acquire land for redistribution only if white owners were willing to sell, but aggressive gangs overwhelmed the orderly plans, and Mugabe gave land away to his followers as an early European king might have done, buying allegiance to the crown. Land redistribution had not initially been Mugabe's priority, but ZANU politicians pursued it relentlessly; by 1990 there was a new class of landowners including government ministers, members of parliament, new civil servants, and military and police officials.[54]

Land *reform* as distinguished from land expropriation never succeeded in Zimbabwe. Originally the government had agreed to buy only
land from willing sellers, but after ten years a law was passed to allow
simple confiscation of any land, at a fixed price and without legal appeal.
White settlers tried to debate the issue and were suppressed; the government eventually announced that land questions were no longer negotiable but a matter of restitution and justice. By the mid-1990s the forcible
acquisitions were being directed even against black-owned farms, with
residents forcibly evicted by riot police. Protests had some effect when it
was shown that the confiscated lands were never actually redistributed to
the poor, but these results were transitory, and after a pause the Mugabe
elite continued to absorb government lands without restraint.[55]

THE VIEW FROM THE CENTER

It is easy to document the egregious ways in which Mugabe's government
of Zimbabwe went downhill for most of his years in office; the more com-
pelling question is why this happened. A return to cognitive complexity
analysis helps in this regard by forcing the observer away from easy con-
demnations and closer to the situation as Mugabe himself faced it. As a
start, the following set of operational rules can be considered. They are
written from what might be Mugabe's point of view as he faced his newly
acquired domain in light of his personal history and the general state of the
nation as it appeared to him, recalling the history Cecil Rhodes had contributed to the indigenous people's collective memory. As rational choice
theory emphasizes the importance of the individual actor's goals, the code
begins with a hypothesized definition of Mugabe's goals, then moves on to
the practical necessities surrounding that objective – in other words, what
Mugabe believes about his world and the people who inhabit it.

1. *Goal*: That the country of Zimbabwe shall be governed by its
   indigenous people without outside interference, either direct or
   indirect.
2. *Belief*: Outsiders will invariably govern in their own interest.
3. *Belief*: To gain the support of the people, the government must do
   what the people want.
4. *Belief*: Otherwise the people will support someone else.
5. *Belief*: The people want land and wealth, and vengeance.
6. *Belief*: The people are all I have if I am to stay in power; and I have
   no power to change the people.

7. *Conclusion:* I will defend the people who are loyal to me, and them only.
8. *Conclusion:* I will dramatize their legitimacy by providing justification for their gains.
9. *Conclusion:* In my own behavior I will dramatize our joint legitimacy, our joint glory.

A frequent reaction by outsiders when they are introduced to the history of Mugabe and Zimbabwe is to say he is clearly power mad, which leads back to Lord Acton's theory and gives a superficial satisfaction in having explained the man: power tends to corrupt, absolute power tends to corrupt absolutely. Since Mugabe's Zimbabwe is a perfect story of corruption, this explanation has a certain sentimental appeal. But such simple explanations are made from the top down and allow the observer to escape the richer lessons that emerge from getting more bottom-up detail.

The first proposition in Mugabe's code states an almost standard hope for a people that has suffered invasion and oppression, the desire to govern themselves. America's founding fathers felt the same when they decided to throw out King George. What gives this obvious goal particular bite in Mugabe's cognitive landscape is the set of secondary propositions within which it has been embedded.

The second statement, that outsiders invariably govern in their own interest, reflects a particularly vivid experience in Zimbabwe, that the settlers accorded no rights at all to the local people. Rather than providing any routes of upward mobility, Rhodesia could only allow, if someone happened to get some education, that they could follow a teaching career, and that preferably in another country. The second of Mugabe's beliefs should be recognized as straight out of Anthony Downs, and quite rational; indeed it suggests Downs's theory is not just a theory of democracy but of all politics everywhere; the necessity is to find out what people want and then do it. History may, however, give them extremely violent wants, a point the rational choice theorists tend to overlook.

Where its inclusion in Mugabe's cognitive map amplifies the original Downsian theory is that the followers need not be the whole citizen body but may be a selected few, exactly those who have a particular intensity to their demands. In this sense there are no strongmen, tyrants, or dictators, but only men trying to ride the tiger they have mounted. In practical terms, no one rules alone, in defiance of his associates on the political lattice. Every leader of every group must, if he or she is to stay in office, be supported by someone. The appropriate question is not whether the citizens, as a group, are the supporters of a given regime, but *which groups* support the regime. Mugabe's most obvious supporters are the aggressive, the angry, and the greedy; these are those he must satisfy, and a program of law and order will not suffice for such a base.

Mugabe's next belief in the cognitive list captures this truth: that his supporters, who fought by his side through guerilla and civil war, wanted land, vengeance, and access to the lifestyle enjoyed by the former colonial elites. It is important to highlight what their demands did not include; no one was asking for good government in any general sense, and at any rate Mugabe was in no position to offer it. Eleven years in prison and academic degrees acquired by correspondence do not prepare a man to administer a country, particularly in the absence of an educated elite to manage the many executive programs and agencies that normal government requires.

The final belief listed, that Mugabe had no power to change the people he had inherited but needed them to stay in power, emphasizes his position in his party as fragile, something he had to work every hour of every day to maintain. This leads to the three final elements of the cognitive system, that Mugabe will use loyalty as his sole criterion for the distribution of all goods, including honor; if men supported him, Mugabe would protect, defend, and praise them. The final point follows from Goffman's theatrical metaphor: staying on top of a self-organized political system structured like Zimbabwe involves intricate attention to one's followers but also a constant dramatic display of one's personal legitimacy, one's right to rule over the sacred contours of the beloved nation.

RECONSIDERING SOCIETY

This simple map, looking at Zimbabwe's leader from his bottom-up perspective, could work itself out in practice in sometimes appalling ways. This was most apparent in the farm invasions and land expropriations that continued throughout his tenure. While it was not clear that Mugabe would have pursued land redistribution on his own, the importance of land as patronage to those who supported his party seems to have been decisive. It recalls Tilly's theory of early Europe; violence in Zimbabwe was everywhere, and those who used it most effectively were those who prospered. Originally war veterans' groups organized themselves as a way of surviving in a chaotic landscape; later many young men would call themselves war veterans even though they had not participated in the guerilla wars, because the term served to justify their activities.

Mugabe stood behind these and other supporters steadfastly, manipulating legislation in their favor, granting amnesties, and ignoring or intimidating courts that ruled against him. Associated with support for acquisition of wealth by a new elite was their inclusion in the political system; at one point Mugabe had forty-two ministers – although the World Bank said fifteen would suffice – and he gave out Mercedeses and plush retirement packages to all participants.[56]

In terms of Zimbabwean democracy, its campaigns and elections, Mugabe's behavior suggested a background philosophical belief that might be added to the basic cognitive map suggested earlier, in that he clearly felt all politics, if not indeed all life, was zero-sum: whatever one player gained, the other player lost. Elections were held more or less regularly, but arrangements were manipulated in terms of missing polling places, stuffed ballot boxes, gerrymandering, and similar practices. Worse was the regime's behavior during campaigns, where opposition rallies were banned, hoodlums were sent to disrupt those that were held anyway, and opposition leaders were attacked by thugs or jailed.

Mugabe took the election results seriously, however, and if a district failed to vote for his party, it would be punished by not receiving aid in times of famine or drought. His reasoning on this was flawlessly rational and emphasizes how innocently American rational choice theorists use the term, never taking it to Mugabe's logical end point, that if all the people get government aid, no matter who they vote for, then why would anyone vote for him?

Attention is often given to Mugabe's Marxism, which he was said to have picked up in university and demonstrated in his admiration for Ceaucescu, North Korea, and more recently China; yet he never showed any interest in benefiting the Zimbabwean peasant. He made a distinction, in looking around the lattice, between two types of agents – *chefs* and *povos*, the elites and the masses – and the importance of the masses seems to have been entirely in whether or not they voted correctly. Programs to actually give land to the poor disappeared early in his tenure, and no support was given to teach them how to make a living on such land if they acquired it.

He considered laborers on white farms as enemies because they associated with the colonial masters, and distrusted even schoolteachers, perhaps because he had been one himself. At one point white businesses were invaded in the name of their exploitation of labor, but this was brief. Various campaigns, instead, were directed at dissidents and "rubbish," defined as anyone who did not support him, *murambatsvina* and *gukurahundi*. What is striking is the degree to which Zimbabweans kept organizing new protest parties, the frequency with which districts voted against him, and the stubborn way judges ruled against the government.[57] It reinforces Mugabe's central cognitive point, that just holding on to his authority was his major challenge in governing.

The cultural side of his cognitive interpretation of the world was a major element in Mugabe's strategy for ruling, and its structure emphasizes one of complexity theory's major ideas, that choices made by one group of people at one point in time will have unintended consequences for other groups, acting on the choice open to them at a later point in time. Colonialism educated the people on whom it imposed itself, and each colonial regime affected its host countries in slightly different ways. In Rhodesia the legacy was: (1) arbitrary confiscation of property, supported (2) by a legal system that legitimized and enforced racial bias, and (3) the creation of an aristocratic lifestyle for members of the favored group and peonage for the rest.

Mugabe repeatedly uses this pattern as a justification for outrageous behavior by his Zimbabwean regime, and he does not see why his critics do not appreciate the parallel. The British did not rule by law, according to his interpretation, because their law was biased law, created to uphold entrenched attitudes about master races. Public response drives him to denial of such statements, but Mugabe clearly believes it and seeks to impose it, not racially, but under the euphemistic principle that good things must be given only to those "who support the struggle." This struggle, as described by one supporter, may be to take the society "back to zero," to the days before it was corrupted by outsiders.[58] Leaving aside the legal issues, or indeed the moral ones, the attitude is a tribute to the power of self organization as a motivating force in history.

THE PAST CARVED INTO THE PRESENT

One of the peripheral but interesting sidebars of complexity theory is the idea of *unintended consequences*, a technical term that has proved its relevance by turning up in everyday conversations outside academia. The theoretic roots of the unintended-consequences explanation are neither understood nor noticed, and it is frequently used to suggest that events are too mysterious to predict. Careful consideration of the elements of complexity theory can be used to reduce the level of mystery in the surrounding political world however. By focusing attention on individual people, on their experiences and their reactions to those experiences, from the bottom up, the observer can uncover processes and ideas that drive individual behavior and the events that follow from individual choices.

The phenomenon that is Robert Mugabe is a small illustration of unintended consequences in operation. On the surface, the international media can only see frightened but brave young white farmers, driven off their carefully cultivated lands by marauding bands of Zimbabwean thugs. The story seems clear, that lawlessness reigns in the country and the injustice is enforced by random violence, all under the aegis of one monumentally perverse leader.

The Zimbabwe story is not this simple. The analysis of the country's recent history and its architectural impact within the political intelligence of its long-term president and his variegated supporters demonstrates that the situation is not lawless, nor is it random. In effect, Mugabe has inverted the legal system imposed on the country by the colonial settlers, and its application is anything but random. If the colonials ruled the country in their own interest, disparaging the original inhabitants' rights, then Mugabe will rule in the interest of the indigenous people against the rights of those whom he thinks of as the invaders.

The phrase "unintended consequences," despite its origin in complexity theory, is surprisingly top-down in terms of its explanatory quality, rather implying that the events so described are inherently mysterious, not accessible to any sort of straightforward explanation. When the term is correctly used from the bottom up, however, the meaning can be obvious; indeed, the logic is almost syllogistic in its simplicity. IF a stronger group attacks a weaker group and takes all its resources, from its land to its dignity, THEN the weaker group will be angry; and IF that weaker group finds that circumstances change and come to favor it, THEN that formerly weak group will take revenge.

The appreciation of the long-term interrelatedness of actions taken over time is a particularly useful contribution of complexity theory because it organizes events and games logically, so that the observer can better appreciate the way in which events circle outward, as waves expand from a stone tossed into a quiet pond. Consequences are unintended only because players forget that justice is double-edged. Consequences are unintended because players forget to study their opponents, and fail to recognize that their opponents may learn from hard experience and later, in victory, apply the hard laws they have learned from their losses.

Tversky and Kahneman, in the behavioral decision studies discussed earlier in this chapter, point out that the simple criterion question of "what do I want now?" as a guide to decision making is flawed in that it may lead to cognitive inconsistencies in terms of whether the individual's desires, at one point in time, accurately reflect the pleasure or pain the decision will bring about. The issue is central to self government, as seen earlier in Thomas More's well-run island where all pleasures were evaluated solely on whether or not the future consequences were beneficial or harmful.

From a more modern perspective, Tversky and Kahneman propose a "predictive" criterion of rationality to improve the quality of decisions; instead of "what do I want now?" they shift to "what will I feel then?" in order to substitute a different frame within which to consider a possible action. They conclude that "the framing of acts and outcomes can also reflect the acceptance or rejection of responsibility for particular consequences," and that the deliberate manipulation of frames is "an ethically significant act" and an instrument of self-control.[59] Cognitive psychology in this case supports conclusions already suggested by micro-sociology about the practice and the constraints of self government: that political intelligence needs to take into account the lessons it teaches its opponents.

7

The Complexity of Simplicity

If politics is everywhere around us, and can be played at high or low levels, and if everyone is a participant, consciously or unconsciously, in this political process of allocating values, then it becomes relevant to study how the universal process acts on the individual person, how the individual person acts on his or her companions in the battle, and what the individual person does to himself or herself in terms of the choices made. In respect to personal self government, the last point is important and often overlooked; people need to be conscious of their own self government in order to be able to participate sensibly with the people around them.

In terms of the individual's self government, this concluding chapter begins with three old bottom-up classics that situate the innovations of complexity theory firmly in traditional yet nontraditional concerns about the circumstances and constraints of political identity and the hazards of sovereignty. A single non-philosophical chapter is taken from Plato's grand study of the republic and its virtues to show the importance of different types of individual persons in constituting types of regime, and to emphasize the dialectical interaction of person and regime as virtue leads to vice and vice to a reconsideration of virtue. Completing Plato's empirical argument from a modern perspective is Machiavelli's study of the prince, also known as the self-governed man and a guide to the oppressed. Finally Karl Marx explains what politics is.

Returning then to a central theme of the book, namely the importance of game theory as a tool useful in the pursuit of self government at both the individual and social levels when enriched with the micro-sociological detail of prior chapters, particular attention is given to its capacity to describe the invisible – to show, that is, not only what happens but what does not happen when political people interact with one another. These examples dig under the surface of events to provide explanation of why individual actors behave in sometimes perplexing ways. The general answer is that the participants in a particular scrimmage defined their payoffs in a way the observer may not have appreciated without the guidance of the game matrix. The chapter and the book conclude with a case study of Nelson Mandela and his South Africa, showing how closely the two meanings of self government may intertwine.

AFTER THE PHILOSOPHER KING

No one described better than Plato the dialectical process in which individual behavior impacts social conditions for other people, how their reactions spiral off to affect still other people, and how the impact of their behavior is relevant both at the psychological and the sociopolitical levels to all of the participants who continue to be present and to take part in the ongoing activity. Plato seems an unexpected precursor of complexity theory because his work is generally considered high philosophy rather than science of any sort, but when his attention went in an empirical direction, the result was science in the innovative pattern described in this book, complexity theory as the micro-observation of micro-behavior.

The intelligent observation of the other people who are spread across the lattice that surrounds the governing individual is another of the famous footnotes to Plato, those discoveries that the Greek philosopher made centuries ago and which keep being rediscovered in subsequent periods. Plato was a formidable observer of empirical human behavior, when he was not otherwise occupied, and his analysis in Book VIII of *The Republic* is directly relevant to the understanding of government in general as well as of self government in particular.[1]

Plato's basic point is not always fully clear because it is so basic that it can be overlooked. *The Republic* is based on the principle that the nature of government is a direct reflection of the character of the men who compose it, that these characteristics vary in systematic ways and lead to substantially different types of regime, and that change occurs as different men react to each other across time. Or, as Plato more vigorously put it, change occurs as different men fight their way through history, being simply themselves but being important in bringing their values into and out of political prominence. This is pure complexity theory, *avant la lettre*, and deserves attention.

In the context of the overall argument contained in Book VIII of Plato's *Republic*, the decline of the ideal state may seem like a simple just-so story, but if, with honest apologies to philosophers, the tale is wrested from its larger metaphysical environment and asked to stand alone, the sequence Plato describes can be seen as a case of bottom-up analysis, rich in explanatory import. Plato's distinctive methodological choice in explaining "how things fall apart" is his interdependent decision model, populated by actors guided by substantively different motives defined by the well-known metals classification, where the best people are gold, the next best are silver, and everyone else is brass and iron.[2]

The collapse of the perfect state begins, according to Plato, with a mathematical miscalculation, but the more important empirical sequence begins, bottom up, with a representative philosophic man who, finding himself surrounded by lesser mortals, opts out of the ruling group so not to be bothered by having to endure their vulgarity. Plato's account emphasizes that this decision, which the philosopher took in consultation with no one but himself, directly affects his wife, who intended to achieve social status by marrying him and has now, by his retirement, been deprived of her former prestige; other wives make her aware of this loss if she fails to notice it on her own.[3]

As the philosopher's wife complains about his thoughtless choice that has so negatively affected her position in the world, a second interdependence occurs in that their son hears her charges and is ashamed that his father is no longer honored in society. Plato shows how the problem circles outward further as the family servants are affected by the philosopher's decision; because he no longer supports them in their quarrels with other men's servants, they are angry and badger the son to be *more of a man* than his simpleton father.[4]

IT IS A WISE CHILD WHO . . .

After this basic psychological start on the process of change, Plato then begins tracing the further generational learning cycle that pushes change onward, step by step as the children age and take on adult interests. For the philosopher's son, the situation caused by his father's retirement results in severe cognitive dissonance: he admires his father's learning but does not like the social scorn now associated with him. The son therefore adopts a middle position in terms of behavior and social status; as a youth he is spirited and loves victory, as a man he is haughty and loves honor; finally the mature son becomes entangled in litigation and loses everything.[5] Educated by this unexpected loss of stature and privilege, the next generation, impoverished and frightened at the speed with which honor can disappear, turns to pure moneymaking.

Plato expresses a certain respect for the man that now emerges: he is hardworking, stingy, fulfills only his necessary desires, has no education, and makes war badly because he is not willing to spend money on it.[6] At the personal level, his soul is factional, with conflicting desires, but he tries to restrain any desire for excess. His worst problem, according to Plato's account, is his love of wealth; this creates a divided city, the rich who rule and the poor who eventually will bring down the whole structure.

The more immediate unintended consequence of the government of the stingy rich is that their self-discipline cannot be passed on to their children, according to the Platonic story. The youth must be forced into consumerism because unless the youth are licentious, they will not need to borrow the money the rich profit by lending them. This creates two cities, the rich rulers' children and the indigent poor; one lazy and soft, the other lean and hard. When the revolution comes, the poor win and the glories of democracy ensue.[7]

Plato describes democracy as "probably the fairest of the regimes ... like a many-colored cloak decorated in all hues"; democracy is also convenient in studying the wider spectrum of regimes, according to Plato, because it displays within itself all the other ways a city can be ordered, so that people can choose their government "like a man going into a general store." Such a regime is praised by Plato in ambiguous terms; his approbation is always conditioned with such clauses as "for the moment" and "it would seem"; and compliments are double-edged, as where democratic regimes dispense "equality to equals *and unequals* alike."[8]

When Plato inspects the young man whose character fits the democratic regime, the picture he paints is of a person raised (by his oligarchic father) without proper education and seduced into self-indulgence by those who want to sell him pleasures; he is a youth who has become a battlefield between contradictory values: insolence argues with virtue, moderation loses to wastefulness, shamelessness is called courage, and anarchy rules.[9] With luck, the youth grows up and may settle at some middle point, fostering all the human desires equally, whether they are necessary or frivolous.

The conclusion follows: "[T]here is neither order nor necessity in [the democratic son's] life, but calling this life sweet, free, and blessed he follows it throughout." Such a people, Plato concludes, are accustomed to being overindulged by their leaders and will be very hard on those rulers if *any* restraint is placed on them; neither the good doctor nor the good beekeeper can have any effect on this sort of citizen.[10] But the democratic regime is the only one that allows for philosophy, because in its freedom the individual may by study become self-governed, superior to the surrounding city.

Academic political philosophers rightly call this chapter in *The Republic* the "outline of a political *science*,"[11] a large and plausible claim from the viewpoint of complexity theory, but mainstream political scientists have never seen Plato's discussion as at all relevant to the modern world; and this is understandable, since nothing in Book VIII has anything to do with the standard concerns of academic political science in terms of democracy, elections, or common methodological techniques for assessing citizen attitudes. What Book VIII shows, however, is that Plato was a better scientist than he may have been given credit for. As the work of Goffman and Garfinkel has shown, from a sociological direction, there is important political impact in even the most everyday events, like a servant complaining that his master is insufficiently aggressive. These basic patterns spread easily across whole societies and mold them, as Plato argued.

For the appreciation of self government, the important points of Plato's analysis are: first, that political regimes are both *creators of* certain types of people, and are *created by* certain types of people; and second, that the change in regime patterns follows a sociological logic, where the unintended effects of various behaviors lead to new circumstances and those circumstances change the next generation. This will be familiar from the *Social Construction of Reality* and Bourdieu's *habitus*, but Plato's interest in who is winning, *within the individual,* is philosophically and scientifically different.

ON THE DARK SIDE

There is one further character in Plato's list of governments, the tyrant, and it is important to include him in the analysis because the sociological and economic theorists included in the present study tend to have an important bias toward the benign – toward sociopolitical behavior in restaurants, doctor's offices, fishing villages, schools, and other reasonably peaceful small groups. Yet most real-world societies also contain serious hostilities between ethnicities, races, genders, and ideologies. Self government would be seriously incomplete if it did not take such hard-core disagreements into account, and a closer study of the micro-nature of the tyrant can be useful.

Plato deals with the tyrant[12] in terms of a distinction between necessary and unnecessary human needs: the necessary and therefore allowable needs are basic: water, food, sleep, all in moderation. All other needs are for Plato unnecessary, including all the passions, and the tyrant in his definition is committed wholesale to satisfying all the unnecessary passions at the expense of everyone else. If there are only a few such men in a city, they do "small evil deeds": they "steal, break into houses, cut purses, go off with people's clothes, rob temples, and lead men into slavery ... bear false witness and take bribes." In private life such tyrants act either as masters to their followers or sycophants to more powerful men from whom they need favors.[13]

Plato then goes on casually to mention a point readers will recognize from earlier chapters of the present book on self government: that for observers to understand such men, they must not judge on external appearances or masks, but must be *able to get underneath the surface* and see what is really going on. "Would I also be right in suggesting," Plato inquires of Glaucon, "that man should be deemed fit to judge them who is able with his thought to creep into a man's disposition and see through it – a man who is not like a child looking from outside and overwhelmed by the tyrannic pomp set up as a facade for those outside, but who rather *sees through it* adequately?"[14] This "seeing through" the surface is exactly the point essential to self government, because getting the underlying structure is central to understanding events.

Beyond this point, Plato's interests return to the philosophical question of human happiness rather than the political question of survival in the face of such tyrants when they are in office, leaving the reader with a picture of tyranny in the individual as a total chaos of uncontrolled impulses and a tyrannical regime as the antithesis of self government, since only one man rules. Some centuries later Machiavelli would put a different spin on the matter by reconsidering tyranny as politics and turning it into the very center of his theory. He did this by redefining men's natures and moving out of Plato's eternal worldonto an everyday lattice subject to constant practical threats and sometimes dreadful opportunities.

FORTUNE FAVORS THE BOLD

Machiavelli is well known for a serious vigor in the discussion of strategy; *The Prince* is replete with cases of magnificent dinners after which the host has all the guests massacred, or of loyal officials who carried out unpopular policies and whose bodies were displayed, chopped into bloody pieces, in the marketplace to assuage the anger of the public. Machiavelli is frequently unable to constrain his admiration for the effectiveness of such actions.[15] Yet other readers see *The Prince* as an early treatise on game theory, based on the tenet that the first rule is to protect the self from danger and achieve one's purposes, and that even where it may be impossible to achieve the original goal, honor is accorded to those who play well.

Machiavelli's analysis begins with the short but incisive bit of text that serves as his contribution to political sociology: "[I]n every city there are these two different humors which have their origin in the desire of the people to be free of the orders and oppression of the great and the desire of the latter to order about and oppress the people."[16] There is some controversy among academics as to just what audience Machiavelli is addressing as he goes on to give advice for behavior under such circumstances; perhaps, it may be argued, the advice is directed to everyone.

The curriculum laid out in *The Prince* has been interpreted in many ways. This is just what makes a classic book classic; it speaks afresh to every new contingency in which a reader might become involved. As a manual of self government, the book summarizes in dramatic form much of the social science included in the present essay on complexity. Whether he is speaking to the man seeking power in Florentine politics of the 1500s or to those in danger from more recent power holders, Machiavelli lays out the basic principles concisely.

From the self government perspective, his primary thesis is the importance of relying only on the self: beware of being given power or office, he says, because inexperience will mean such power is quickly lost.[17] Unless the individual acts on personal initiative, and studies the results carefully so they become personal lessons, goals cannot be held even if attained. Machiavelli's assumption, in the entire analysis of *The Prince*, is that the other players are not innocuous tenants of the political lattice, but are predators and may become, at any moment, dangerous adversaries. His advice, therefore, is couched in terms of wars and how to win them, and this provides a sharp edge to the discussion which is particular to hardball political science.

Before moving on to human-related issues of interpersonal strategy, Machiavelli advises study of the landscape itself, knowing where the dead ends are, the location of the valleys where ambush is easy, and making note of high grounds that should be taken before the enemy is able to secure them and dominate the field. Even in time of peace the individual should be well organized, well armed, and in good physical condition. Luck is fickle, Machiavelli observes, but this does not mean forethought, care, and prudence are unnecessary; a river in flood cannot be controlled, but in quiet times preparations can be made to avoid its ravages.[18]

PEOPLE SHOULD NOT BE BUT SEEM

In respect to social behavior, Machiavelli's advice recalls the dramaturgical model of Erving Goffman discussed in Chapter 4 because it emphasizes the difference between how one's actions appear and what they actually entail in terms of self-protection. Some habits that appear virtuous will bring ruin, he cautions. There are some sensible examples of this principle; for instance, one must appear generous but must not give away resources that may be needed for reaching more important personal goals; similarly, kindness should be rationed, lest it lead to others' bad behavior. But Machiavelli takes the principle into rough country, believing that breaking one's word has accomplished great things, and action is more effective than debate: a belief that leads him to the conclusion that proceedings in law courts may fail, and that individual *action* is more effective.[19]

What justifies such apparently lawless behavior, for Machiavelli? Men will not keep faith with you, he argues, so you are not bound to keep faith with them. This comes in conjunction with the advice about lions and foxes, that one must be a lion to frighten wolves and a fox to avoid traps. Acting only like the lion is stupid, he says: you should not stick to your word when it would be to your disadvantage or when circumstances have changed. The wise man must appear to have all the virtues, must appear to be "compassionate, faithful to his word, kind, guileless, and devout ... indeed he should be so. But his disposition should be such that, if he needs to be the opposite, he knows how."[20] Many people may privately agree with this advice; for the self-governed it is important that Machiavelli states it honestly, as others do not.

The self must be protected also from friends and flatterers, who are not to be trusted, according to Machiavelli's advice. One needs information from such people, but if they feel free to give you advice, you will lose prestige, so allow such intimacy only when you explicitly ask for it. But beware: when things go well, such people are all yours, yet when trouble comes, they disappear like the wind. The importance of this point seems to explain Machiavelli's constant warnings against hiring mercenary troops, which, because they are bought, can be lured away by anyone who offers them a better price, and can carry your secrets into the enemy's camp.

True honor is earned, according to Machiavelli's ontology, only by personal excellence, by the ability to conceive great projects and the capacity to carry them through. While Machiavelli's tactics may sound extreme in their harshness, on the other hand he does not waver in his respect for achievement, for actually getting things done in a hazardous political world. In terms of complexity theory, it is interesting how Machiavelli situates his advice at the strategic level: one acts not for the general good, which in a postmodern world is unknowable, but for one's own honor, worthy of acclamation by the observers. It is a neat summary of self government's balancing between the individual and the group.

CAN ALL SIDES BE RIGHT?

The political problem of who is right and who is wrong, in any particular struggle, is perhaps the fountainhead of self government, if considered in the abstract. The debate is usually one-sided: the speaker is right and the world is wrong. Pulpits are ascended, anathemas are bandied about, virtue is torn into sufficient pieces to cover everyone in any way connected to the controversy. When such cases are treated not in the abstract, from the top down, but from the bottom up, the picture gets clearer and it is more difficult to render a one-sided verdict.

To illustrate this point, one last classic work can be brought in to complete the commentaries of Plato and Machiavelli by focusing with a sociological artistry on an economic debate. The writer is Karl Marx, and he is considering the length of the working day; his conclusion is not what everyone might expect from the conventional interpretation of Marx's commitments, nor indeed is it the opposite of what people might expect. In the important question of which side to be on, Marx proposes an unheard-of third possibility. Perhaps, he says, everyone is right. And that, miraculously, is the definition of politics.

Marx is an unexpected example of an agent-centered theorist, and his use of the same bottom-up or complexity model defined here is counterintuitive because his general theory is usually thought of as a grand historical sweep from feudalism through capitalism, then socialism into communism, and is often considered quasi-Hegelian, based on a process that unfolds automatically or naturally from inherent principles. But Marx also had a very bottom-up theory, and an interest in analytic reduction that led him to a lattice-based world as defined by complexity theory where battles never culminate but rage on and on, across time and history.

A short example can be found in *Das Capital*, tucked within economic theory of a high and controversial nature that can be ignored here, where the concern is not to evaluate economic schools, but to show how the bottom-up perspective brings out clearly the nature of the mixed-motive controversy we call politics. Marx does this in his consideration of the length of the working day, and the plight of an ambitious but fairminded capitalist who wants to make a profit but wants it understood by all observers that his profit is legitimate, respectable, even public spirited.[21] Marx rejoiced, as he sometimes did in his writings, by playing with the situation in cheerfully dramatic form: he describes a debate among concrete individual people about what they are doing and what each is thinking about what the others are doing. The facts are simple. If cotton is to be made into yarn, someone must bring together a certain amount of cotton, a certain type of machinery, and certain quantities of human labor.[22] Marx lays this out on a little spread sheet as follows:

	6 *hours*
Price of 10 pounds of cotton	10 shillings
Cost of wear on machinery	2 shillings
Six hours labor	3 shillings
Value of yarn	15 shillings

The problem with this calculation is, as Marx's capitalist unhappily concludes, it provides no profit; the price that he can properly ask for the product is exactly equal to the investment he has made, and the capitalist feels this is inappropriate. Perhaps there are profits in scale? Since the laborer can certainly work a longer day, everything can be doubled.

	12 *hours*
Price of 20 pounds of cotton	20 shillings
Cost of wear on machinery	4 shillings
Twelve hours labor	6 shillings
Value of yarn	30 shillings

This does not fill the requirement either; the value of the yarn, the value he is entitled to receive, is no greater than the costs. The capitalist complains that he had the best of intentions in setting up the factory, that he produces goods of value to society and is entitled to some remuneration for all this. The capitalist even argues he does supervisory work, although here Marx widens his view to include the actual factory foremen who are in the audience at this little drama, and the foremen laugh scornfully at his claim to have had any direct role to play in production.[23]

FOLLOW THE LAWS OF THE MARKET!

Deprived of all audience sympathy, Marx's capitalist gets annoyed and calls on the fact that, in the marketplace, anything has two values, its use value and its market value; a potato has as its use a certain *fixed* amount of nourishment, but its market value is different from this and may vary depending on how good the potato crop was. Since human labor also has these two values, in use and in exchange, Marx's capitalist finally sees the solution to his problem and, according to Marx, the capitalist laughs with delight at the discovery.[24]

	12 *hours*	12 *hours*
Price of 20 pounds of cotton	20 shillings	20 shillings
Cost of wear on machinery	4 shillings	4 shillings
Twelve hours labor	6 shillings	3 shillings
Value of yarn	30 shillings·····················>	27 shillings

The difference between 30s. and 27s. is 3s. = Surplus value, Capital has been created!

Because laborers can be paid at their *market* value, while doing a long day's work at their *use* value, it is possible for Marx's capitalist to make the profit he has been seeking, and to do it entirely within the rules of the classical marketplace, which recognizes that if something is abundant, its value goes down. And in practical terms, if any laborer objected to the salary he was being paid, he was entirely free to leave and there were hordes waiting at the factory gates, glad to take over his job at the lower pay rate. So the capitalist, by understanding the laws of the economic marketplace, has created value, "a live monster that is fruitful and multiplies."[25] The profit can be reinvested and the capitalist system can multiply without end.

The interdependent decision model takes Marx a step further, and as is frequently the case with bottom-up models, the results may surprise people who think they know which side Marx was on. The capitalist's ingenious invention of surplus value is Marx's economic concern, but he then moves on to the political ramifications. Unnoticed in the background of the little drama described earlier, a worker has been listening to the discussion and finally, for the first time, joins in with his own point of view, that his labor (which depends on his health and strength) is his capital, and as such he is entitled to use it wisely. If the factory owner uses up the laborer's capital so that he dies by age forty, the worker is not getting a fair return on his physical capital. The laborer thus demands, in the same spirit that the capitalist demanded a profit, that under the immortal laws of the free market he has a right to a normal working day.[26]

All readers familiar with the stereotype of Marx's sympathies will here jump to the conclusion Marx will be on the side of the laborer, but this is exactly wrong. Only a few pages later in *Das Capital*, Marx describes the contradiction between the capitalist and the worker as a true antinomy, right against right, and concludes that under these circumstances only political interaction can decide the result. "There is here ... an antinomy, right against right, both equally bearing the seal of the law of exchanges. Between equal rights [politics] decides."[27]

This eminently neutral conclusion is borne out later in *Capital* when Marx investigates the reasons why the working day was eventually shortened. It was not out of anyone's kindness of heart. In political fact, the shorter hours were approved in the English House of Commons because they got the votes of the Tories, who voted with the Chartist advocates of the change. Why did the Tories vote to benefit the lower classes? The landowning aristocracy took this position because earlier their Whig opponents had abolished the so-called Corn Laws, which covered all grain crops and which kept prices high for the domestic producers and profited the landowning, agricultural Tories. The Chartists, therefore, found the Tories "panting for revenge," delighted to vote against the Whigs.[28] The ancient law of hardball politics was played out: don't get mad, get even.

SEEING WHAT DOESN'T HAPPEN

Marx's definition of politics could not be clearer; right may be on both sides. To follow the implications of this difficulty, analytical game theory can be exceptionally revealing because it is designed to assist in the description of human interactions in a manner that is more sharply focused than casual discussion makes possible. When human interdependencies are laid out in a game matrix, there is an additional benefit in that the matrix shows not only what is happening but also what is not happening – but might. What people *do* is not all there is; there are roads not taken, and political wisdom consists in trying to understand this potential world.

The game matrix pushes the observer toward recognition of unnoticed possibilities because each player is assumed, by the shape of the matrix, to have at least two options. This produces alternatives of at least four cells, as strategies intersect, and each cell can be hypothesized to have different payoffs to each player in each of the four cells. What the observer would not be aware of, without the completed matrix, would be the *reasons why* a particular choice was made by each player.

This does not mean, it should be emphasized, that everyone calculates a game matrix before taking any action; people act, as Goffman, Garfinkel, Tversky and Kahneman, and others have demonstrated, on habit, intuition, and speculation. But many times the choice will prove unrewarding, and the actor himself might consider whether further thought were necessary; or a perplexed observer might wonder "what on earth" led someone to make an incongruous or self-defeating choice. Laying out a game matrix, hypothesizing payoffs for each side, and inspecting those payoffs can give an unexpected advantage, explaining what a player might have done if the payoffs had been seen by that player as different. The matrix, in other words, provides insight into the invisible. Since self government occurs in the presence of earlier self organization, and since that earlier self organization is usually invisible, game matrices can be revealing both of the problem and the possible solutions.

This can be illustrated with some cases discussed earlier. Take Tilly's case of warmaking as the foundation of the modern European state; it can be set up with two choices, to make war or to not make war. Tilly's contention is simple, in game terms.

		State A	
		Make War	Don't Make War
	Make War	? ?	−10 +10
State B	Don't Make War	+10 −10	0 0

The question-marked results in the upper left would be filled in, for specific combatants, depending on the strength of each participant and whom each of them guessed might win in a contest between them. The question whether to avoid war entirely would be based on a similar calculation; the choice for either side not to make war would be based on the hope that the other player would also avoid war. Tilly's basic argument is the NE-SW diagonal, that anyone who just stands there when the other player chooses war will definitely lose out. The flavor is similar but more interesting in Scott's case.

		The State	
		Impose Taxes	Don't Impose Taxes
	Pay Tax if Asked	10 / −10	−10 / 10
The Citizen	Don't Pay Taxes	−10 / 10	0 / 10

The payoffs as stipulated here ignore any benefits the state might provide, such as road building or police services, and direct attention solely to the revenue issue. With agreeable citizens in the upper left cell, the citizen loses whatever is taken by the state; in the upper right cell, the state loses what is in effect a "revenue opportunity" by not taxing a citizen who is willing to comply. Noncompliant citizens, in the bottom two cells, always profit; but the state loses face if it tries to tax and is scorned. The matrix is educational in positing that the relation between the state and the citizen, rather than being a purely legal or civic relation, may better be pictured as two semi-cooperative opponents, eyeing one another warily across the universal strategic lattice.

Recall next the placid island society invented by Thomas More and used in Chapter 2 to illustrate a transparent society where the political surface seems effectively determined by the habits and customs of the sociopsychological infrastructure. That people are naturally good is not More's assumption; the islanders as he postulates them are as ornery and grouchy as anyone else. So why does stability prevail? Two matrices explain.

		Citizen I	
		Break a Rule	Follow the Rules
	Condemn Vice	−10 / −5	5 / 0
Citizen II	Praise Virtue	−5 / +5	10 / 10

The relevant point about More's island community is that everyone lives in full view of everyone else, and most people follow the approved customs. If, however, anyone gets out of line, it is immediately noticed and condemned: in the upper left cell this costs the enforcing citizen something by imposing an unpleasant duty, but it costs the violator more.

If, as shown at the lower left, the good citizen simply praises those with virtue, ignoring the sin, the violator still loses social capital because he is out of line with the island's consensus. More's description of the island's affairs suggests that, most of the time, activity is as described in the lower right, where virtue meets praise; but he is aware of the other possibilities and acts to control them.

What keeps the island's leaders in line? It can be seen as a variation on the same theme.

| | | Leaders | |
		Act Autocratically	Serve People Quietly
Citizens	Quick to Anger	−5 +10	+10 0
	Slow to Anger	+10 −5	+15 0

The island citizens, according to More's account, may be more surly in respect to their leaders than to each other; it is the main reason the treasury is stored in a public fashion so no suspicions can arise. The matrix shows that this is beneficial in avoiding autocracy; if the people were slow to anger, autocracy might be rewarded (lower left cell). But the payoff of +10 for putting down a potential autocrat (upper left cell) encourages vigilance, and the leaders prefer the payoffs in their right-hand column, where the payoffs indicate that suspicious citizens may be a slight nuisance (payoff of +10) and more peaceful folk make it easier to rule (+15).

The case of Italy, where corruption flourished so massively under Silvio Berlusconi, leads to a natural question, the answer to which is transparent in game terms but is not always obvious to citizens of any country: Why do opposition political groups not put a stop to such corruption?

| | | Berlusconi | |
		Act Honestly	Corrupt Practices
Opposition Leaders	Anti-Corruption Laws	+10 −10	−100 +10
	No Corruption Laws	+10 +20	+100 +30

The matrix shows roughly, with the numbers intended only to indicate general levels of payoff to each of the players, that the problem with anti-corruption laws is that they also cost the opposition substantial losses. If the laws curb Berlusconi (upper right cell), then the joy at cutting him down somewhat mitigates the opposition's personal losses, as well as seriously damaging Berlusconi; but if he avoids the prosecutors and escapes (upper left cell), the opposition will be hurt by its own loss of corrupt revenues. Without any laws (bottom two cells), Berlusconi returns to corruption at +100 rather than the +10 payoff for honest business dealings, and the opposition also gains, even more if Berlusconi chooses corruption and increases the inflow of bribes to all leaders, including the opposition.[29]

Another interesting question, again not restricted to Italian politics, is why opposition groups are unable to iron out their differences and form alliances against popular candidates who win simply because other forces cannot get together. Consider the following explanation, based on the intuitively plausible hypothesis that egotism plays a substantial role in all politics, from autocratic to democratic.

		First Opposition Leader	
		Unite with Second Leader	Remain Alone
Second Opposition Leader	Unite with First Leader	−5 −5	+5 -1
	Remain Alone	-1 +5	+3 +3

This matrix is an example of the difference in the way participants view the game and the way observers may see it. Unity seems to be, in the abstract, a good thing, leading to political success in voting or in coalition formation. From the inside, however, the picture is different: unity (upper left cell) means loss of autonomy and individuality, and worse still, in the unified group the other politician may turn out to be stronger than oneself. In the two cases where one politician is willing to unite and the other refuses, the one who rejects the offer seems to win (+5) in the battle over face. If both refuse to unite, both save face but lose any opportunity to win in the wider vote against some popular rival.

BRINGING SELF GOVERNMENT TOGETHER

Self government is not a brick, not a compact or clearly defined object that can be possessed, given as a gift, seized, or stored safely in a vault. It is a process based on an ability to see through the myriad spectacles, ambiguities, and uncertainties of everyday events, and is directed toward the practical goal of finding personal and perhaps social coherence in relation to those events, finding and occupying an area of defensible ground in a wide and diverse political lattice.

The project would be hopeless without a recognition of what has been called here the haecceity of politics, the thesis that everyone, even in the most petty details of everyday life, works constantly in a world of inter-dependent decision where the motives of the participants may vary across a wide spectrum from total selflessness to screaming egotism. To survive under such circumstances requires care, because the field contains opportunities and dangers, most of which can only be met through an increased ability to understand how other people define their worlds and their purposes, and on the basis of this knowledge to rearrange the self to most effectively meet what may ensue.

That everyone is socially constructed is central to the understanding and conduct of self government because it links the two sides of the equation. A group's self government is broadly dependent on the capacity of its members for individual self government, and the individual's personal psychological architecture will reflect that of those who inhabit the surrounding web. Human interaction across this lattice is not a well-defined game with clearly posted rules and standardized players, but a creative ongoing interplay in which human choice may change all the parameters in midstream.

Social science has over recent years cumulated around basic ideas that provide leverage in dissecting this apparently unmanageable flow. There is a natural process of self organization where people take on roles and are guided by audience reaction in playing those roles; where preexisting rules may be inadequate and people invent solutions using the invisible and unstated depths of the group's common experience; where existing rules can be used in new ways in the ongoing pursuit of social capital; and both rational calculation and the adaptive model of reward-seeking in an unpredictable environment are used to guide individual choices.

A real-world example can show how these two processes sometimes work themselves out in history, seen from the micro level, from the bottom up, in a process of dynamic political logic. The choice of Nelson Mandela and South Africa is not intended to suggest that either achieved self government: the man was imperfect as all human beings are imperfect, and the country's new democracy was and remains imperfect as all democracies remain imperfect. But the case is edifying because at the time it happened, none of the participants, of whatever color or kind, knew how it would turn out, or where it would end. It was a game of skill, and those who could see through the spectacle to the structure underneath played better than those who did not.

AS A YOUNG MAN

Nelson Mandela, the first black president of the nation of South Africa,[30] reports that it was not until he was in his early twenties, in Johannesburg, when he first met a white man "who treated me as a human being."[31] That fact alone illustrates how group self government and individual self government are related; they work together, and no group can be governed without the active participation of sovereign individuals. It is sometimes assumed that when there are injustices in the world, time will cure them and everyone needs to be patient until that happy outcome occurs. Bottom-up history explains vividly how unlikely is such natural justice.

With a greater sensitivity to the haecceity of politics, that subtle cultural interdependence that is the essence of human behavior, it is possible to recognize that change, whether for good or evil, rarely comes by itself but is created by people who either seize power when no one is looking, as in Rousseau's *Origin of Inequality*, or by people who stand up for their rights, as in Marx's drama of the working day. The rest, as Marx concluded, is politics.

After a lifetime of struggle for black rule in South Africa, including eighteen years on the infamous Robben Island and more years after that in Africaner prisons, Mandela is revered by many observers as a kind of political saint who prevailed over a malevolent environment through wisdom, generosity, and greatness of spirit. This may certainly be true but it underestimates the difficulty that inheres in the details.

If positive change is to occur in any human situation, there are many individual days to work through, many difficult people to deal with, many unpredictable problems to solve, many threatening possibilities to escape, and many hopes to sustain. It takes Machiavelli's qualities of both the lion and the fox to achieve what Mandela achieved, and his story can provide a vivid example of how the two meanings of self government are woven together in the real world.

Mandela was born in 1918, the son of a Tembe chief in Transkei and a member of the royal family, though in a minor line. Shortly after his birth, Mandela's father was de-chiefed for refusing to attend a hearing called by a local white magistrate. The father was stubborn, a trait the young Mandela thought he inherited, and proud, "with no sense of inferiority toward whites." Despite the loss of family wealth, the young Mandela had a rich rural childhood; because the family was polygamous and the older children had left, he was the favorite of all, and had in effect four mothers to care for his needs.[32]

His father died when the boy was nine, and Mandela was sent to the tribal regent to be raised and educated, welcomed into the royal family but not quite a full part of it. He learned much about kingship by watching the regent dispense justice, and he always valued the virtues of judgments he saw implemented at these tribal meetings.[33] He also learned to compare himself to others: less aggressive, he avoided team sports for individual ones; less quick to learn, he worked harder than other students did.

Mandela was spoiled in his social life in school, admired, stylish, and popular. He was stubborn to a fault, being thrown out of school for heading up a student rebellion over an issue no grander than the food service. In light of his royal background, the authorities urged him to recant, but he refused, and by this choice quite ruined his plans for a civil service career, which required a college degree. Mandela also described himself, in retrospect, as an ungrateful youth. When it came time to marry, the regent selected a bride for Mandela, as was customary, and Mandela ran off to the city rather than follow the wishes of the man who had raised him like a son and paid for his education.[34] When the regent got him and his cousin jobs at a mine outside the city, Mandela bragged about his independence and was eventually fired. But his environment chastened him; he attended law school without distinction and encountered racism everywhere in the city. As a law clerk in a white office, he was "conscientious, never devious, tidy in person and in mind."[35]

A young prince in appearance, tall and invariably well dressed once he could afford it as a result of his law practice, Mandela began to change further in response to changes in the environment as the Dutch Afrikaners began to mobilize and seek control through the apartheid system, against the less oppressive British attitudes. Blacks were slow to recognize the threat, seeing Afrikaners as "tram drivers, ticket collectors, police men," and Mandela himself was "stunned" by their moves, still believing peaceful reconciliation was possible.[36] This would mark an enduring split in the African National Congress between the black nationalists who wanted nothing to do with the whites and those like Mandela who continued to believe in multiracialism. As black defiance grew, the government became more harsh, which drove out the black moderates and left the ANC more radical.[37]

THEATER AND THE T-MAZE

With Oliver Tambo, who would be his closest ally, Mandela established the first black African law firm in the country, serving rural clients and developing a theatrical style in court that led the white lawyers to try to disbar him; but a white judge found in his favor, teaching him that fair treatment sometimes happened. Increasing government bans pushed Mandela toward greater militancy; his dramatic and rousing speeches led other ANC members to see him as immature and too warlike. By 1955, there were mass arrests of black activists for high treason, and the extended trial of Mandela and other defendants brought increasing prominence to him as the preeminent black ANC leader; when the white judges declared everyone not guilty in 1961, the intensity of the struggle increased. Mandela took a brief, armed, underground role as the Black Pimpernel, but the organization demonstrated little skill at terrorism, with not even a pistol at their secret headquarters in Lilliesleaf.[38] After seventeen months in hiding, Mandela was arrested by the South African police in August 1962, and his career as a symbol of the black struggle began.

Mandela lived up to his role, making his first appearance in court in a Xhosa leopardskin *kaross*, carrying his people's history, as it were, on his back. Then the authorities invaded the ANC headquarters, capturing all the written evidence the group had never gotten around to destroying, and the whole group went on trial for their lives. Mandela made a famous speech just before the sentence was announced, saying he had fought against white domination and black domination, had sought a democratic and free society with all races living together in harmony, and it was an "ideal which I hope to live for and achieve." He concluded quietly, "But if needs be, it is an ideal for which I am prepared to die."[39] On June 11, 1964, the judgment was pronounced – life imprisonment – and Mandela and his associates were sent directly to Robben Island. International political opinion supported them, but the British and the Americans wanted friendly relations with Praetoria, and attention turned elsewhere.

Prison was particularly brutal because the warders and the prisoners were members of different races, and one race believed the other was barely human. The central group of seven ANC prisoners had, however, already developed strength and maturity in the anti-apartheid struggle and worked together on Robben Island, basically to try to protect themselves from the brutality of the guards and the prison conditions, but then also to govern themselves effectively. Isolated from other prisoners, the ANC men appointed a High Organ of four men, including Mandela, to decide on policy toward the authorities and internal discipline, with a communications committee to smuggle messages to other parts of the prison; when non-ANC groups complained, they broadened the committee to deal with common issues.[40] The social support the group provided rescued many prisoners from terminal depression.

Gradually the prisoners developed strategies of befriending the guards, learning about the discriminations to which the Dutch settlers had been exposed, and working to educate them. The ANC leaders also mixed deliberately with the regular prisoners, and prisoners from other political groups, learning about their problems and debating issues of strategy in the fight against apartheid. Mandela particularly played this role, speaking Afrikaans with the warders and making friends with them despite the odds; when marched by six guards to a meeting with an outside visitor, he cheerfully introduced them, by name, as his honor guard.[41]

Mandela would also act like a government on his own, writing complaints to prison officials that sounded "like an official report from the head of a department." On occasion he would be even provocative; it took the High Organ weeks of debate to quell his idea that prisoners should not be made to stand up in the presence of warders, or respond to being called by their first names.[42]

Mandela would play conscious politics with the prison officials. When the Commissioner of Prisons sent three judges to the island to see him about recent atrocities by the guards, Mandela asked that the prison commandant be present while he described the brutal beatings. The commandant, furious at Mandela's revelations, threatened him with harm in the judges' presence, and Mandela announced calmly, "If he can threaten me here, in your presence, you can imagine what he does when you are not here." Mandela's strategy worked to improve prison conditions, and would eventually also improve the commandant's attitude toward the black prisoners, confirming Mandela's theory that even evil men could be changed, that they behave like brutes "because they are rewarded for" brutal behavior.[43]

NERVES OF STEEL

Even in the close confines of Robben Island Mandela acted the leader. He was a friend to everyone, knowing their family histories and their problems, giving tactical and strategic advice. But he was a close friend to no one; "behind his kind and gentle manner" was a "steeled and hardened" person, according to one friend. When younger, he had been angry at the system, but over time he had become "cold and analytical."[44] This quality could surface in a display of vehement anger when someone behaved improperly, but it was theatrical and deliberate, not emotional. The performance was, of course, high politics, a case of fully playing a role that was necessary in the long and ambiguous sweep of events that led toward an uncertain future.

He could even be dangerous to friends and associates: he argued harshly with anyone who was not well informed, and he was in no way inclined to suffer fools gladly. One friend said, apparently taught by rough experience, that "Nelson can be vicious" in his Socratic method, and leaves his opponent battered and humiliated because he demands that people "look at both sides of the question, to attempt to give an objective and honest answer to it."[45] Finally the prison would be organized along the lines of a university, with different courses, reading groups, and constant debates.

These characteristics would be important, as the South African situation developed independently of the Robben Islanders, with structural divisions among different white groups, different black nationalist groups, and the apartheid government's growing recognition that the system could not prevail because the economic sanctions imposed from outside were hurting, and international admiration for Mandela and his cause had so strongly increased. As Mandela was removed from Robben Island and placed in sequentially more comfortable prisons, he was also isolated from his prison friends and had the added difficulty of keeping the ANC together in the face of younger members' fears that he would go over to the state and sell them out. When the government finally agreed to negotiations, after a long period when Mandela alone represented his movement's moral stature and imperative, his Machiavellian skills were tested at the highest level.

Because of Mandela's stature, he was a political target for South African state officials, many of whom were impressed by his dignity and character but also perhaps misled by his reasonableness; they misinterpreted his civility to mean weakness and thus hoped that he could be manipulated to weaken the black cause from within. Against all odds, however, he stuck to his three major demands. He would not renounce violence (since the government had not done so), would not break with the communists (who had long supported black justice), and would not abandon majority rule (essential to overthrow the old system).[46]

When F. W. de Klerk won the country's presidency and began to make concessions, prisoners began to be released, and finally on February 11, 1990, Mandela himself was free. After almost two chaotic years of domestic violence, the negotiations over a new constitution began and reached a deadlock. It was a Schelling moment of "pure" bargaining, defined as occurring when the issue is solely the strength of will, of who will blink first. While some in his own party waffled, fearing to insist on their full demands, Mandela had background information that de Klerk's government officials were split, and that some had decided they could live with majority rule, so Mandela held firm. He said of de Klerk, "This chap, I have had enough of him. We hold the line here today." When de Klerk gave in, ANC observers were impressed. "Mandela has nerves of steel," Ramaphosa recalled. "He can be very brutal in a calm and collected sort of way."[47]

Beyond this political triumph the story becomes conventional, with elections, forming governments, and making policy, and need not be pursued further here. The real interest of Nelson Mandela's trajectory through South Africa's transition is the way he illustrates both sides of the self government equation. On the one hand, he and a group of men of which he was not entirely the leader managed, from an isolated island in the south Atlantic Ocean, to hold together themselves and the movement around which their lives centered. Gradually Mandela grew, among these men, into the first among equals, recommended by his gradually developed capacity to govern himself.

WHY CHANGE HAPPENS

In terms of the social scientists included here, Mandela's success can be described as a central simplicity within a surrounding complexity. It was said of Mandela that he always knew what stage he was on, and always played his role flawlessly – was indeed conscious of the stage and the audiences, as a leader needs to be. Beneath the dramaturgical level, he managed to see other people as they saw themselves and earn their respect because of this deep courtesy. In terms of games, he was a natural master, playing fiercely against prison authorities, subtly with government leaders, honestly with his own allies, firmly with himself. He was aided by the fact, as war strategists point out, that "a good cause is a sword as well as armour" but his talent for high politics was decisive.[48]

In retrospect, Mandela's political task may have seemed easy, a fight against egregious injustice that he was naturally going to win, but this is a mistake and deprecates the chaos of the events through which the participants fought. At the time it was not clear to any of the different sides involved in the South African conflict what the problem was or what the range of solutions might be, where resources might come from, or who among one's allies saw most clearly the route into a future obscured by the fog of war.

Mandela entered the battle with a variety of advantages and some serious human disadvantages; he would change in many ways over his long lifetime, from the slightly spoiled scion of a royal family through a long and frequently bitter maturity during which his deliberate self-discipline made him a formidable player on an international stage.

His story illustrates both sides of self government, how the individual achieves it and how individuals come together, sometimes, to work toward a wider sociopolitical goal. Seen in terms of complexity's lattice, Mandela was created by his neighbors in their reaction to the child and the youth of royal bearing: having four mothers tends to strengthen the soul, being a strong character tends to evoke admiration, high style attracts prominence, hard work and humility gain respect. The white world taught him he was black, with all the encumbrances that entailed; yet a white lawyer took him in, and white judges would find cases in his favor.

The country of South Africa changed around him as the Afrikaners began the movement toward apartheid, a movement itself caused by the neighborliness of the lattice in that the Dutch settlers, disillusioned with the British and fearful of the native peoples, sought to protect themselves. The harshness of their final regime created radicals where before there was disorganization. Complexity theory explains this action and reaction pattern across time as a series of games that defined new roles and new tactics and strategies for both sides, a full political battle in Marx's sense because, as Mandela would continually emphasize, the Boers had also felt extreme injustice.

It is important also to bring into the historical account the divisions among the white authorities over the period. Individuals would reach out to black people in defiance of the general racism; one long court case against black leaders dragged on for years while everyone tried to figure out just what should be done with them; when Mandela and his colleagues were sent to Robben Island, white sympathizers assured them they would be out by Christmas; when finally de Klerk lost in the showdown with Mandela over majority rule, it was because the lattice had shifted under de Klerk's feet: his own advisors had lost sympathy with the hard line he was demanding.

SELF GOVERNMENT TOGETHER

What stands out in this dynamic rolling flood of human behavior is a small group of seven black men, sent not to the gallows but to Robben

Island, and quite deliberately setting about to govern themselves, with desperate intelligence, facing a merciless world and hoping for an almost impossible future world where the majority of South Africans would rule. None would have survived without the others; white colleagues were imprisoned alone, isolated in regular prisons, and collapsed mentally from the unmitigated brutality of guards who considered them racially disloyal.

But the Mandela contingent governed themselves: they worked out their priorities, first protection against the vicious guards and the malevolent prison officials, then intellectual control through sharing books and ideas, then reaching out to other black groups with whom they disagreed to increase understanding and possible sympathy on both sides, then taking responsibility for the ordinary criminals, giving them education and skills for use when they were released. Finally they turned even to sympathizing with and educating the prison guards, young men at the bottom of the social system, who would not have taken such jobs had they had any other options.

Throughout the pedestrian miseries of eighteen and more years, the core ANC group around Mandela lived their lives together as their personal values dictated, and set a pattern of dignity and decency that the authorities could not but notice. Biographers note that international officials were usually astonished by meeting Mandela; they had expected a rabid menace to human society and instead found themselves with a distinguished, educated, civil, and even redoubtable gentleman of color, who might understand them better than they understood themselves.

At a personal level, Mandela's development was central to the group's overall self government. To those who witnessed the final stages of the apartheid struggle it may seem surprising that he was once a hothead, who allowed himself to be expelled from college simply to defend a principle, who went to court in leopard skins, who agitated even in the lostness of Robben Island for such respectful treatment for the prisoners that the High Organ was hard-pressed to talk him out of it. Recognition of his central role would be shown when he and three others were eventually removed from the island, apparently to prevent their leadership role.

Yet Mandela was continually analytic in his imprisonment and his appreciation of how the national political currents were crashing over everyone's heads. He kept up as much correspondence with international leaders as the prison authorities would permit, to force them to recognize that the struggle could not be ignored. When he was eventually separated from all his colleagues in a new prison and forced to live quite alone, he took it as an opportunity to analyze the situation fully without being biased by other opinions. He made odd alliances, meeting with the hard-line P. W. Botha when still in jail, finding they both distrusted de Klerk and rather liked each other.[49]

In the final stages of negotiations with the apartheid government, a particular mark of Mandela's contribution was the high quality of the younger men who were attracted to the cause by Mandela's remarkable stature. Most revolutions are thought of from the top down, as a unified group of people with a unified point of view, but from the bottom up this has always been untrue.

In black South Africa there were different groups everywhere, frequently on opposite sides of the struggle, many being bribed by the government with political status in the townships; there was not even agreement on whether Mandela's multiracial solution was acceptable. It took a self-governed person to survive such challenges, and South Africa created him, through the hostility that led him to become what he became. It is an educational lesson in the simplicity of complexity.

Notes

1. The Simplicity of Complexity

1. The recent proposition that the United States could best be described as an oligarchy was raised in a publication of the official organ of the American Political Science Association, *Perspectives on Politics* (Winters and Page 2009) and was amplified in Winters (2011). The oligarchs were defined not just as the rich but the super-rich whose primary concern was to defend their massive accumulations of wealth. A statistical test of various democratic theories (Gilens and Page 2014) showed similarly that majoritarian models failed to explain the data, while the economic elite theory was highly effective.
2. Downs 1957, 23–24.
3. Schelling 1960.
4. Schelling 1978, 147–155; his segregation model is available on Netlogo, which can be downloaded free from the web.
5. Axelrod (1997), Cederman (2003), Lustick et al. (2004); for a purely political case, see Laver and Sergenti (2014). A good recent summary of the method by one of its founders is John Holland (2014).
6. Schelling 1960, 54–55.
7. The original announcement to the public of the Game of Life was by Martin Gardner (1970); for a fuller discussion, chapter 2 in Sigmund (1993) is both lucidly technical and philosophically charming.
8. Epstein and Axtell 1996.
9. Epstein and Axtell 1996, 45–48, 25; eternal life on Sugarscape was shortly modified by the addition of death, to make the model more interesting.
10. The points in the paragraph are found, sequentially, in Epstein and Axtell 1996, 36, 42–43, 94–137, 54, and 82–83.
11. Waldrop (1992) is the classic history of the movement.
12. Rousseau's *Second Discourse* (Masters 1964, 141).
13. On the well-known "democratic deficit," see Norris (2011); on government failure, see Schuck (2014); for a cool-eyed argument that Americans do not

want democracy anyway, see Hibbing and Theiss-Morse (2002); and for two books that seek to get beyond current democratic ideas, consider Crouch (2004) and Rosanvallon (2008).

14. Thomas Hobbes *Leviathan*; Berger and Luckmann 1967.
15. Scott 1998, 11.
16. Scott 1998, 12.
17. Scott 1998, 14.
18. Scott 1998, 19, 15.
19. Scott 1998, 21.
20. Scott 1998, 23.
21. Scott 1998, 33–34.
22. Scott 1998, 36.
23. The American Political Science Association, the professional group for the entire profession, used to publish every ten years a summary of political science research for the prior decade; in 2002, the entire volume was devoted to the state, a topic many thought had gone out of date in the nineteenth century; see Katznelson and Milner (2002). On Hegel, the most directly relevant text is his *The Philosophy of Right*.
24. There are different versions of Tilly's essay; see Tilly (1982) and Tilly (1985).
25. Tilly 1985, 169, 170.
26. Tilly 1985, 172–175; Tilly 1982, 1.
27. Tilly 1985, 175, 183, 177, 179.
28. Haecceity means "thisness" and attempts to capture the everywhere, everyone, every minute aspect of human political interactions; the term is taken from Garfinkel (1967).

2. The Haecceity of Politics

1. On haecceity, see the last endnote to Chapter 1; Garfinkel's general approach is discussed fully in Chapter 4.
2. Downs (1957) *An Economic Theory of Democracy* 6–7.
3. Downs 1957, 7.
4. Downs 1957, 40.
5. Downs 1957, 77–79, 208–209.
6. Downs 1957, 82.
7. Downs 1957, 87.
8. Downs 1957, 28–29.
9. Downs 1957, 55, 94.
10. Downs 1957, 96.
11. Downs 1957, 109–111.
12. Downs 1957, 116–117.
13. Downs 1957, 160–161.
14. Downs 1957, 162, 224.
15. The paradox was brought to contemporary attention in Arrow (1951), 93–96.
16. The major work on the Prisoner's Dilemma in political science is Axelrod (1997).

17. Axelrod (1997, 20–26) concluded that Tit for Tat was the best overall strategy, although defecting the first two rounds (in a computer simulation rather than the sheriff's office) could alert a sharp player to whether its adversary were a natural sucker and could be permanently exploited.
18. More's work is in the public domain and available in many varieties, all of which are similar. Page citations are to the Ogden version listed in the bibliography (More 1949), along with chapter titles for reference to other editions, most of which use similar headings.
19. More 1949, "Their Economy and Occupations," 33–36.
20. More 1949, "Their Magistrates," 32.
21. More 1949, 32.
22. More 1949, "Their Traveling and Foreign Trade," 43.
23. More 1949, "Their Social and Business Relations," 40.
24. More 1949, 38.
25. More 1949, 37.
26. More 1949, "Their Country and Agriculture," 29.
27. More 1949, "Their Cities and especially Amaurot"; and "Their Social and Business Relations" 39–40.
28. More 1949, "Their Economy and Occupations," 33–34.
29. More 1949, "Their Social and Business Relations," 42.
30. More 1949, "Their Moral Philosophy," 47–48; "Their Warfare," 64.
31. More 1949, 65–67.
32. More 1949, "Their Punishments, Their Legal Procedure, and Other Matters," 59.
33. More 1949, "The Religion of the Utopians," 72.
34. The marsh Arab community in Iraq was first disrupted in 1958 with the revolution that overthrew the monarchy; after the First Gulf War in 1991, Saddam Hussein's government, in retribution for a failed uprising, effectively destroyed the marshes by building an "immense canal" to drain the area. After the U.S. invasion of Iraq in 2003, tribesmen breached the dikes and some of the ecology began to restore itself; estimates of possible restoration of the marshes range from 20 to 80 percent (Anderson introduction to Thesiger 2007, 8, 10.)
35. Wilfred Thesiger, *The Marsh Arabs,* first published in 1964 by Longmans, Green, in 1967 by Penguin Books, and published as a Penguin Classic in 2007.
36. Thesiger 2007, 75; and see the photographs of the almost gothic buildings that could be constructed from this simple material.
37. Thesiger 2007, 47, 37–40.
38. Thesiger 2007, 117, 50, 37, 30, 97.
39. Thesiger 2007, 28.
40. Thesiger 2007, 103–104, 198–199.
41. Thesiger 2007, 28, 68, 38, 134.
42. Thesiger 2007, 71, 133.
43. Thesiger 2007, 172–181 for a rounded picture of the family of one of his local canoe men; references to family connections can be found at every stop in Thesiger's wide-ranging travels.

44. Thesiger 2007, 209–214 on the hazards of blood and the feuds it might generate.
45. Thesiger 2007, 125.
46. Thesiger 2007, 121–122.
47. Thesiger 2007, 165–166.
48. Thesiger 2007, 73, 209–214.
49. Thesiger 2007, 32, 65.
50. Thesiger 2007, 83, 35.
51. Thesiger 2007, 33, 81.
52. Thesiger 2007, 75.
53. Thesiger 2007, 176.
54. Thesiger 2007, 183, 42–43, 108–110.
55. Thesiger 2007, 164, 41–43.
56. Thesiger 2007, 105–107.
57. Thesiger 2007, 111, 123.
58. Thesiger 2007, 82, 91.
59. Thesiger 2007, 64.
60. Thesiger 2007, 134–135.
61. Thesiger 2007, 177.
62. Wittgenstein (1981).
63. The classic work used here is Peter Berger and Thomas Luckmann, *The Social Construction of Reality* (1967).
64. Berger and Luckmann 1967, 29.
65. Berger and Luckmann 1967, 53–55.
66. Berger and Luckmann 1967, 56, 62.
67. Berger and Luckmann 1967, 61–62.
68. Berger and Luckmann 1967, 58–59.

3. The Complexity of Self Organization

1. For an eminently clear introduction to basic game theory, with a foreword by one of its modern founders, Oskar Morgenstern, see Morton Davis's *Game Theory: A Nontechnical Introduction* (1973).
2. Richard P. Feynman, *Six Easy Pieces,* 1995, 24.
3. In Davis 1973, page x.
4. Simon's first step was described in *Administrative Behavior* (1947), which reinterpreted public administration in empirical or behavioral terms; his work on human problem solving and bounded rationality is found in Simon (1997), and his contribution to complexity theory can be found in *The Sciences of the Artificial,* especially the 1996 revised edition.
5. See William H. Riker, *The Theory of Political Coalitions* (1962), 32.
6. Olson 1965, 17.
7. Olson 1965, 48.
8. Buchanan and Tullock 1962, 76.
9. Buchanan and Tullock's discussion is more subtle than this but makes a similar point; see 136–142.

10. Schelling's autobiography can be found on the Web by searching his name combined with Nobel Prize Biography.
11. The quotations are from Schelling's *Strategy of Conflict*, 1960, 16 and 17, respectively.
12. Schelling 1960, 16, 17.
13. Schelling 1960, 22.
14. Schelling 1960, 146.
15. Schelling 1960, 21.
16. Schelling 1960, 28.
17. Schelling 1960, 17.
18. Schelling 1960, 57.
19. Schelling 1960, 56–57.
20. Schelling 1960, 117.
21. Schelling 1960, 169.
22. Schelling 1960, 14–15.
23. Mehta 2004, 56.
24. Mehta 2004, 56.
25. Mehta 2004, 112.
26. Mehta 2004, 59–60.
27. Mehta 2004, 98.
28. Mehta 2004, 99,101.
29. Mehta 2004, 99, 101, 102.
30. Mehta 2004, 100.
31. Mehta 2004, 104.
32. Mehta 2004, 85–86, 104.
33. Mehta 2004, 88.
34. Mehta 2004, 41.
35. Mehta 2004, 73.
36. Mehta 2004, 43.
37. Mehta 2004, 71.
38. Mehta 2004, 72–73.
39. Mehta 2004, 77.
40. Mehta 2004, 78.
41. Mehta 2004, 74–75.
42. Mehta 2004, 82, 85.
43. Mehta 2004, 85–86.
44. Mehta 2004, 86, 61.

4. The Social Complexity of Games

1. B. F. Skinner, *Science and Human Behavior* (1953); see his interesting discussion of this issue on pages 18–22.
2. Erving Goffman, *The Presentation of Self in Everyday Life* (1959); and Harold Garfinkel, *Ethnomethodology* (1967).
3. Goffman 1959, 3.
4. Goffman 1959, 36–40.

5. Goffman 1959, 249.
6. Goffman 1959, xi.
7. Goffman 1959, 16.
8. Goffman 1959, 2–3.
9. Goffman 1959, 1, 5–8, 252.
10. Goffman 1959, 9.
11. Goffman 1959, 10, 12–13.
12. Goffman 1959, 85–98.
13. Garfinkel 1967, vii, 3, 10.
14. Garfinkel 1967, 76.
15. Garfinkel 1967, 26, 41.
16. Garfinkel 1967, 88–94, 104–115.
17. Elaine Sciolino, *Persian Mirrors* (2000).
18. Sciolino 2000, 136.
19. Sciolino 2000, 133.
20. Sciolino 2000, 147.
21. Sciolino 2000, 135.
22. Sciolino 2000, 142–143.
23. Sciolino 2000, 137.
24. Sciolino 2000, 350.
25. Sciolino 2000, 175–184.
26. Sciolino 2000, 184.
27. Sciolino 2000, 347, 348.
28. Sciolino 2000, 5.
29. Sciolino 2000, 6–7.
30. Sciolino 2000, 4–5.
31. Sciolino 2000, 35.
32. Sciolino 2000, 35.
33. Sciolino 2000, 37, 34.
34. Sciolino 2000, 30.
35. Sciolino 2000, 359, 360.
36. Sciolino 2000, 198–199.
37. Sciolino 2000, 39.
38. Sciolino 2000, 197.
39. Sciolino 2000, 251.
40. Sciolino 2000, 284.
41. Sciolino 2000, 288, 284–285.
42. Peter Hessler, *River Town: Two Years on the Yangtse* (2002).
43. Hessler 2002, 4.
44. Hessler 2002, 337.
45. Hessler 2002, 9, 80–83.
46. Hessler 2002, 169.
47. Hessler 2002, 44, 50.
48. Hessler 2002, 70, 68.
49. Hessler 2002, 117–118.
50. Hessler 2002, 205.
51. Hessler 2002, 100–105.

52. Hessler 2002, 254.
53. Hessler 2002, 178.
54. Hessler 2002, 374–379.
55. See the exemplary discussion in Charles Lave and James March, *An Introduction to Models in the Social Sciences* (1975).
56. Lave and March 1975, 317.
57. Lave and March 1975, 294–297.
58. Lave and March 1975, 298–299.
59. Lave and March 1975, 282–284.

5. The Complexity of Change

1. Axelrod 1997, 52.
2. Garfinkel 1967, 68.
3. Pierre Bourdieu, *The Logic of Practice* (1990).
4. Bourdieu 1990, 148–161.
5. Bourdieu 1990, 53–54.
6. Bourdieu 1990, 53 *emphasis added.*
7. See Chapters Three and Four *supra* on these three authors.
8. Joseph LaPalombara, *Democracy Italian Style* (1987); Alexander Stille, *The Sack of Rome: Media + Money + Celebrity = Power = Silvio Berlusconi* (2006).
9. Gabriel Almond and Sidney Verba, *The Civic Culture: Political Attitudes and Democracy in Five Nations* (1963).
10. Almond and Verba 1963, 402–403, 102, 228.
11. LaPalombara, *Democracy Italian Style* (1987).
12. LaPalombara 1987, 1.
13. LaPalombara 1987, 11–12.
14. LaPalombara 1987, 60–74.
15. LaPalombara 1987, 46–52, 99.
16. LaPalombara 1987, 105–113, 125–126.
17. The term became famous from the work of Edward C. Banfield, *The Moral Basis of a Backward Society* (1958).
18. LaPalombara 1987, 26–27.
19. LaPalombara 1987, 28.
20. LaPalombara 1987, 147.
21. LaPalombara 1987, 155, 153–154, 197.
22. Stille 2006, 3–4.
23. Stille 2006, 4–6.
24. Stille 2006, 24.
25. Stille 2006, 26, 27.
26. Stille 2006, 28.
27. Stille 2006, 30.
28. Stille 2006, 29–30.
29. Stille 2006, 31.
30. Stille 2006, 31–34.
31. Stille 2006, 65.

32. Stille 2006, 59.
33. Stille 2006, 54–55, 57, 75, 55.
34. Stille 2006, 63.
35. Stille 2006, 59.
36. Stille 2006, 59–60.
37. Stille 2006, 76, 78.
38. Stille 2006, 76–78.
39. Stille 2006, 99–100, 107, 108.
40. Stille 2006, 111.
41. Stille 2006, 112, 113.
42. Stille 2006, 90, 93.
43. Stille 2006, 121.
44. Stille 2006, 136.
45. Stille 2006, 135–136, 154.
46. Stille 2006, 156–163.
47. Stille 2006, 185.
48. Stille 2006, 186, 190, 194, 196.
49. Stille 2006, 247, 275.
50. Stille 2006, 127.
51. Stille 2006, 176, 194, 242, 320, 322.
52. Stille 2006, 277–279, 283, 285.
53. Stille 2006, 288.
54. Stille 2006, 305–310, 326, 276.
55. Stille 2006, 42, 244.
56. Stille 2006, 61.
57. Stille 2006, 19.
58. Stille 2006, 23, 252.
59. Stille 2006, 254–256.
60. Stille 2006, 288.
61. Stille 2006, 226–227.
62. Stille 2006, 221–222.

6. The Complexity of Political Intelligence

1. Clausewitz's *On War* (1832) is the classic discussion, especially chapter III, "The Genius for War."
2. See the discussion of Schelling's argument in Chapter 3.
3. The major exponent of this approach was Milton Friedman.
4. Newell and Simon's (1972) *Human Problem Solving* is illustrative of this approach in the political sciences.
5. See Downs, Riker, Olson, Buchanan, and Tullock as discussed earlier; the essential point was that whether what they wrote was or was not correct, it was usually stated with sufficient clarity that the critic was able to argue intelligently with its conclusion, rather than left simply mystified by the ambiguities of the language used so that no real discussion was possible.
6. Downs 1957, 5.

7. The argument was laid out in two articles by Amos Tversky and Daniel Kahneman in the prestigious journal *Science*: "Judgment under Uncertainty: Heuristics and Biases" (1974); and "The Framing of Decisions and the Psychology of Choice" (1981). Kahneman was awarded the 2002 Nobel prize in economics "for having integrated insights from psychological research into economic science, especially concerning human judgment and decision-making under uncertainty"; Tversky died in 1996, and the prize is not awarded posthumously.

8. Tversky and Kahneman 1981, 457.

9. See Davis (1973) on repeated cases in which experimental subjects do not play games the way game theorists expect (and predict) they will do.

10. Tversky and Kahneman 1974, 1124.

11. Tversky and Kahneman 1974, 1126.

12. Tversky and Kahneman 1974, 1125.

13. Tversky and Kahneman 1974, 1125, 1130.

14. Tversky and Kahneman 1974, 1127.

15. Tversky and Kahneman 1974, 1127–1128.

16. Tversky and Kahneman 1981, 453.

17. On the lawyers, see Ariely (2008), 71; on the credit surcharge, see Tversky and Kahneman (1981), 456.

18. On day-care parents, see Ariely (2008), 76–77; on medical reactions, see Ariely (2008), 173–175.

19. Ariely 2008, 240, 243.

20. Ariely 2008, 456.

21. For an accessible discussion of programming issues in the area, see Karl Sigmund's *Games of Life: Explorations in Ecology, Evolution, and Behaviour* (1993).

22. Robert P. Abelson and J. Douglas Carroll, "Computer Simulation of Individual Belief Systems" (1965).

23. Abelson and Carroll 1965, 28.

24. Abelson and Carroll 1965, 24.

25. Abelson and Carroll 1965, 24, 26, 27.

26. Abelson and Carroll 1965, 25.

27. Abelson and Carroll 1965, 25.

28. Abelson and Carroll 1965, 26, 28.

29. Abelson and Carroll 1965, 26.

30. Abelson and Carroll 1965, 27.

31. Abelson and Carroll 1965, 28.

32. Abelson and Carroll 1965, 25.

33. This is the genetic algorithm method; see Holland 2014.

34. Abelson and Carroll 1965, 29–30.

35. Ithiel De Sola Pool and Allan Kessler, "The Kaiser, The Tsar, and The Computer: Information Processing in a Crisis" (1965).

36. Pool and Kessler 1965, 31.

37. Pool and Kessler 1965, 31.

38. Pool and Kessler 1965, 31, 32.

39. Pool and Kessler 1965, 32.

40. Pool and Kessler 1965, 35–36.
41. Pool and Kessler 1965, 35.
42. Pool and Kessler 1965, 37.
43. Meredith, Martin, *Mugabe: Power, Plunder, and the Struggle for Zimbabwe* (2007).
44. Meredith 2007, 19–26
45. Meredith 2007, 37.
46. Meredith 2007, 38.
47. Meredith 2007, 42–43.
48. Meredith 2007, 45–46.
49. Meredith 2007, 48, 49.
50. Meredith 2007, 50.
51. Meredith 2007, 52.
52. Meredith 2007, 112–113.
53. Meredith 2007, 114–117.
54. Meredith 2007, 118, 121.
55. Meredith 2007, 122–123, 125, 127.
56. Meredith 2007, 127.
57. Meredith 2007, 177, 214, 235, 66.
58. Meredith 2007, 180, 175, 232.
59. Tversky and Kahneman 1981, 458.

7. The Complexity of Simplicity

1. The translation used is Bloom's (1968), with text references in the traditional Stephanus system so that readers can locate citations in any translation of the work.
2. Republic 415 a-b.
3. Republic 549.
4. Republic 549–550.
5. Republic 550, 553.
6. Republic 555.
7. Republic 555–558.
8. Republic 557d, 588c, emphasis added.
9. Republic 560.
10. Republic 561d, 564.
11. Bloom 1968, 414.
12. The tyrant is discussed in Book IX of the *Republic*, and the discussion is predominantly philosophical rather than empirical, so that the political consequences are not fully worked out.
13. Republic 573c-e, 575b, 575e.
14. Republic 577a, emphasis added.
15. Prince chapter VIII.
16. Prince chapter IX.
17. Prince chapter VII.
18. Prince chapters XIV, XXIV–XXV.

19. Prince chapters XV, XVII, XVIII.
20. Prince chapter XVIII.
21. Marx 1967, 184–195.
22. Marx 1967, 186–190.
23. Marx 1967, 193.
24. Marx 1967, 193–194.
25. Marx 1967, 195. It needs to be recalled that Marx was *in favor of capitalism,* without which, he felt, there would be no wealth to distribute when socialism came around; the "live monster" was essential to the good life, in other words. This point has largely been lost in the stereotypes used to describe Marx's theory.
26. Marx 1967, 233–234.
27. The standard translation uses "force" instead of "politics" here, but since Marx's text goes on to refer to the "struggle" between the capitalist and the laboring classes, politics seems closer to the author's intention (Marx 1967, 235).
28. Marx 1967, 283.
29. The pattern is not exclusive to Italian politics; very few politicians in any country are noted for imposing severe restrictions on the gifts that can be accepted legally by elected officials.
30. The history is taken from Anthony Sampson's *Mandela: The Authorized Biography* (1999); the quotation is from page 34.
31. Sampson 1999, 34.
32. Sampson 1999, 6, 7.
33. Sampson 1999, 11.
34. Sampson 1999, 35.
35. Sampson 1999, 33.
36. Sampson 1999, 52.
37. Sampson 1999, 67.
38. Sampson 1999, 156.
39. Sampson 1999, 171, 192.
40. Sampson 1999, 210–211.
41. Sampson 1999, 213.
42. Sampson 1999, 220, 280.
43. Sampson 1999, 222.
44. Sampson 1999, 242.
45. Sampson 1999, 234.
46. Sampson 1999, 376.
47. Sampson 1999, 459.
48. Liddell Hart 1991, 322.
49. Sampson 1999, 385–386.

References

Abelson, Robert P., and J. Douglas Carroll. 1965. "Computer Simulation of Individual Belief Systems." *The American Behavioral Scientist* 8:9 (May) 24–30.

Almond, Gabriel, and Sidney Verba. 1963. *The Civic Culture: Political Attitudes and Democracy in Five Nations*. Princeton: Princeton University Press.

Ariely, Dan. 2008. *Predictably Irrational: The Hidden Forces That Shape Our Decisions*. New York: Harper.

Arthur, W. Brian. 1994. *Increasing Returns and Path Dependence in the Economy*. Ann Arbor: University of Michigan Press.

Arrow, Kenneth J. 1951. *Social Choice and Individual Values*. New York: Wiley.

Axelrod, Robert M. 1997. *The Complexity of Cooperation: Agent-Based Models of Competition and Collaboration*. Princeton: Princeton University Press.

Banfield, Edward C. 1958. *The Moral Basis of a Backward Society*. Glencoe: Free Press.

Berger, Peter L., and Thomas Luckmann. 1967. *The Social Construction of Reality: A Treatise in the Sociology of Knowledge*. New York: Anchor.

Bonabeau, Eric, Marco Dorigo, and Guy Theraulaz. 1999. *Swarm Intelligence: From Natural to Artificial Systems*. New York: Oxford University Press.

Bourdieu, Pierre. 1990. *The Logic of Practice*. Stanford: Stanford University Press.

Brams, Steven J. 2011. *Game Theory and the Humanities: Bridging Two Worlds*. Cambridge, MA: MIT Press.

Brunner, Ronald D., and Garry D. Brewer. 1971. *Organized Complexity: Empirical Theories of Political Development*. New York: Free Press.

Buchanan, James M., and Gordon Tullock. 1962. *The Calculus of Consent: Logical Foundations of Constitutional Democracy*. Ann Arbor: University of Michigan Press.

Cederman, Lars-Erik. 2003. "Modeling the Size of Wars: From Billiard Balls to Sandpiles." *American Political Science Review* 97:1 (February) 135–150.

2005. "Computational Models of Social Forms: Advancing Generative Process Theory." *American Journal of Sociology* 110:4 (January) 864–893.

Clausewitz, Carl von. 1968. *On War* (1832). Edited with an Introduction by Anatol Rapoport. Baltimore: Penguin Books.

Crouch, Colin. 2004. *Post-Democracy*. Malden: Polity Press.

Davis, Morton D. 1973. *Game Theory: A Nontechnical Introduction*. With a foreword by Oskar Morgenstern. New York: Basic Books.

De Marchi, Scott, and Scott E. Page. 2008. "Agent-Based Modeling." In Janet M. Box-Steffensmeier, Henry E. Brady, and David Collier (Eds.) *The Oxford Handbook of Political Methodology*. Oxford: Oxford University Press, pages 71–94.

Downs, Anthony. 1957. *An Economic Theory of Democracy*. New York: Harper and Row.

Epstein, Joshua M., and Robert Axtell. 1996. *Growing Artificial Societies: Social Science from the Bottom Up*. Washington, DC and Cambridge, MA: Brookings Institution and the MIT Press.

Evans, Peter B., Dietrich Rueschemeyer, and Theda Skocpol (Eds.). 1985. *Bringing the State Back In*. New York: Cambridge University Press.

Feynman, Richard P. 1995. *Six Easy Pieces: Essentials of Physics*. Reading: Helix Books.

Fukuyama, Francis. 1992. *The End of History and the Last Man*. New York: Free Press.

Gardner, Martin. 1970. "The Fantastic Combinations of John Conway's New Solitaire Game 'Life.'" *Scientific American* 223 (October) 120–123.

Garfinkel, Harold. 1967. *Studies in Ethnomethodology*. Englewood Cliffs: Prentice-Hall.

Gilens, Martin, and Benjamin I. Page. 2014. "Testing Theories of American Politics: Elites, Interest Groups, and Average Citizens." *Perspectives on Politics* 12:3 (September) 564–581.

Gintis, Herbert. 2000. *Game Theory Evolving: A Problem-Centered Introduction to Modeling Strategic Behavior*. Princeton: Princeton University Press.

Goffman, Erving. 1959. *The Presentation of Self in Everyday Life*. New York: Doubleday Anchor.

Hessler, Peter. 2002. *RiverTown: Two Years on the Yangtze*. New York: Harper Perennial.

Hibbing, John R., and Elizabeth Theiss-Morse. 2002. *Stealth Democracy: Americans' Beliefs About How Government Should Work*. New York: Cambridge University Press.

Holland, John H. 2014. *Complexity: A Very Short Introduction*. New York: Oxford University Press.

Katznelson, Ira, and Helen V. Milner (Eds.). 2002. *Political Science: State of the Discipline*. New York and Washington, DC: Norton and American Political Science Association.

LaPalombara, Joseph. 1987. *Democracy, Italian Style*. New Haven: Yale University Press.

Lasswell, Harold. 1958. *Politics: Who Gets What, When, How?* Cleveland: Meridian.

1960. *Psychopathology and Politics*. New York: Viking Press.

Lave, Charles A., and James G. March. 1975. *An Introduction to Models in the Social Sciences*. New York: Harper and Row.

Laver, Michael, and Ernest Sergenti. 2012. *Party Competition: An Agent-Based Model*. Princeton: Princeton University Press.

Liddell Hart, B. H. 1991. *Strategy* (Second Revised Edition). New York: Meredian Books.

Long, Norton E. 1962. "The Local Community as an Ecology of Games." In *The Polity*. Chicago: Rand McNally, pages 139–155.

Luce, R. Duncan, and Howard Raiffa. 1957. *Games and Decisions: Introduction and Critical Survey*. New York: John Wiley and Sons.

Lustick, Ian, Dan Miodownik, and Roy J. Eidelson. 2004. "Secessionism in Multicultural States: Does Sharing Power Prevent of Encourage It?" *American Political Science Review* 98:2 (May) 209–229.

Machiavelli, Niccolò. 1961. *The Prince*. Translated with notes by George Bull. New York: Penguin Classics.

Marx, Karl. 1967 [1867]. *Capital: Volume I: A Critical Analysis of Capitalist Production*. Edited by Frederick Engels. New York: International Publishers

Masters, Roger D. (Ed.). 1964. *The First and Second Discourses of Jean-Jacques Rousseau*. New York: St. Martin's.

Mehta, Suketu. 2004. *Maximum City: Bombay Lost and Found*. New York: Vintage.

Meredith, Martin. 2007. *Mugabe: Power, Plunder, and the Struggle for Zimbabwe*. New York: Public Affairs.

Migdal, Joel. 1988. *Strong Societies and Weak States*. Princeton: Princeton University Press.

Miller, John J., and Scott E. Page. 2007. *Complex Adaptive Systems: An Introduction to Computational Models of Social Life*. Princeton: Princeton University Press.

More, Thomas. 1949. *Utopia* (Translated and edited by H. V. S. Ogden). Arlington Heights: Crofts Classics.

Newell, Allen, and Herbert Simon. 1972. *Human Problem Solving*. New York: Prentice Hall.

Norris, Pippa. 2011. *Democratic Deficit: Critical Citizens Revisited*. New York: Cambridge University Press.

Olson, Mancur, Jr. 1965. *The Logic of Collective Action: Public Goods and the Theory of Groups*. Cambridge, MA: Harvard University Press.

Ostrom, Elinor. 1990. *Governing the Commons: The Evolution of Institutions for Collective Action*. Cambridge: Cambridge University Press.

Parsons, Talcott and Edward A. Shils (Eds.). 1951. *Toward a General Theory Of Action: Theoretical Foundations for the Social Sciences*. Cambridge, MA: Harvard University Press.

Plato. 1968. *The Republic of Plato*. Translated, with notes and an interpretive essay by Allan Bloom. New York: Basic Books.

Pool, Ithiel De Sola, and Allan Kessler. 1965. "The Kaiser, the Tsar, and the Computer: Information Processing in a Crisis." *The American Behavioral Scientist* 8:9 (May) 31–38.

Popkin, Samuel L. 1979. *The Rational Peasant: The Political Economy of Rural Society in Vietnam.* Berkeley: University of California Press.

Putnam, Robert D. 1993. *Making Democracy Work: Civic Traditions in Modern Italy.* Princeton: Princeton University Press.

Richards, Diana (Ed.). 2000. *Political Complexity: Nonlinear Models of Politics.* Ann Arbor: University of Michigan Press.

Riker, William H. 1962. *The Theory of Political Coalitions.* New Haven: Yale University Press.

Rosanvallon, Pierre. 2008. *Counter-Democracy: Politics in an Age of Distrust.* New York: Cambridge University Press.

Rousseau, Jean Jacques. 1964. *The First and Second Discourses* (Edited by Roger D. Masters). New York: St. Martin's Press.

Sampson, Anthony. 1999. *Mandela: The Authorized Biography.* New York: Vintage Books.

Scharpf, Fritz. 1997. *Games Real Actors Play: Actor-Centered Institutionalism in Policy Research.* Boulder: Westview.

Schelling, Thomas C. 1960. *The Strategy of Conflict.* Cambridge, MA: Harvard University Press.

1978. *Micromotives and Macrobehavior.* New York: Norton.

Schuck, Peter H. 2014. *Why Government Fails So Often: And How It Can Do Better.* Princeton: Princeton University Press.

Sciolino, Elaine. 2000. *Persian Mirrors: The Elusive Face of Iran.* New York: Simon and Schuster Touchstone.

Scott, James C. 1976. *The Moral Economy of the Peasant: Rebellion and Subsistence in South East Asia.* New Haven: Yale University Press.

1985. *Weapons of the Weak: Everyday Forms of Peasant Resistance.* New Haven: Yale University Press.

1998. *Seeing Like a State: How Certain Schemes to Improve the Human Condition Have Failed.* New Haven: Yale University Press.

2009. *The Art of Not Being Governed: An Anarchist History of Upland Southeast Asia.* New Haven: Yale University Press.

Sigmund, Karl. 1993. *Games of Life: Explorations in Ecology, Evolution, and Behavior.* New York: Oxford University Press.

Simon, Herbert. 1997. *Models of Bounded Rationality (Volume 3).* Cambridge, MA: MIT Press.

Simon, Herbert A. 1969/1996. *The Sciences of the Artificial.* Cambridge, MA: MIT Press.

1947. *Administrative Behavior: A Study of Decision-Making Process in Administrative Organization.* New York: Free Press.

Skinner, B. F. 1953. *Science and Human Behavior.* New York: Free Press.

Stille, Alexander. 2006. *The Sack of Rome: Media + Money + Celebrity = Power = Silvio Berlusconi.* New York: Penguin Books.

Thesiger, Wilfred. 2007. *The Marsh Arabs.* London: Penguin.

Tilly, Charles. 1982. "Warmaking and Statemaking as Organized Crime." Working Paper 256, Center for Research on Social Organization. Ann Arbor: University of Michigan.

1985. "Warmaking and Statemaking as Organized Crime." In Peter B. Evans et al. (Eds.) *Bringing the State Back In*. Cambridge: Cambridge University Press, 169–187.

Tucker, Robert C. (Ed.). 1978. *The Marx-Engels Reader* (2nd edn.). New York: Norton.

Tullock, Gordon. 1965. *The Politics of Bureaucracy*. Washington, DC: Public Affairs Press.

Tversky, Amos, and Daniel Kahneman. 1974. "Judgment under Uncertainty: Heuristics and Biases." *Science* 185:4157 (September 27) 1124–1131.

1981. "The Framing of Decisions and the Psychology of Choice." *Science* 211:4481 (January 30) 453–458.

Waldrop, M. Mitchell. 1992. *Complexity: The Emerging Science at the Edge of Order and Chaos*. New York: Simon and Schuster Touchstone.

Winters, Jeffrey A. 2011. *Oligarchy*. New York: Cambridge University Press.

Winters, Jeffrey A., and Benjamin I. Page. 2009. "Oligarchy in the United States?" *Perspectives on Politics* 7:4 (December) 731–751.

Wittgenstein, Ludwig. 1981. *Tractatus Logico-Philosophicus*. London: Routledge and Kegan Paul.

Index